CULTURAL POLITICS

The Shakespeare myth

CULTURAL POLITICS
general editors Jonathan Dollimore and Alan Sinfield

Writing Ireland: colonialism, nationalism and culture
David Cairns and Shaun Richards

Poetry, politics and language *John Barrell*

The Shakespeare myth *Graham Holderness*

Garden-nature-language *Simon Pugh*

in preparation

Opera, ideology and film *Jeremy Tambling*

Teaching women *Ann Thompson and Helen Wilcox (editors)*

Drama in South Africa *Martin Orkin*

The politics of romanticism *Nigel Leask*

Empire boys *Joe Bristow*

Georgette Heyer and Jane Austen: representations of regency England
Roger Sales

Writing, postmodernity and femininity *Carolyn Brown*

Strategies of contemporary women writers *Maggie Humm*

Teaching Shakespeare *Stephen Glynn (editor)*

Counter-cultures in 1980s popular music *Steve Redhead*

Gender, race, Renaissance drama *Ania Loomba*

Pre-Raphaelite art and literature *Marcia Pointon (editor)*

Bakhtin and cultural criticism *David Shepherd and Ken Hirschkop (editors)*

Gay culture and politics *Simon Shepherd and Mick Wallis (editors)*

Lesbian identity in twentieth-century women's writing *Gabriele Griffin*

The Shakespeare myth

edited by Graham Holderness

MANCHESTER UNIVERSITY PRESS

distributed exclusively in the USA and Canada by ST. MARTIN'S PRESS, New York

Published by Manchester University Press,
Oxford Road, Manchester M13 9PL, UK
Distributed exclusively in the USA and Canada
by St. Martin's Press, Inc.,
Room 400, 175 Fifth Avenue, New York, NY 10010, USA

British Library cataloguing in publication data
    The Shakespeare myth.——(Cultural politics).
        1. Shakespeare, William, 1564–1616
        Criticism and interpretation
        I. Holderness, Graham II. Series
        822.3'3   PR2976

Library of Congress cataloging in publication data applied for

ISBN 0–7190–1488–3 hardback

To the memory of the
REVEREND FRANCIS WILLIAM GASTRELL

Photoset in Linotron Joanna by
Northern Photototypesetting Co, Bolton

Printed in Great Britain
by Hartnolls (1985) Limited, Bodmin, Cornwall

Contents

Illustrations appear between Parts One and Two (pp. 110 and 111)

Acknowledgements

For permission to reproduce illustrations, gratitude is due to Tesco Stores Ltd.; the International Shakespeare Globe Centre; Whitbread Flowers; Wight Collins Rutherford Scott Ltd.; the BBC and the *Radio Times*.

The recurrence throughout this volume of one particular name will sufficiently indicate that Christopher J. McCullough's role in the genesis and evolution of this book has been more than that of a contributor.

G.H.

One can conceive of very ancient myths, but there are no eternal ones; for it is human history which converts reality into speech, and it alone rules the life and death of mythical language. Ancient or not, mythology can only have an historical foundation, for myth is a type of speech chosen by history.

Roland Barthes, *Mythologies*, trans. Annette Lavers
(London: Paladin, 1973), p. 110

Our objective was the effigy of Shakespeare in Leicester Square: a spot, I think, admirably chosen . . . for the sake of the dramatist, still very foolishly claimed as a glory by the English race, in spite of his disgusting political opinions.

R. L. Stevenson, 'Zero's tale of the explosive bomb', from *The Dynamiter*, 1885
(London, Heinemann, 1923), p. 121.

Foreword: **Cultural materialism**

The break-up of consensus in British political life during the 1970s was accompanied by the break-up of traditional assumptions about the values and goals of literary culture. Initially at specialised conferences and in committed journals, but increasingly in the mainstream of intellectual life, literary texts have been related to the new and challenging discourses of Marxism, feminism, structuralism, psychoanalysis and poststructuralism, and juxtaposed with work not customarily accorded literary or artistic standing.

Some recent developments offer a significant alternative to traditional practice; others are little more than realignments of familiar positions. But our belief is that a combination of historical and cultural context, theoretical method, political commitment and textual analysis offers the strongest challenge and has already contributed substantial work. We call this *cultural materialism*.

There are (at least) two ways of using the word 'culture'. The evaluative use has been more common when we are thinking about 'the arts' and 'literature': to be 'cultured' is to be the possessor of superior values and a refined sensibility, both of which are manifested through a positive and fulfilling engagement with 'good' literature, art, music and so on. The analytic one is used in the social sciences and especially anthropology: it seeks to describe the whole system of significations by which a society or a section of it understands itself and its relations with the world. Cultural materialism draws upon the latter, analytic sense, and therefore studies 'high' culture alongside work in popular culture, in other media and from subordinated groups.

'Materialism' is opposed to 'idealism': it insists that culture does not (cannot) transcend the material forces and relations of production. Culture is not simply a reflection of the economic and political system, but nor can it be independent of it. Cultural materialism therefore sees texts as inseparable from the conditions of their production and reception in history; and as involved, necessarily in the making of cultural meanings which are always, finally, political meanings. Hence the series title: Cultural Politics.

Finally, cultural materialism does not pretend to political neutrality. It does not, like much established literary criticism, attempt to mystify its perspective as the natural or obvious interpretation of an allegedly given textual fact. On the contrary, it registers its commitment to the transformation of a social order that exploits people on grounds of race, gender, sexuality and class.

The Cultural Politics Series seeks to develop this kind of understanding in a sequence of volumes that has intellectual coherence, but no restrictive format. The books will be both introductory and innovatory: introductory in that they will be clear and accessible; innovatory in their application of distinctive perspectives both to established topics and to new ones. In the tradition of Shelley, Arnold, Eliot, the Leavises and Williams, though often in terms very different from theirs, culture and politics are again at the centre of important intellectual debates.

Jonathan Dollimore
Alan Sinfield
University of Sussex

Preface: 'All this'

Those still fortunate enough, in Thatcher's Britain, to have access to a £20 note, will find in the design of its inverse side an appropriate emblem of the Shakespeare myth. The figure of Shakespeare there represented is a familiar icon: a pedestal embossed with the faces of Henry V, Richard III, Elizabeth I, and surmounted by a pile of books, upon which the pensive bard leans an insouciant elbow. The supportive pedestal expresses monumental authority, the figure relaxed contemplation and nonchalant mastery; while the bound volumes, and the manuscript page to which the figure points, appropriate and secure the dramatist's work for the literary rather than the theatrical arts.

When we consider the provenance of this image, we find it to be rooted in the very heart of the Shakespeare myth. The statue represented is the sculpture by Peter Scheemakers, commissioned by public subscription and erected in Westminster Abbey as a memorial to the national poet in 1741.[1] More to our purpose, it formed a centrepiece, in the form of a leaden copy executed in a mass-production statue factory at Hyde Park Corner, of one of the ritual celebrations in David Garrick's 1769 Shakespeare Jubilee, the great formal inauguration of bardolatry as a national religion, which 'marks the point at which Shakespeare stopped being regarded as an increasingly popular and admirable dramatist, and became a god' (Deelman, p. 7). Before this figure Garrick proclaimed his great bardolatrous *Ode*, concluded by a choral song of joy:

> We will, – his brows with laurel bind
> Who charms with virtue human kind:
> Raise the pile, the statue raise,
> Sing immortal Shakespeare's praise!
> The song will cease, the stone decay,
>   But his Name
>   And undiminished fame,
> Shall never, never pass away.[2]

The device on the banknote transacts a complex exchange of values: the currency of Shakespeare as a cultural token enhances the material worth of the promissory note; while the high value of the note itself confers a corresponding richness on the symbol of high art and national culture. A banknote is both a sign of value and a legal contract, a 'bond' between citizen and State: the exchange of such symbolic tokens represents both a constitutive material activity and a cultural process of bonding and socialisation. It is not possible, in a bourgeois society, not to want money: desire is thus initially provoked, and subsequently deflected (rather than satisfied) by an apparent redistribution of cultural property. The fortunate holder of a Shakespearean banknote possesses both monetary wealth and aesthetic richness; and by virtue of that possession is integrated, both materially and culturally, into the hegemonic ideologies of bourgeois society.

A spherical bubble, resembling those in cartoon strips, emanates from the pile of books, and encloses an inset detail of a tableau from *Romeo and Juliet*. The choice of scene is predictable: the so-called 'balcony scene'. from which all the play's familiar catch-phrases ('But soft! what light through yonder window breaks!'; 'Romeo, Romeo, wherefore art thou Romeo'?; 'A rose by any other word would smell as sweet'; 'Parting is such sweet sorrow') are derived. The choice of play must seem at first glance curiously inappropriate: is not this drama the great poetic protest of romantic passion against mercenary morality and commercialised relationship? Utterances of elevated and idealised passion – 'Beauty too rich for use, for earth too dear' – juxtapose incongruously and with ironical effect against the sordid and banal symbols (£20) of monetary value.

Verona, like the Venice of *Othello* and *The Merchant of Venice*, is one of Shakespeare's images of bourgeois society. The constitutive structure of that society is the great competitive rivalry between the houses of Capulet and Montague; its dominant value that transformation of all human purposes and activities into objects, which Marx defined as the central principle of bourgeois culture: the tendency for all things and human relationships to become objectified ('reification') as a consequence of the commodity production endemic to the bourgeois economy. Love between a Capulet and a Montague signifies the precise antithesis of the feud, a symbolic gesture of concord and mutual affection with power to negate the antagonisms and contradictions of dynastic struggle and commercial rivalry.

But paradoxically, the poetry which seeks to transform bourgeois society becomes a characteristically reified product of that society's culture: idealised and romanticised out of all dialectical relationship with society, it takes on the seductive glamour of aestheticism, the sinister and self-destructive beauty of decadent romance. The 'death mark't passage' of the lovers' *liebestod* is the culmination of a process of abstraction and refinement which gradually transforms 'passion' into 'poetry', 'love' into 'literature'; and becomes not a subversion of bourgeois society but a paradoxical ratification of its power. The close of the play sees the lovers finally transformed into reified aesthetic objects – the statues which Montague and Capulet will raise to the memory of their son and daughter. Such objects, which combine in themselves aesthetic perfection and material value, are the decorative curiosities of bourgeois society rather than forces for revolutionising its corrupt and mercenary power. Just as the potentially revolutionary force of reciprocal desire is not annihilated but appropriated and converted by the bourgeois world of Verona: so the potentially radical powers of a drama capable of such interrogation and disclosure is transformed, by the operations of cultural reproduction, into a classical monument, simultaneously eloquent of values both commercial and cultural; simultaneously expressive of both material and ideological power.

'Where, in all this', as Muriel Bradbrook lamented when reviewing *Political Shakespeare* in *The Guardian*, 'are Shakespeare's plays?' *The Shakespeare Myth* is a contribution to that growing body of theoretical, historiographical and textual work here urbanely elided, by a *grande dame* of the academic establishment, as 'all this'. Bradbrook's elegiac interrogative attempts to insinuate into implicit acceptance a concensus, as to what 'Shakespeare's plays' may be understood to mean, which scarcely any longer exists: implying that in this new brand of criticism, certain familiar and unmistakeable cultural objects are dissolved into currents of polemical theory, so that an authentic and authoritative presence becomes lost, a great heroic monotone is drowned in the polyphonic chatter of modern critical voices. For such complacent observers the true object can, in fact, never wholly disappear: it remains, somewhere, immanent in its inviolable identity, 'towering over' the petty mediations of interpreters and critics:[4]

> . . . he doth bestride the narrow world
> Like a Colossus, and we petty men
> Walk under his huge legs, and peep about
> To find ourselves dishonourable graves.
>
> (*Julius Caesar*, I.ii.133–6)

That 'colossus' is the subject of this volume, the principal purpose of which might be defined as a demonstration of how this 'Shakespeare myth' functions in contemporary culture as an ideological framework for containing concensus and for sustaining myths of unity, integration and harmony in the cultural superstructures of a divided and fractured society.

In order to map the contours of this myth it is necessary to recognise that both 'Shakespeare's plays' and their legendary author exist and function in more varied and complex forms than a scholarly monograph on the design of the frons scenae, or the latest explication of flower-imagery in The Winter's Tale. It is both inevitable and appropriate that initial resistance to the cultural authority of 'Shakespeare' should have emanated from within the field of English studies: since the Victorian reconstitution of Shakespeare as the paradigmatic liberal–humanist functioned as a founding-father for the discipline of English itself; and may even, if Alan Sinfield is correct, be the last frail bond holding the ramshackle apparatus of 'Literature' together.[5] There now exists a substantial and invaluable body of work offering counter-readings of Shakespeare's texts and re-locations of Shakespeare's 'reputation'. The texts have been re-read in the light of post-structuralist linguistics, historiographical research, psychoanalytic theories and feminist sexual politics; and criticism itself has been exposed as the ideological operateur that strategically reconstitutes a hegemonic Shakespeare.[6] But the domination of radical Shakespeare criticism by 'Eng. Lit.' specialists has no foundation in the object of the inquiry, and no justification in terms of the broad political objectives of the movement: it derives rather from the structure of the very discipline its practitioners seek to disturb and transform. Furthermore, it has been too easy for radical 'English' specialists to take advantage of the academic apartheid of 'disciplines' to root their polemical stances in apparently alternative grounds: opposing the liberal–humanist hegemony of 'Literature' with the instinctive materialism of historiography, the educational progressivism of 'drama', the natural libertarianism of theatrical performance. While it is true that the dialectical juxtapositions available within an 'interdisciplinary' framework can afford opportunities for radical intervention, these 'alternative' disciplines to which radical teachers and critics have turned do not in fact represent inherently progressive discursive formations, but rather parallel structures of cultural hegemony with firmly-entrenched establishments and dominant ideologies.

It is therefore incumbent upon a new critical intervention into the Shakespeare debate to resist the dead hand of 'English', to break from the conventions of textual 're-reading', and to address directly those fields of discourse and those institutional practices in which the cultural phenomenon of Shakespeare operates with some form of signifying power. The contributors to this volume were encouraged to look behind and beyond the 'plays' as commonly constituted and presented, the narrowly-defined forms of literary text, historical phenomenon and theatrical production: and to recognise 'Shakespeare' wherever and

whenever that authorial construction is manifested,
as television advertisements, comedy sketches, St
tourist attractions, the design on a £20 note or a nar
homoerotic 'physique' magazine. These broader o
pursued by drawing contributors not only from
studies but from departments of drama, education, adult education
communications studies. The common theoretical objective is the
analysis and disclosure of those discursive formations and cultural
institutions which throw these manifestations of the Shakespeare myth
into active and strategic play, and manipulate them into some form of
ideological constraint or composure.

In addition, the essays are complemented by interviews with
prominent cultural practitioners of Shakespeare in education, theatre,
the press, and television. Although the interviews were conducted in a
combative spirit, they should not be read simply as expressions and
exemplifications of the cultural establishment identified and attacked in
the essays; as the presence among the interviewees of socialists like
Michael Bogdanov and Sam Wanamaker should testify. The relationship
between the arguments advanced in essays and the views articulated in
interviews is in practice, as the reader will soon discover, rather more
complex and dialectically interdependent than a mere confrontation of
radical and establishment positions.

In terms of form, then, this book has some unusual features, which
perhaps require a note of explanation. Its principles of organisation lie at
a point of intersection between the monograph, the critical anthology
united by a common problem, the collection of essays linked by a
uniform approach, and the volume of edited interviews with
professional practitioners. In practice these diverse influences have
cohered to shape an infrastructure of considerable formal coherence (an
attempt to render this explicit by an elaborate system of cross-
referencing had to be abandoned as impossibly cumbersome, though
the most useful parallels have been preserved) while at the same time the
polyphonic medium is productive of great cultural difference and
ideological contradiction. As a form this methodology clearly has
analogies with the circularity of liberal–humanist pluralism: but in the
interests of securing genuine debate and interaction, such complicity
seems worth risking – particularly if the alternative is an elevation of
ideological correctness over practical intervention, theoretical purity
over political engagement.

Cultural materialism has established itself primarily as a politicised
form of historiography: it should also be recognised, as the second half of
Political Shakespeare demonstrated, as a radical form of cultural sociology. It

_resses the past in order to re-read culture in the context of its true ustory, and to interrogate the constructions of intellectual and artistic work effected in different societies in different periods. It must also, if its political pretensions are to be realised, address the present: since it is there, in the perpetual strategic mobilisation of the past, that the politics of culture are activated, the endless battle for cultural meaning joined. The call of the contemporary is inescapable: the artistic and intellectual acts of the present cannot be regarded as ephemeral exhalations from the shrine of an immortal divinity; for in those acts, cultural materialism insists, the meanings of the present and the past are simultaneously made. For every particular present, Shakespeare is, here, now, always, what is currently being made of him. In writing of that making, we are not merely offering, in a formalised shape, the provisional and undecided hesitancy of a review: we are writing an immediate, continuous and politically active history.

Graham Holderness

Notes

1 Christian Deelman, The Great Shakespeare Jubilee (London: Michael Joseph, 1964), pp. 69–70.
2 Martha Winburne England, Garrick's Jubilee (Bowling Green, Ohio: Ohio State University Press, 1964), p. 252.
3 See Graham Holderness, 'Romeo and Juliet: empathy and alienation', Shakespeare Jahrbuch, 123 (1987).
4 See Inga-Stina Ewbank, Times Literary Supplement, (25 April 1986), p. 451.
5 Alan Sinfield, 'Political Shakespeare', Times Educational Supplement (26 April 1985), p. 24.
6 For examples of all these see Jonathan Dollimore and Alan Sinfield, eds., Political Shakespeare, (Manchester: Manchester University Press, 1985); John Drakakis, ed., Alternative Shakespeares (London: Methuen, 1986); Patricia Parker and Geoffrey Hartmann, eds., Shakespeare and the Question of Theory (London: Methuen, 1986); and Terry Hawkes, That Shakespherian Rag, (London: Methuen, 1986).

Discursive fields

Bardolatry: or,
The cultural materialist's guide
to Stratford-upon-Avon
Graham Holderness

Stratford will help you to understand Shakespeare. (F. J. Furnivall)[1]

In the spring of 1936 the Directors of the Stratford-upon-Avon Festival Company received the following cable: *'Please send earth Shakespeare's garden water River Avon for dedication Shakespeare Theatre, Dallas, Texas, July 1st'*. The 'Shakespeare Theatre' referred to was a 'replica' of the Globe playhouse erected for the Great Texas Fair; it had previously served as the centre-piece of a mock 'English village' constructed for the World's Fair in Chicago. Stratford knew how to respond to what might seem to us a bizarre request. A group of citizens and actors gathered in the garden of Shakespeare's birthplace to meet the American Vice-Consul. In a solemn ceremony a handful of that rich dust was disinterred and placed with ritual formality into a small box made of charred wood – a relic from the Shakespeare Memorial Theatre which burned down in 1926. The party then repaired to the premises of the Stratford rowing club on the banks of the Avon. Mr Fordham Flower, descendant of the brewing family which endowed the Shakespeare Memorial Theatre, accompanied the Vice-Consul on a small raft to the middle of the river. Into the sacred stream they dipped a small bottle made of aluminium (light metal, like brewing, being an important local industry) and bearing Shakespeare's coat-of-arms. Both sacred earth and holy water were conveyed to New York, free of carriage charges, by the Cunard Line: thence to Dallas, where in a ritual of libation the *ersatz* Globe was consecrated by the sprinkling of Stratford earth and Avon water; and the superflux exposed to the general veneration of Dallas.[2]

In praise of Shakespeare

These rites, based on an attenuated form of relic-worship, are the liturgi-
cal properties of a religion: bardolatry, the worship of Shakespeare.
Visitors to the Great Texas Fair in 1936, as they watched the pageant of
Queen Elizabeth I and her morris-dancers, and were ushered into the
replica Globe for a severely truncated performance of a Shakespeare play
(the forty-five minutes traffic of that particular stage)[3] were invited into
communion with a ritual enacting an idealised English past: a past linked
to the present in transhistorical and transcontinental continuity, by the
power of these vatic, totemic images.

   Though there were a few isolated prophets, bardolotry as an organised
evangelical movement scarcely existed before David Garrick's Stratford
jubilee in 1769. Crowds followed the corpse of Ben Jonson to Westminster on his death in 1637, and Francis Beaumont was thought to deserve a
place in the Abbey; Shakespeare had been laid to rest in 1616 in a
relatively little, obscure grave in the chancel of Stratford church. He was
not even eligible for a place there on the strength of his poetry or
theatrical achievement (in 1623 Puritan-tinged Stratford corporation paid
Shakespeare's company, the King's Men, not to perform in the Guild-
hall)[4] but as a local landowner and lessee of tithes.[5] None the less by the
mid eighteenth century Stratford was certainly the centre for some kind
of tourist industry, run by some pretty unscrupulous local entrepreneurs.[6] In the garden of New Place, the house Shakespeare bought
and lived in on his retirement, the famous mulberry tree, reputed (by an
aptly-named Thomas Sharp) to have been planted by the Bard's own
hand, had certainly acquired by this period sufficient sacrosanctity to
form an object of tourist interest and attraction.[7] In 1756 the Rev. Francis
William Gastrell, an irascible cleric who had acquired the property, was
so exasperated by 'the frequent importunities of travellers', and so
annoyed with the tree itself (an object of hoary and ancient growth,
which was obstructing the free play of sunlight and engendering rising
damp in the walls of his house) that he had it chopped down; whereu-
pon it very quickly began, like the wood of the true cross, to increase and
multiply into innumerable relics and souvenirs.[8] This legendary product
of Bardic husbandry soon became available from all good local craft-
shops in the form of 'many curious toys and useful articles'.[9] In 1759
Gastrell knocked the house down as well, and thus entered history as
one of the great cultural vandals.[10]

   Another Stratford entrepreneur and founder of the tourist industry was John Jordan, who set up a rival trade in curios from the wood of a crab-apple tree under which Shakespeare (who was, according to beer-mats supplied by Flowers' brewery, 'extremely fond of drinking hearty draughts of English ale') was reputed to have lapsed into unconsciousness during a pub-crawl.[11] John Ward's anecdote, describing Shakespeare's death from the consequences of a piss-up with Drayton and Ben Jonson, neglects to mention what was being drunk at the time: and there seems to be no other evidence of Shakespeare's bibulous preferences. But by this period the Stratford brewing trade was sufficiently well-established to retrospectively determine the Bard's particular tipple, and to connect in a single commercial dimension the diverse products of local business enterprise.

The bardolatrous trade

This was the great age of forgery and fabrication in the Shakespeare industry, and Stratford was the site of a great deal of healthy commercial competition. Jordan for example ridiculed the pretensions of 'the Birthplace' in Henley Street to authenticity, calling it 'a most flagrant and gross imposition';[12] and it was Jordan also who decided that the house known as 'Mary Arden's house' at Wilmcote was the domicile of Shakespeare's mother. The attribution is an arbitrary fantasy: but along with the Birthplace, New Place, Hall's Croft and Anne Hathaway's Cottage, Mary Arden's house occupies its place as a station on the route of bardolatrous pilgrimage.

By 1800 the Birthplace was partly a butcher's shop and partly an inn called the Swan and Maidenhead,[13] a sign replete with romantic connotations for the devotees of Queen Gloriana and the Sweet Swan of Avon. Here, as Ivor Brown observed, it was possible to get Bed, Board and Bard under one roof: but the sign itself was taken down and deconstructed in 1808 by a drunken company of Warwickshire yeomanry, who felt it inappropriate that the only maidenhead left intact in Stratford should be a wooden one. The butcher's shop was then occupied by a Mrs Hornby, who traded in bardolatry as well as bacon by exhibiting a collection of relics, including a legendary piece of furniture reputed to be Shakespeare's own chair. Curiouser and curio-ser, the chair was fabulous in more senses than one: since although every visitor paid to cut a piece off, it never grew any smaller. A rival widow who actually owned the building then took over the pub, and decided to evict Widow Hornby and appropriate the bardolatrous trade for herself. Widow Hornby decamped, but took her relics with her, and set up in competition in a house across the road. 'These rival dowagers', a contemporary eyewitness records, 'parted on envious terms; they were constantly to be seen at each others' doors abusing each other and their respective visitors, and frequently with so much acerbity as to disgust and even deter the latter from entering either dwelling'.[14]

These images of nineteenth-century Stratford appropriately map the contours of the Shakespeare myth: an atmosphere of unscrupulous opportunism, commercial exploitation and gross imposture; the *laissez-faire* environment of a cultural industry in which the free play of market forces determines all values. The reverential Victorian pilgrim journeying to Stratford in search of a religious communion with a more settled, more tranquil, more certain past, found himself instead in the crossfire of a Widows' War, and probably felt disposed to wish a plague on both their houses. You could wander through medieval streets and observe Tudor buildings: but the *values* you came in search of – truth, authenticity, the assurance and consolation of a vanished golden age, the transcendent illumination of transhistorical genius – were not after all to be discovered, visibly embedded in an uninterrupted continuum of time and space, like fossils in the strata of rocks; the past itself was the site of a furious battle between competing appropriators, rival enterprises within a cultural industry.

Shakespeare lives

The cultural and commercial antagonisms of the Victorian period were ultimately reconciled by the formation of a monopolistic organisation, the Shakespeare Birthplace Trust, which now represents the authentic clerisy of the Shakespeare religion: Stratford itself its church, and its high priest Dr Levi Fox. No fraudulent claims are now made, no original chairs or pieces of mulberry tree sold in local souvenir shops. Stratford contains, as well as the 'Shakespearean Properties' and innumerable commercial adjuncts to the tourist industry, the Royal Shakespeare Theatre, country home of the most prestigious British theatre company; and the Shakespeare Centre, a highly-respected research institute. Tourism is regarded by some serious (and perhaps cynical) scholars and theatrical practitioners as the bread-and-butter trade on which the more elevated superstructures of culture can be erected, in an age when State subsidy of the arts and education is that much harder to come by.[15] How then are these cults and rituals of bardolatry to be understood in the

present? what relation do they have, if any, to the position of Shakespeare within the apparatus of British culture?

Tourists are still lured to Stratford by the deployment of an overtly
religious language of pilgrimage and worship. 'It is the fame of the
properties associated with William Shakespeare and his family, that
makes Stratford-upon-Avon a Mecca for visitors from all over the world',
writes Levi Fox in the current guidebook.[16] 'Anne Hathaway's cottage,
the home of Shakespeare's wife before her marriage, is one of England's
most famous buildings. The reason is not far to seek. Apart from its
literary and romantic associations as the scene of Shakespeare's youthful
courtship, it is a property of outstanding architectural appeal which for
generations has been a shrine of international literary pilgrimage.' A 1951
guidebook to Anne Hathaway's cottage was confident that *As You Like It*
contains an 'unmistakable reference' to this cottage, in Celia's lines about
their holiday home in the Forest of Arden.[17] In the current official
Stratford guidebook the claim is moderated, but Levi Fox still preserves
its substance: 'it has been suggested that Shakespeare's description of the
situation of Celia's home in *As You Like It* was inspired by the poet's
recollections of his wife's early home.' These lines were of course originally delivered on a bare, unlocalised stage on London's Bankside; and the
'Arden' of the play is the Ardennes of northern France rather than the
forest which once existed in Warwickshire, and which may or may not
have adjoined the cottage in which Anne Hathaway, whom Shakespeare
may or may not have married, may or may not have lived. But bardolatry
trades in certainty, not in the slippery elusiveness of documentary fact:
the buildings have acted as objects of pilgrimage and shrines of worship
for generations, and that in itself is an assurance of their value.

And what values are these buildings in practice commandeered to
express? Pure, unimpeded images of an idealised historical past. The
photographs in the guidebooks appear purified of any association with
the complex, sordid present; isolated as timeless symbols of a neat, tidy,
innocent world: 'so venerable', as Matthew Arnold said of Oxford, 'so
lovely; so unravaged by the fierce intellectual life of the century'.
Guidebooks from the 1950s appear to have used prewar photographs,
and one even offered the monuments of Stratford transmuted into the
pastel tints of a series of English watercolours. An idealised 'English' past,
picturesque and untroubled, is thus embodied and incorporated into
commodities for sale to national and international markets, the transaction simultaneously satisfying both cultural and commercial demands.
These publications, as Roland Barthes said of the *Blue Guide*, 'answer in

fact none of the questions which a modern traveller can ask himself while crossing a countryside which is real *and which exists in time*. To select only monuments suppresses at one stroke the reality of the land and that of its people, it accounts for nothing of the present, that is, nothing historical, and as a consequence, the monuments themselves become undecipherable, therefore senseless'.[18]

Tourism as pilgrimage

The modern tourist, as a growing body of sociological work has shown, is a direct descendant of the medieval pilgrim. Both are engaged in a ritualised passage to a sacred site; both are in search of the icons of their culture: relics, pieces of the true cross, burnished with age but sanctified by the miracle of survival through time. Pilgrims, Donald Horne argues in his fine study *The Great Museum*, were the first mass tourists, and sightseeing and souvenir collecting the inescapable material dimension of their spiritual quest. In marxist terms, tourism is a commercial exchange process whose symbolic centre is the fetishism of objects: and museum relics and treasures can certainly be said to possess such a holy, magical aura.[19]

The symbolic function of a souvenir or photograph is partly acquisitive[20] – you exhibit it to show that you've been there, done that place – but it also operates, like the medieval relic, as the embodiment of an experience: a trigger for memory, with a magical capacity to release recollection; a mnemonic device designed to preserve memory from the wastage of time. In an age of mechanical reproduction, photography familiarizes the objects of tourism to such a degree that one wonders why anyone should still want to visit the *Mona Lisa* or the Parthenon or the leaning tower of Pisa at all. Oral tradition is likely to preserve the 'magic' of an unseen place intact; visual tradition (photography) should gradually bleed away that magic, imperceptibly but relentlessly wearing away the sacred aura. Yet in practice the impulse to visit a place in person, to see it with one's own eyes 'as it really is' seems to grow rather than diminish. When we arrive we observe the 'reality' of a place in a context prescribed by visual tradition, 'discovering' that the place is after all synonymous with the photographs; and our own snapshots obediently reproduce the images of the guidebooks. We may attempt to intervene by including ourselves or our companions in the frame with an object of pilgrimage; but we succeed only in ratifying the power of the monument. We may seek to appropriate the object to our own personal vision: in practice we appear merely as adjuncts to the object, illustrations of its magical power to draw reverential or irreverent attention. Our attempts at authentic personal experience become incorporated into a powerful, quasi-religious ideology.

In a riverside park at Stratford stands a statuary group: in the centre a large pedestal surmounted by the figure of Shakespeare, sitting like patience on a monument, smiling at the bus station. He is surrounded on four sides by the creatures of his imagination: Lady Macbeth, Falstaff, Prince Hal, and of course Hamlet, staring philosophically at the obligatory skull. The bronze statue of the prince is coated with green verdigris; but not so the skull. The corruption of time which ought more properly to encrust the dead than the living form, is absent from the skull: effaced by the reverential touching of generations of pilgrims. The iconic emblem of Hamlet holding the skull is the most universal Shakespearean image: frequently confused with the 'To be or not to be' soliloquy, it stands for the transcendent wisdom of the prince of poets. The great contemplative genius gazes stoically, with meditative calm and philosophical resignation, through the mysteries of life and death.

Pilgrim's progress

The touristic component of the Shakespeare industry has a history coterminous with the origins of the plays themselves. Much of the most significant evidence in existence about the Elizabethan and Jacobean theatres originates from the recorded observations of travellers. The only visual documentary record of an early Elizabethan public playhouse is the familiar sketch made by the Dutchman, Johannes de Witt. The recorded observations of tourists provide much more information about the theatres than any home-grown, native evidence: the Germans Samuel Kiechel, Thomas Platter, Paul Henzner; the wide-eyed Venetian Busino, who visited the Fortune in 1617; the French ambassador who took his wife to the Globe to see *Pericles* in 1607; the Spanish ambassador who went to the Fortune in 1621, and afterwards banqueted with the players; and a stream of titled dignitaries who patronised the playhouses, such as Prince Lewis Frederick of Württemberg, Prince Otto of Hesse-Cassel, Prince Lewis of Anhalt-Cöthen and Duke Philip Julius of Stettin-Pomerania.[21] Normally these eye-witness accounts have been used as objective documents of theatre history: but it is useful also to look *at* as well as *through* them, and consider the inbuilt distortions necessarily endemic to such testimonies.

There is more foreign than domestic evidence for simple reasons: foreign travellers noted what they saw because they found it remarkable; they recorded what they saw because they were educated, literate observers of an only partially-literate culture; and because as travellers they were keeping diaries and writing letters and dispatches to their families or employers back home. Native observers could not be expected to share this shock of confronting the striking and original; many, being illiterate, could hardly have written it down if they had; and many lettered native observers were prejudiced on moral or religious grounds against the theatre, and so produced accounts with an opposite bias to that of the enthralled foreign tourists. For the manifest disparity between foreign and native accounts lies in the preponderance among visiting observers of extravagant praise, rapturous wonder and enthralled excitement. Such native sources as there are differ remarkably in their strikingly phlegmatic matter-of-factness. John Stow's *Survey of London* mentions the existence of theatres in the city with deadpan impassivity: 'Of late time . . . hath been used comedies, tragedies, interludes, and histories, both true and feigned; for the acting whereof certain public places as the Theatre, the Curteine etc. have been created'.[22] Fynes Moryson in his *Itinerary* seems to wonder what all the fuss was about: he refers to certain 'peculiar theatres', drawing 'strange concourse of people', the latter 'being naturally more newe-fangled than the Athenians to heare newes and gaze upon every toye'.[23] It would be interesting to speculate to what extent the rapturous wonder of foreign tourists fuelled the characteristic rhetoric which later retrospectively reconstructed the Elizabethan 'Golden Age'.

It is very probable that the surviving evidence for the presence of foreign tourists within the audiences of Elizabethan public playhouses reflects a disproportionate emphasis, and that in practice they were numerically insignificant. It seems very likely that theatrical entrepreneurs would do what they could to inveigle foreign travellers to the theatres; and the plays often of course contained matters of international interest, and satirical portraits of other nationalities. But the early public playhouses presumably drew for their clientele primarily on a local metropolitan audience. None the less, an important consequence of the establishing from the 1570s of a centralised metropolitan theatrical profession occupying purpose-built theatres in or around London, was the provision of a specific cultural venue to which tourists might be drawn. As the theatre became incorporated, notwithstanding complex and pervasive conflicts of interest, into the new political and cultural hegemony of the metropolis, so the drama became a prestigious possession of the new national state; as Thomas Heywood testified: 'Playing is an ornament to the city, which strangers of all nations, repairing hither, report of in their countries, beholding them here with some admiration: for what variety of entertainment can there be in any city of Christendom, more than in London?'[24] The economic dependence of the RSC, at Stratford and the Barbican, on international tourism, began there: far from being victims of such commercial exploitation, Shakespeare's plays helped to bring it into being. Shakespeare belonged to a new class fraction of bourgeois entrepreneurs which shaped the drama as a privately-owned and State-subsidised cultural industry, and decisively effected the radical separation of theatre from the general texture of social life.[25] That class helped to establish a cultural pattern in which every spectator is encouraged to become a tourist: who may well undertake a lengthy journey to a metropolitan theatre, who is required to attend at the dramatic event with reverence and possibly some incomprehension – and who returns with a souvenir programme as a mnemonic preservation of a sacred experience.

Those 'national' theatres are still with us today: and any one familiar with their repertory will be aware to what extent they still trade in that same 'admiration' noted by Heywood; to what extent they still cater to the wide-eyed, open-mouthed 'wonder' exhibited by foreign and native visitor alike at displays of meretricious 'stage magic' and meaningless spectacle. The gullible appetite for 'miracles' of staging, lighting, music and theatrical effect derives ultimately from bardolatry. One is driven to sympathise with Mr Gradgrind, with his injunction 'never wonder': though 'wonder' is not perhaps incompatible with understanding, it can too easily be opposed against it: as a mode of contemplation it has too much in common with inert religious quiescence, and too little with alert and vigilant curiosity. It is, after all, one of the blessings which, according to our national church, great writers transmit to us from above: at the canonisation of D. H. Lawrence in Westminster Abbey, prayers were accordingly offered to 'God, whose spirit inspires artist, prophet, and sage, bestow thy blessing, we beseech thee, on those who speak to us for our beguilement, and provoke us to thought, to reflection and to wonder'.

The Shakespeare myth

This is the spiritual heart of the Shakespeare myth: and the institutions of bardolatry and quasi-religious worship are the structures holding that myth in place. Myth is not a non-existent fantasy or ideological conjuring-trick: it is a real and powerful form of human consciousness, holding some significant place within a culture. It is not possible to banish such a myth by appealing to provable facts, such as those of Shakespeare's biography, or the texts of the plays themselves: the myth itself also has to be subjected to analysis, its ideological content disclosed, and its hegemonic position challenged by the invoking of alternative perspectives.

It is often believed that only primitive societies have myths: but the figure of Shakespeare is actually very similar to the 'culture heroes' of anthropology: figures which may be legendary heroes, fabulised historical characters or mythological deities; but which exhibit, throughout the countless mythologies of world culture, certain common structural characteristics. Consider for example the legend which arose in the eighteenth century about Shakespeare's youthful poaching of deer in Sir Thomas Lucy's park: a crime which reputedly resulted in his fleeing to London. Those scholars who demonstrated that Sir Thomas Lucy had at the time neither park nor deer were missing the point: the historical details were merely narrative properties necessary for mythologising Shakespeare as a culture-hero, exhibiting the characteristic pattern of a misspent youth, and the confrontation with a persecutor who thrusts the youth into exile. But the most relevant structural pattern here is a problem of identity: a mystery about the hero's true parentage – he is never the person he appears to be. Folklore, fairly tales and romances abound in figures who are brought up by peasants, shepherds, servants; but whose true parents are kings and queens, aristocrats or gods. Who was Robin Hood – son of a Saxon yeoman, or of Robert, Earl of Huntingdon? Who was Jesus of Nazareth – son of a carpenter or offspring of God? Who was William Shakespeare – Francis Bacon or the Earl of Oxford? son of a provincial glover or a scion of the aristocracy or *haute bourgeoisie*?[26]

Ultimately it is this myth that explains the old quarrels about the true authorship of Shakespeare's plays. Shakespeare was the son of a Stratford small businessman: but England's greatest poet must surely have had a more exalted parentage. So he became Lord Bacon, the Earl of Oxford, Sir Walter Raleigh, Queen Elizabeth herself. These controversies still rumble on in the peripheries of the scholarly word: but the basic *mythos* recently surfaced at one of the centres of Shakespeare scholarship and criticism. The old myth-makers used to employ arcane cabbalistic ciphers to locate the initials of Bacon among Shakespeare's writings; the modern mythologist comes armed with the more formidable tools of computer programmes and statistical analysis.

In November 1985 Gary Taylor, joint editor with Stanley Wells of the prestigious *Oxford Shakespeare*, offered to the public interest a supposedly 'lost Shakespearean love poem': an untitled lyric discovered in a seventeenth-century anthology, and now familiarly known by its opening words, 'Shall I die?'. The poem is attributed to Shakespeare in the anthology, and Taylor believes the ascription to be reliable. Furthermore, he subjected the poem to computerised tests of vocabulary and syntax, which seemed to him conclusive proof of authorship. This 'discovery' was fed to the press and fêted with substantial media 'hype', and headlines of the 'How Gary discovered the Bard's lost poem' variety.[27] A battle of wits then ensued between those who agreed that Taylor was correct and those who didn't. The terms of the debate were scholarly: is the manuscript ascription to Shakespeare reliable, and are the language-checks trustworthy? – and critical: is the poem good enough to have been written by Shakespeare? The methods of scholarship were both defended and denounced, and the general critical opinion has been that the poem is so 'bad' that it must either have been written by someone else, or by Shakespeare in a spirit of parody.[28] As the wrath of the literary–critical establishment, incensed at the attribution to the Bard of a bad and boring poem, fell on him, Gary Taylor began to appear in the progressive light of a scholar displacing the grounds of textual inquiry from bardolatry to scientific method.

The whole debate has however been framed by the Shakespeare myth, because it has centred on only one question: did Shakespeare write the poem or not? The poem may or may not have been written by William Shakespeare: but a preoccupation with the validating qualities of authorial authority leads to the wrong questions being asked. If we were to approach the poem in terms of its genre and cultural function rather than with a hypothesis of individual authorship, it would be possible both to raise and answer a different set of questions: concerning the formulaic rather than individualistic methods of composing lyric poetry in the Renaissance, the dependence of certain kinds of poetry on the context of musical setting, the intertextuality of a poem's position within a personal manuscript anthology, and so forth.[29] In the kind of debate precipitated by 'Shall I die?' (and sustained by a revival of the claims of *Edmund Ironside*), the myth of Shakespeare as culture hero, as transcendent genius and omniscient seer, is continually reaffirmed.

The true content of that myth, which can be decoded from a long history of intellectual struggle around the problem of identity, is that the concept of individual authorship on which most Shakespeare criticism is based is a misleading way of addressing the work of an Elizabethan/ Jacobean dramatist; perhaps, following Foucault, a mythical concept in itself.[30] The theoretical problematic is analogous to the cultural pattern of the tourist industry: everything in Stratford must be definitively assigned to the personal possession of the Bard or it becomes worthless and irrelevant. The theatre must be 'Shakespeare's' theatre, an exhibition of Elizabethan England must be 'The World of Shakespeare'; and signs directing the traveller to 'The Birthplace' betray, by their striking anonymity, the monopolistic character of Shakespeare's authorship of Stratford.

Those scholars who speculated that Shakespeare might perhaps have been somebody else, or a group of authors, were asking the wrong questions; but they were at least grappling with a genuine problem. We cannot rely, when addressing the work of a Renaissance dramatist, on the apparent clarity and simplicity of a direct, controlling relationship between author and written text. These plays were made and mediated in the interaction of certain complex material conditions, of which the author was only one. When we deconstruct the Shakespeare myth what we discover is not a universal individual genius creating literary texts that remain a permanently valuable repository of human experience and wisdom; but a collaborative cultural process in which plays were made by writers, theatrical entrepreneurs, architects and craftsmen, actors and audience; a process in which the plays were constructed first as performance, and only subsequently given the formal permanence of print. As Terry Hawkes observes:

The notion of a single "authoritative" text, immediately expressive of the plenitude of its author's mind and meaning, would have been unfamiliar to Shakespeare, involved as he was in the collaborative enterprise of dramatic production, and notoriously unconcerned to preserve in stable form the texts of most of his plays. A project which seeks to award those texts the status of holy writ . . . [is] the product of a culture which characteristically invests a good deal of intellectual capital in concepts of individuality, personal ownership and responsibility, and maintains a high regard for the printed text as a personal unmediated statement, particularly in the form of "literature".[31]

It is still, however, worth using that £20 note to buy a railway ticket and to take what British Rail engagingly call (in a phrase equally suggestive of aristocratic affiliation and underworld dealings) 'the Shakespeare Connection' to the town of the Bard's birth, with this guide in hand: for

Stratford genuinely can, as F. J. Furnivall suggested in the quotation that heads this essay, help us to understand Shakespeare – though in a sense rather different from that he and many others have traditionally intended.

Notes

1 F. J. Furnivall, 'Introduction' to his edition: *Gervinus' Commentaries*, 1875; quoted in Louis Marder: *His Exits and his Entrances: the Story of Shakespeare's Reputation* (London: John Murray, 1963), p. 251.

2 See Ivor Brown and George Fearon, *Amazing Monument: a Short History of the Shakespeare Industry* (London: Heinemann, 1939), pp. 9–11.

3 See Brown and Fearon, *Amazing Monument*, p. 140; and below, pp. 21–2.

4 See Christian Deelman, *The Great Shakespeare Jubilee* (London: Michael Joseph, 1964), p. 34; and Brown and Fearon, *Amazing Monument*, p. 28.

5 Deelman, *Shakespeare Jubilee*, p. 15; Brown and Fearon, *Amazing Monument*, p. 28.

6 Deelman, *Shakespeare Jubilee*, pp. 34–5.

7 See Thomas Davies, *Memoirs of the Life of David Garrick* (London, 1781), 2, p. 218; Brown and Fearon, *Amazing Monument*, p. 57; and Marder, *Exits and Entrances*, pp. 235–6.

8 Robert Bell Wheler, *History and Antiquities of Stratford-upon-Avon* (Stratford, 1806), p. 138; Brown and Fearon, *Amazing Monument*, pp. 58–60; Marder, *Exits and Entrances*, pp. 236–7; and Martha Winburne England, *Garrick's Jubilee* (Bowling Green, Ohio: Ohio State University Press, 1964), p. 9.

9 Deelman, *Shakespeare Jubilee*, pp. 48–9.

10 Wheler, *Antiquities*, pp. 137–8.

11 Brown and Fearon, *Amazing Monument*, pp. 66–7.

12 *Ibid.*, p. 146.

13 William Smith, *A New and Complete History of the County of Warwick*, 1829; quoted in Brown, *Amazing Monument*, p. 149.

14 Washington Irving gives an unrivalled account of Widow Hornby in his essay 'Stratford-on-Avon'; Haskell Springer, ed., *Sketch Book*, in *The Complete Works of Washington Irving* (Boston: Twayne Publishers, 1978), pp. 210–11. See also Brown and Fearon, *Amazing Monument*, pp. 151–2; and Marder, *Exits and Entrances*, pp. 241–3.

15 See Deelman, *Shakespeare Jubilee*, p. 6.

16 Dr Levi Fox, *The Shakespearian Properties* (Stratford-upon-Avon: Shakespeare Birthplace Trust, 1981).

17 Wilfrid J. Osborne, *Anne Hathaway's Cottage* (Stratford-upon-Avon: Shakespeare Birthplace Trust, 1951), p. 4.

18 Roland Barthes, *Mythologies*, 1957, trans, Annette Lavers (London: Paladin, 1973), p. 76.

19 See Donald Horne, *The Great Museum: the Re-presentation of History* (London: Pluto Press, 1985).

20 See Susan Sontag, *On Photography*, 1977, (Harmondsworth: Penguin, 1979).

21 See E. K. Chambers, *The Elizabethan Stage* (Oxford: Oxford University Press, 1923), 2, pp. 367–9.

22 John Stow, *A Survey of London*; quoted in Chambers, *Elizabethan Stage*, 2, p. 263.

23 Fynes Moryson, *Itinerary 1617*; quoted in Andrew Gurr, *The Shakespearean Stage, 1574–1642*, 2nd edition (Cambridge: Cambridge University Press, 1980), p. 10.

24 Thomas Heywood, *An Apology for Actors*, (London, 1612), sig. F3.

25 See Graham Holderness, *Shakespeare's History*, (Dublin: Gill and Macmillan, 1985), pp. 158–60. Cook's 'privileged playgoer' thesis, notwithstanding its one-sided distortion of the evidence, obviously has implications for this argument: see Ann Jennalie Cook, *The*

Privileged Playgoers of Shakespeare's London (Princeton, N.J.: Princeton University Press, 1981); and for a corrective critique, Martin Butler, Theatre and Crisis (Cambridge: Cambridge University Press, 1984), pp. 293–306.

26 See Alfred Harbage, 'Shakespeare as culture hero', Aspects of Shakespeare (Oxford: Oxford University Press, 1966).

27 See, e.g., The Sunday Times (24 November 1985).

28 See for example correspondence in the Times Literary Supplement (24 and 31 January 1986).

29 See Erica Sheene and Jeremy Maule, 'Shall I Die?', Times Literary Supplement (17 January 1986).

30 Michel Foucault, Language, Counter-memory, Practice, (Oxford: Blackwell, 1977), p. 124.

31 Terence Hawkes: That Shakespeherian Rag (London: Methuen, 1986), pp. 75–6.

I am grateful for the advice, enthusiasm and support of John Drakakis, Jonathan Dollimore, Terry Hawkes, Russell Jackson and Alan Sinfield.

Sam Wanamaker
interviewed by Graham Holderness

(This interview was conducted in January 1986, before the out-of-court settlement of the dispute between The Globe Trust and Southwark Council discussed in the subsequent essay.)

Could you first give a brief history of The Globe reconstruction project?
The project began about 1970 with the concept of rebuilding The Globe on or close to its original site. From the incorporation of that first charitable trust it took something like two or three years to convince the existing Southwark local council that this was a good idea. They agreed in principle to the scheme, and suggested that the only way in which it could be done was through some joint arrangement between the Trust, a private developer and the council. The developers themselves had considered the possibility of the Globe, but did not want to be involved with a charity: they wanted to control it themselves on a purely commercial basis. The council had been in discussion with the owners of adjacent land who were seeking commercial redevelopment of their site for offices; they came to an agreement with the property developers to pool land for the Globe. Planning permission for offices was conditional on this arrangement; and we succeeded in pushing the offices back from the river-front to give the Globe the prime position. Agreements were signed after a year of negotiations, just before the local elections.

Meanwhile fund-raising had proceeded in America; academics and others interested in the project, from Britain, North America and other parts of the world, became involved to advise on the reconstruction of the Globe; international conferences were held, and a brief given to an architect by scholars and academics who volunteered their time and participation. The basic idea was to make a faithful reconstruction based on specialist research in the Renaissance theatre.

At the elections a new left-wing council overthrew the old guard labour establishment. A minority political group, which had been opposed to the Globe project on the grounds that it was élitist, touristic and irrelevant to local needs, thus became the majority. They wanted the site designated for public housing, and openly declared their intent to break the previous council's agreement with The Globe Trust. They were able to discover a small paragraph in the original terms which could be used as a justification for breaking the agreement: we were advised that the council were acting illegally, and resolved to sue them in a court action scheduled for hearing in mid-June (1986).

Which aspects of the project then were particularly offensive to the new local council?

The office development. Part of the hostility created against our project was that we were seen as part of a speculative, exploitative development of the land for private profit. Unfortunately the previous council had indicated that the only means of building the Globe was to enter into such a joint scheme: which would enable the property development company to make a 'community-benefit' contribution in the form of giving away some of their land to a charitable institution. We ourselves were very much opposed to the offices and I was actually seen as the enemy of the developers, since I wanted the prime site for the Globe. This was the main target of their attack, apart from personal hostility to myself as an American actor, an alien uninterested in the local people and unlikely to benefit them.

You are suggesting that prospects for building housing on the site are poor. Many people have the idea that the dispute between the Globe and Southwark council is a conflict between 'high culture' and housing needs.

In the North Southwark Development Plan (which has not been approved by government, and against which there are many local objections) the council have designated that land for housing and open space, although we have perfectly valid planning permission. The left take no account of the costs, and propose simply to pass them over to the government. Their only concern is to win acceptance for their view of the site's most beneficial function – and on that I have a very strong difference of opinion with them. We agree that there should be housing close by: but to take the prime sites that have national and international significance and value – when housing could be built elsewhere – is the destruction of cultural and social values, and of a potential public amenity accessible to all. If you build council houses on the river front you are effectively preventing other people from taking advantage of a national (or London) amenity.

If we could turn now to the specific relationship between the Globe and the local community: could you say in detail how you think the people of Southwark would benefit from the scheme?

My own background is, as you know, working-class, and my political convictions left; in all my professional life I've tried to do things which would have a direct relationship with 'the people', based on the premise that theatre can be a great force for social change. In America I was involved with the politicised theatre, which during the war dealt with fascism, nazism, racism, all the social problems of the time. My first steps in Southwark were to seek out local community organisations: I found only one, run by a chaplain from Southwark Cathedral, composed mainly of local business people. I also approached the council's planning department and local firms to solicit advice and co-operation. Some of these interests joined our advisory group to discuss the general development of the area. We were seeking the kind of community participation that would keep us informed of and sensitive to local needs. When we started in 1972 with an open-air season of plays sponsored by John Player, we incorporated into the programme activities directly for local people – childrens' events, lunch-time theatre for office-workers, an open-air pub to which people could bring their children, firework displays, an itinerant theatre group that performed in the squares of local council flats. We had a local community committee, we always saw ourselves as having two faces: one looking north, across the river to the wider world beyond; the other facing south to the locality, and to the people of Southwark and the other south London boroughs. We never abandoned the belief that we were local, national and international in character.

There appear to be several different motives underlying this reconstruction. There is a scholarly and academic ambition to re-establish as accurately as possible the physical conditions which produced Elizabethan drama. There is a theatrical practitioner's interest in a replica Renaissance theatre usable for dramatic experimentation. There is an educationalist's wish to provide a demonstrative model of a Renaissance institution for pedagogic purposes. There is an antiquarian concern to develop a museum of the Elizabethan/Jacobean stage. Lastly, there is the proposition to inaugurate a new tourist centre, a kind of out-post (or rather in-post) of Stratford, competing directly with the London tourist industry, acting – in the words of your newsletter The Southwark Globe – as 'a Mecca for the millions of Shakespeare lovers from all over the world'. Now the putative site of the original theatre is hardly a necessary adjunct to any of these save the latter. Isn't it the case that it is really the tourist centre that represents a commercially viable and potentially profitable enterprise? And while the phoney religion of the tourist industry may be economically necessary, won't it be culturally and perhaps politically damaging to the project's other aspirations?

The economic crisis through which Britain has been passing since the war has been a crisis more severe than that experienced by other nations such as Germany and Japan, and has also been affected by the terrible transition from an imperialist power to a second- or third-rate nation. These economic and political changes have had far-reaching cultural consequences: among them a growing awareness that public funding for educational or cultural or artistic projects is likely to be increasingly restricted or denied. We recognised at once that this project could not depend on public funding and would have to rely on private contributions towards an educational and charitable purpose. Furthermore, other comparable institutions like the Metropolitan Museum in New York or the museums in this country hope to attract great numbers of people to spread awareness and further the purposes of the institution. Some of these institutions are also institutions of education, research and training: for example the British Museum or the Folger Shakespeare Library are great research centres, but they experience no incompatibility with these functions in attracting millions of visitors and tourists every year. Many institutions incorporate different purposes, scholarly and popular, which are not incompatible but rather cross-fertilising. Stratford-upon-Avon, through the Shakespeare Birthplace Trust, combines an academic organisation with a touristic one. We see no contradiction there whatsoever: the tourists will help to support the project and protect it from dependence on public funds (an anxiety of the local authority); and without State subsidy what other means is there? We don't believe that popular entertainment and scholarly research are at all incompatible.

You grew up in an extremely internationalist community, the child of Jewish Ukrainian immigrant workers in Chicago; and have lived an international life since leaving America. Do you believe that the Globe will represent a genuine ground of international solidarity and friendship? To what extent is tourism itself likely to accomplish this?

I certainly do. What is common about the peoples of the world is a common culture, whether of language, history or religion; certainly in music, painting, sculpture, drama, common elements are expressed. The genius of great literary figures (among which Shakespeare must stand very high, if not pre-eminent) consists in their ability to express the human condition in a form recognisable to all people. The fact of Shakespeare's plays being translated into some 95 languages indicates his significance for many disparate peoples. If we are looking for forces to bring people together whatever their language, social status, culture, educational level; and if we seek within English culture a fitting representative figure manifesting the language and people, where else would we look but to Shakespeare and a few other great writers? Whoever

studies Shakespeare is coming to an understanding of English language
and English culture. You may say that the peasant in the field isn't
studying Shakespeare: but given the opportunity of some confrontation
with and experience of Shakespeare, he would identify himself with the
human aspects with which Shakespeare deals. I feel very strongly – and
I'm saying nothing original here – that culture and art are primary means
of drawing people together, into mutual understanding and the transgression of barriers. It was this aspect of the project that intrigued me in
the first instance, and which I recognised had to be international in spirit
and scope. Many thousands of foreign students have come here to this
site because of Shakespeare and the Globe theatre; and we have the only
facility in the area capable of instructing them about the site and its
significance in the history of dramatic literature. And it was on that basis
that I was able to convince certain distinguished and influential people
internationally to support the project; which in turn earned us respectability and some of the money necessary to build the Globe.

*A lot of cultural workers on the left would argue that this view of Shakespeare as
representative of a universal human nature is inevitably conservative in its ideological
effects. Do you think working with Shakespeare can have the opposite effect, of making
people politically conscious?*

One of the things that we as an organisation have from the beginning
insisted on is the necessity of making Shakespeare accessible to those
so-called 'peasants in the field'. Here in Southwark Shakespeare is part of
the popular heritage; yet many people don't know about that heritage.
Without a sense of the past and pride of origin people lose dignity and
self-respect. They point to certain local heroes – Michael Caine and
Tommy Steele from Bermondsey for example; actors or footballers are
regarded with proprietary pride by the people of these localities. But
much experimental work is required to make Shakespeare accessible.
Joe Papp in New York did Shakespeare with black or Puerto Rican actors
in order to link culture directly with the social problems of those ethnic
or racial groups, reaching out to unlock opportunities previously denied.
Why should Shakespeare be available only to the educated? Why
should that door remain closed? The value of Shakespeare to the
contemporary struggle for social improvement is that his work has a
great potentiality for contributing to that struggle.

*You describe the popular–cultural phenomenon of the 'local hero': but isn't this a
process whereby individuals are respected to the degree that they escape their class and
community? Should we still be thinking of Shakespeare as an individual genius – a figure
which in some ways reinforces the individualism of bourgeois culture; or rather thinking of*

the collective achievements of Renaissance popular culture? And shouldn't the Globe be sustaining those democratic traditions rather than reverencing the individual genius?

Tyrone Guthrie (and before him William Poel) long ago recognised the extent to which Shakespeare had been corrupted by the presentation of his plays: and experiments were made in the use of a simpler theatrical form, the open thrust stage for which the plays were originally written. Theatre architecture changed considerably – especially from 1945 – to break away from the artificility of the proscenium arch. The theatre at Stratford was built as a conventional proscenium-arch theatre: but ever since its inception in 1930 attempts have been made to alter and modify the stage and return it to a 'Globe-type' theatrical space. The early theatre with its open stage, and before it the platform in the inn-yard or the booth-stage in the street, offered an accessible event available to all: a show like the circus or other forms of popular street-entertainment. We have lost the popular public theatre through these changes in theatrical architecture. The closed space of the new theatre became the prerogative of the bourgeoisie, who in the older theatres (despite seat-price differentials, which are still there in the football-stadium or the bull-ring) shared the same space with the common people. The Globe will make the theatre (not only Shakespeare) once again popular, public and accessible: the working-class man will feel less constrained and inhibited there than in the plush, enclosed space of a bourgeois theatre.

Your first encounter with Shakespeare was in a replica Elizabethan theatre, part of a mock 'English village' constructed for the Chicago World Fair. That same replica was subsequently dismantled and transferred to Dallas, Texas, where it was re-erected for a similar event in 1936. The 'theatre' was inaugurated by a ceremony of libation in which Stratford earth and water from the Avon were sprinkled reverently across the stage. To what extent was your initial encounter with Shakespeare more a matter of American bardolotry than of Renaissance popular theatre? What is your own opinion of the quasi-religious aspects of the Shakespeare myth?

My encounter with the Chicago reconstruction was in fact at a time when I was most conscious of my working-class culture: my father was unemployed because of a strike, consequent on his attempts to build a union, and my first experience of Shakespeare was in that context. The experience produced no contradiction, and was not at all bardolotrous; I knew nothing of any ceremony of consecration! I had no interest in Shakespeare, but inherited a taste for the theatre from my father who used to take me to the Yiddish Theatre. I went to the Worlds' Fair: and found there a free spectacle – English morris-dancing and Queen Elizabeth and her courtiers. From there one entered the theatre. I have no

interest in the bardolatry: the quasi-religious ceremony and reverential
verbiage seem to me ludicrous. The source-material itself is so incredibly
rich that people are still mining it, still digging and discovering. I find
myself continually searching and lighting upon wonderful jewels
embedded in the source-material, which is of such richness that constant
recourse and return lead to fresh and marvellous discoveries as you
yourself grow in perception and understanding. And of course the
Globes that were reconstructed in American bore no resemblance to the
real thing! I think it's possible to separate the true value of the material
itself from the nonsense that surrounds it.

But if one considers Stratford-upon-Avon, it's evident that an established respect for
what you call the 'material', evidenced in the work of the RSC and in the Shakespeare
Centre as a research institute, co-exists with the staple currency of the tourist industry
which trades in bardolatry. One feature of that business is a strategy for confusing
Shakespeare with the royal family: images of the past juxtapose the dramatist with Queen
Elizabeth, while in the souvenir shops dolls of Shakespeare and Henry VIII stand beside
Prince Charles and Princess Diana. Idealised images of the British past are thus purveyed
through these objects to the foreign visitor and the native tourist. All this is surely a far cry
from the revival of popular theatre?

In the case of Stratford the commercial aspects are very clear: the
whole town is dedicated to making profit out of Shakespeare and anything that can be attached to him. It's not to be denied that we will also
have a shop: but this factor can be controlled. The Metropolitan Museum
produces comparable artefacts, and part of their income depends on
selling them. The Folger Library, the National Theatre, the RSC all have
their shops. But it is possible to incorporate this activity into your policy
with integrity and honesty. Spin-off interests supply a demand as well as
raise a revenue: people who go to see a play want to buy the text. In my
view there is nothing wrong with this exchange provided what you buy is
not cheapening or reductive but educative. A Shakespeare colouring
book can be educative: can develop a child's experience and memory of
a play, deepening appreciation, opening doors and broadening
horizons.

Some sociologists of tourism have seen an analogy between the medieval custom of
pilgrimage to a sacred site, from which you would acquire a relic; and the modern practice
of tourism, visiting one of the 'Meccas' of a particular national culture and returning with
a souvenir. Would you say that was a far-fetched comparison?

Not necessarily. Anyone who visits another place is a tourist: why
denigrate that? To visit a place or site for its historical associations is to
acquire an experience. To visit the ruins of an important historical centre

is to acquire an experience. To visit a replica or reconstruction is not quite the same, yet such places can acquire the patina of the original. St Paul's Cathedral is a reconstruction; Southwark Cathedral a nineteenth-century building incorporating a few blocks of stone from the original. The new stones acquired the patina of what they'd replaced: and a reconstructed Globe, genuinely and carefully researched, and constructed with fidelity to the known facts, will absorb the spirit of the original theatre. People who come to it – whether in superficial curiosity, reverential love or deep appreciation – will experience something of the past. If they take an object away with them – a photograph, a model, a figure – it will serve as a link with the experience, and act as an enrichment. There's nothing wrong with that.

Theatre, ideology, and institution: Shakespeare and the roadsweepers
John Drakakis

The dumb go down in history and disappear
and not one gentleman's been brought to book:
Mes den hep tavas a-gollas y dyr
(Cornish) —
'the tongueless man gets his land took.'[1]

Regular listeners to that relic of English bourgeois colonialism, *Desert Island Discs*, will have noticed that in addition to inflicting upon an exotically constructed geographical 'other' an array of musical items, the guest 'castaway', who is always a post-industrial descendant of Defoe's Robinson Crusoe, is allowed two essential books: the Bible and *The Complete Works of Shakespeare*. Machiavelli would, almost certainly, have understood the ideological connection between these two essential instruments of colonisation, as indeed would Fulke Greville, when he observed in his *A Treatise of Monarchy* (c. 1600), that 'Religion' was the means whereby "the Sceptre gains / More of the world, and greater reverence breeds – in Foreigners, and homeborn subjects too / Then much expense of blood or wealth can do".[2] Had Althusser's phrase 'ideological State apparatus' been available to Greville in 1600, he may well have been tempted to deploy it: since he goes on in this long poem to offer a disturbing Elizabethan analogue to the more familiar modern notion of the construction of human subjectivity, whereby each individual is both accorded an identity, while at the same time remaining 'subjected' to a higher authority:

Religion's fair name by insinuation
Secretly seizeth all powers of the mind,
In understanding raiseth admiration,
Worship in will, which native sweet links bind

> The soul of man, and having got possession,
> Give powerful will and ordinate progression.[3]

Desert Island Discs attributes to Shakespearean influence, through the telling juxtaposition of the Bible with *The Complete Works of Shakespeare*, what Fulke Greville attributes axiomatically to 'religion' and to its political potential. This tacit acknowledgement of Shakespeare as universal, transcendent, and eternal confers upon a quintessentially English writer – whose 'works' are regarded as a miraculous contingency of his being and detached supreme consciousness – a divine status. Shakespeare, removed thus from human history, becomes for us the 'Absolute Subject' whose all-embracing 'Word' takes its place alongside the Bible as our guarantee of civilisation and humanity, breeding reverence 'In Foreigners, and homeborn subjects too'; that which remains as evidence of his historical existence becomes, in this quasi-religious context, the object of tourist pilgrimages. The deification of the man Shakespeare proceeds hand-in-hand with the valorisation of 'culture', thus masking the ideological practice of production and re-production of Shakespearean texts as agencies of authority and subjection. That a popular radio programme should represent that process in terms of timeless pleasure indicates nothing less than the power of ideology to efface contradiction. In this respect what cultural and political force Fulke Greville attached to 'religion', may, with equal conviction be attached to the Shakespeare canon as we have come to 'know' it through particular forms of cultural representation:

> Forming in conscience lines of equity,
> To temper laws, and without force infuse
> A homeborn practice of civility,
> Current with that which all the world doth use,
> Whereby divided kingdoms may unite,
> If not in truth, at least in outward rite.[4]

Of course, the imposition of cultural and political values may not necessarily result in religion's being entirely successful in *secretly* seizing 'all powers of the mind', and thus internalising them. The 'insinuation' of religion forces a tension between what Greville calls 'truth' and what he defines as 'outward rite' which itself becomes the site of struggle for meaning and political control. In a brilliantly succinct manner he locates here the site of what we have come to know as 'the imaginery': the place within the process of signification itself where ideology is at work constructing human subjects who internalise the values of the dominant social order, and constantly patrolling the boundaries of meaning. It is, significantly, the space occupied by 'mythology', which works to efface the traces of its own determinate historical production.

There is still a resistance to viewing Shakespearean texts as sites of struggle, and as repositories of ideology, at both synchronic and diachronic levels of analysis. Yet such recent events as the televising of 'The Complete Works of William Shakespeare' – the result of a partnership between the BBC and the appropriately named Time-Life TV company, and hence the result of an amalgamation of resource 'from the very highest levels of economic and cultural power'[5] – demand to be read 'against the grain' (to use Walter Benjamin's phrase) as the coded lament of a moribund Tillyardism. Indeed, Benjamin's strategy of viewing what he calls 'cultural treasures' with 'cautious detachment', is directly related to his perception of their deep implication in political process; he argues, 'Whoever has emerged victorious participates to this day in the triumphal procession in which the present rulers step over those who are lying prostrate. According to traditional practice, the spoils are carried along in the procession'. The reading of such cultural artifacts 'against the grain' thus represents an attempt to recover the historical conditions of their production and reproduction.[6] In the case of Tillyard this process is obscured by the inadvertent conflation of the critic's own motivation and the determinate history with which he seeks to engage. Even though we can now read with deep suspicion the final sentence of Tillyard's *The Elizabethan World Picture*, which places a desirable 'Elizabethan habit of mind' against the activities of 'our scientifically-minded intellectuals' who have 'helped not a little to bring the world into its present conflicts and distresses',[7] we have still to contend with the manufacture and periodic mobilisation of a reactionary populism – usually in support of royal weddings and foreign quarrels – which, even at this relatively urbane level, works to obscure historical difference within these texts. Indeed, it would not be an exaggeration in any sense to situate Shakespearean texts at the centre of a 'culture industry': 'obedient', as Adorno and Horkheimer observe in relation to the general category, 'to the social hierarchy', deeply implicated in 'that process of cataloguing and classification' which brings culture 'within the sphere of administration'.[8] As in the case of the BBC Shakespeare (and, more obliquely, *Desert Island Discs*), the growing affinity of 'business' and cultural pleasure, or to use Adorno and Horkheimer's term, 'amusement', accords a specific political significance to the latter sphere of activity, which is 'to defend society'.[9] Viewed within this context, Tillyard's

'Elizabethan habit of mind' is an evaluative rather than a neutrally descriptive phrase, a political judgement representing itself as an historico-aesthetic response, which signals the desire to return to an already romanticised pre-technological past. Here determinate material 'histories' are crudely conflated into History, before being collapsed into that most unhistorical of categories, 'life'.

Many of these issues have recently received an unexpected apotheosis, a surprising drawing together of ideology and institution, in the activities of 'The Shakespeare Globe Trust', brainchild of the actor and director Sam Wanamaker. Here Shakespeare and pyramid selling, 'culture', capitalist enterprise and bureaucracy have converged on what has become literally a 'site of struggle': the Greenmore Wharf site, a derelict parcel of land on the south bank of the Thames in Southwark, near the place where the first Globe theatre is conjectured to have stood.

In a recent High Court judgement, the culmination of a legal wrangle which began in 1982 when a more radical Labour group gained control of Southwark Borough Council, Mr Justice Harman ordered that the site should be leased to The Shakespeare Globe Trust for a period of 125 years at a peppercorn rent; and in an out-of-court settlement the Council agreed to pay Derno Freshwater Estates – the developer involved in the original plan to erect an office-block near the theatre – a sum of £7.2 million in compensation. This recent judgement, the outcome of what appears on the surface to have been a struggle between a self-appointed custodian of 'high culture' (allied with a property developer interested primarily in the commercial potential of the scheme) and a democratically-elected local authority, has signalled the renewal of a fund-raising initiative to secure the £12 million estimated to be the current cost of rebuilding the Globe Theatre. To some extent, the problem appears to be one of attempting to align a cherished dream of providing a monument and a cultural amenity, with a concern which is more unashamedly commercial in its objectives: requiring as it does both the resources of capital and the intellectual approval of an international academic community. The difficulty arises directly from the fact that both sides of the argument are deeply implicated in those very social and economic structures from which they would naively wish to free themselves. If the Southwark Borough Council's desire to designate a prime building site for the purpose of low-cost housing is utopian in its wish to regenerate a local community, then the combined interests of Sam Wanamaker and Derno Estates is far from innocent: as representatives of the alliance of capital and culture, the latter already own part of the site of the current Shakespeare Globe Centre, and would have stood to gain much more under the original agreement by the acquisition of the Greenmore Wharf site.

One important ingredient in the conflict has been the insistence by The Shakespeare Globe Trust that the project is in receipt of a broad-based popular support. Within the larger context of the turbulent politics of the Southwark–Bermondsey constituency over the past few years, such a claim may be read as an enabling strategy rather than as the transparent articulation of genuine grass-roots feeling. Indeed, The Shakespeare Globe Trust's desire to project a 'local image' – involving a certain packaging of Shakespeare as Southwark's 'most famous resident' – has its origins in the political imperative to construct a popular consensus which can then be opportunistically exploited. With the formation of urbane pressure groups, such as The Friends of The Southwark Globe, that process of constructing consensus becomes more amenable to analysis, and to a reading against the grain. Launched as a popular movement in June 1985, within months its impressive list of dignatories were already reported to have proved 'a real asset'; although from the shrill nature of the appeal for more members – 'the more the merrier. If more people join, we can arrange more events'[11] – it is possible to conclude that a truly demotic support was less than forthcoming. Indeed, while academic advisers were talking openly in the months leading up to the formation of The Friends of the commercial aspects of the project as the property developer's 'pay-off', there was also nervous talk of 'stepping-stone' strategies which, as late as September 1985 and beyond, could regard local grass-roots support as a convenient variable in the equation. In this context the formation of The Friends of The Southwark Globe could be seen in structural terms as a strategic neces-sity, designed to supply, should occasion require, a 'popular' base on whose behalf it could then speak. In November 1985 there was still some concern over the lack of local support for the project, a factor emphasised by the crude journalistic exaggerations of the International Globe Centre's publication, *Southwark Globe*, which could argue that 'Support within Southwark is mounting. Support from the rest of London and the UK is mounting. The support from the rest of the world is strong – from as far afield as Russia and South America, from Tokyo to Berlin. And the United States has always been a centre of strong support – both financial and moral.'[12]

Such populist rhetoric is of a piece with an earlier, more sophisticated 'academic' document entitled 'Shakespeare Globe Centre: Planning Prospect', which had been prepared by Professor Philip Brockbank in July 1983 and ratified at an International Conference held at Northwestern University in Illinois in June 1984. Here the practical justification for what is otherwise a respectable, if eccentric, archaeological project is its tourist appeal, expressed in this document in terms of a surprising sentimentalisation of the area's historical significance:

While the Globe Centre will concentrate on its Shakespearean aims, it is to be expected that considerable tourist interest will be excited. The new theatre will contribute much towards making the riverside from Waterloo to Southwark attractive enough to draw Londoners and tourists to the area. It will be an important magnet for both the purposeful and casual visitors, and will help the area to recover some of the importance as a centre of popular civilization that it had in Shakespeare's time.

Much depends, in Brockbank's account, upon the meaning accorded to the problematical phrase 'popular civilization'. The term can be considered (and its difficulties multiplied) in connection with the curiously distorted, but so far unrefuted, view of Elizabethan audiences propounded by Alfred Harbage in his book *Shakespeare's Audience*.[13] In Brockbank's account, the silent transformation of the customary (and often denigratory) phrase 'popular culture' into the more subtle, but deeply contradictory 'popular civilization', is effected as a rhetorical ploy designed to secure, literally from the people, an area which belongs in large part to them. The tacit assumption is that 'popular civilization' is a transportable essence, which the present inhabitants of Southwark *can be taught* to recognise and acknowledge at a price. The benevolently paternalistic plan to allow access to the facilities at reduced rates for local inhabitants seriously risks attracting the allegation that Shakespeare, like other commodified examples of expropriated cultural production will, in Adorno and Horkheimer's words, be made 'accessible for public enjoyment as a park'.[14] Thus, the misrecognition of the Globe Project as the re-appropriation of an essential 'popular civilization' through a commercial re-constitution of the genius of 'Shakespeare', is to do little more than exchange one set of myths for another: a well-meaning, but misguided attempt to reclaim a once vibrant and deeply contradictory art, which was the product of a particular historical conjuncture, for an age of mechanical reproduction. In short, such naive and extravagant claims to historical authenticity are firmly inscribed within the bounds of an ideological practice which justifies political power by according to the unconsciously mediated products of 'popular civilization' a use-value within the framework of an existing hierarchy of social relations.

This protracted process – involving campaigning, persuasion, the lobbying of influential dignatories (it is reported that the Trust's patron, the Duke of Edinburgh, has laid aside an oak in Windsor Great Park 'for a foundation post'),[15] and final recourse to that most potent of ideological State apparatuses, the law – offers an unusually comprehensive gloss on Fulke Greville's perception of how 'civility' may be 'infused' rather than enforced, the subtle means whereby 'divided kingdoms may unite / If not in truth, at least in outward rite'.

At stake here, in a more general sense, is the control of the production of meaning through the public representation of the central issues involved. It is possible to detect in broad outline the dispositions of political power and cultural authority, as opponents of The Shakespeare Globe Trust's proposals are persistently re-inscribed within the margins of the debate. In this way the resistance of the borough council, and the North Southwark Community Development Group, characterised as 'hard left', can be represented as the unwelcome politicisation of a non-political issue.[16] Strategically speaking, this move effectively pre-empts the examination of larger, more complex issues of funding, which would inevitably raise profound questions concerning public (and, indeed, private) subsidy of the arts, and their relevance or validity in what is generally regarded as the third poorest local authority in England. Set against the carefully contextualised obstructiveness of a borough council characterised as a destructive clone of the GLC, The Shakespeare Globe Trust can emerge as a group of disinterested public benefactors, forced to re-constitute their harmless ambitions in terms of an unfamiliar political rhetoric of 'increased employment opportunities', 'educational and recreational facilities', and 'a significant re-vitalization of the neighbourhood'.

In the week preceding Mr Justice Harman's judgment, Christine Toomey entitled her article in The Sunday Times 'Enter Stage Left: the 12 roadsweepers who won't make way for the Globe'.[17] Here an elision of human and political interest was accepted as axiomatic, in such a way as to insinuate an opposition between 'popular culture' (an obstructive, 'leftist' category of human behaviour) and 'popular civilization' of which the Globe is offered as the pre-eminent, if appropriately absent, example. The suitably apostolic number twelve, reduced from the seventeen which had appeared in Lynda Murdin's earlier report in The Standard,[18] were given by Toomey a local habitation and a name; and their spokesman, Charlie Cox, was reported in The Sunday Times' best demotic English to 'reckon' that 'the row is much ado about nothing', and that 'If Shakespeare moves in 'ere, I'm moving out'. In line with earlier, simplified media accounts, the issue was reduced to two alternatives: either the Globe, or 'a roadsweepers' depot', with the leader of the equally obstructive Southwark Council – who, like the roadsweepers, made his entry 'stage left' – reportedly dismissing Shakespeare as 'a lot of tosh', and denying History altogether: 'I have always thought that history was over-rated'. Despite such 'authentic' local additions, the media representations of this conflict can be arranged formally into a distinct genealogy, with each account regurgitating in large part the details and distortions of its predecessors.

Thus far, two possible explanations of the motives of The Shakespeare Globe Trust present themselves. The first, with which Wanamaker, with a background in radical theatre, is known to have some sympathy, is that notwithstanding the deference accorded to dignatories and academic 'authority', at heart the project represents an attempt to expropriate 'Shakespeare' from those very structures of Capital which transform 'culture' into 'profit'. Such a view pre-supposes that the Globe Theatre in its original incarnation was an institution whose values and practices accord directly with a universal democratic instinct which the inhabitants of Southwark are now required to re-learn. A second, less charitable explanation would view the Southwark community as the largely indifferent victim of a cultural hegemony consisting of a power élite supported by an influential right-wing press, whose combined strategy is 'to bring culture within the sphere of administration', thus replacing any respect which it might have commanded, 'by a shallow cult of leading personalities.'[19] In this case 'Shakespeare' functions as the absent member of the array of dignatories who constitute the formal membership of The Shakespeare Globe Trust.

Nor is 'religion' – that force which Fulke Greville observed, 'Secretly seizeth all powers of the mind' – very far away, as the project's 'author' (a term used in its Foucauldian sense in this context), and Shakespeare's fellow 'resident' in Southwark, Sam Wanamaker, made clear in a television programme entitled 'This Wooden O'.[20] For him, one of the primary attractions of the site, and one to which the camera returned lingeringly, was 'The magnificent view of St Paul's Cathedral across the river'. Clearly, in the political unconscious of The Shakespeare Globe Trust, cathedral and theatre function in deep collusion with each other. What unites them is nothing less than the capitalist ethic itself, as

evidenced in the figure of one Adam Osborne, successful emigré businessman and 'fellow sharer' in the Globe Project. In that portion of 'This
Wooden O' which recorded Wanamaker's fund-raising activities in the
United States, Osborne was questioned about the history and cost of his
involvement; he confided: 'I was sold by Sam and now I'm busy trying to
sell other people on the same thing.' A sentimental nationalism – 'I did
grow up as a boy in England, I came over here and did remarkably well
for myself, and I think it's the least I can do' – was brought directly into
alignment with its artistic apotheosis, to provide a compelling motivation: 'It's not just another theatre. It is Shakespeare.'

More revealing is the instance of Harry Helmsley, a multi-millionaire
property magnate ('Everybody is Harry's tenant'), and his wife Leona,
whose joint justification for involvement in the project combined patrio-
tism, cultural imperialism, and universal capitalism, all of which were
openly proferred as knowing no geographical boundaries:

Helmsley: You give the right project and there's no problem about any money.
Interviewer: In spite of the fact that this will end up in England?
Helmsley: It's the same thing.
Leona Helmsley: It's got to be both. It's got to be England, they did say, and America,
    because I love America . . .[21]

The urbane English equivalent of this combination of visceral imperialism and exportable nationalism, is to be found in the comment of Theo
Crosbie, the project's architect, one of whose interests lies, appropriately
enough, in the restoration of church buildings, who described the enterprise as 'Sam's dream of recreating the South Bank in some sort of
civilized form'.

This curious mythologising of Southwark, both in its American and its
English manifestations, serves to emphasise that this site itself admits of
conflicting, not to say contradictory, textualisations: all of which are fully
revealed in the naive articulations of a 'culture industry' which misrecognises itself as combining, as desirable motivations, philanthropy and
'civilization'; but which functions as a multi-national corporation. Moreover, that the view from the Greenmore Wharf site of St Paul's has
something more to recommend it than simple architectural interest is
emphasised by the decision to dedicate it: 'In the name of God, the
creator of all life, we dedicate this site and commemorative sign in
thankful memory for the life and work of William Shakespeare'. Thus, in
a spiritual sense St Paul's is brought to Southwark, with missionary zeal,
in a gesture designed to dispel the detritus of an industrial society, and to

elevate to the realm of mystification what is basically a paternalist, aristocratic politics. That this strategy of de-materialisation can co-exist with the feeling of satisfaction that the support of 'right people' has been secured – 'I think we are now beginning to have the right people in support of the project; and what I mean by 'right people' are the people who represent the Establishment, the power structures in this country and America'[22] – offers a momentary glimpse of the operation of an ideological practice, confident of its own power, in which the myth of 'Shakespeare' is deeply imbricated. The deep structure of these seemingly spontaneous strands of what advertises itself as a naively empirical process, stands revealed in Wanamaker's own thinking as elements in the operation of a hegemony. His brilliantly opportunistic courting of the American financial aristocracy is appropriately effected through the resuscitation of the most regal of Renaissance dramatic forms, the court masque: the means whereby monarchical authority could participate directly in the representation of its own power: 'I wanted to go back to the old masque idea where royalty and the aristocracy of the sixteenth and seventeenth centuries used to put on performances, charades, or masques, and they did it for their own entertainment.'[23] Thus ever does 'popular civilization' disclose the conditions of its existence within the dispositions of power.

Given such statements of intention and strategy, it is more than a little surprising to find that the defence to which supporters of the Globe project consistently return is that they are 'giving Shakespeare back to the people'. The assumption upon which this, at best, naively a-historical assertion is based is that there is an essential 'Shakespeare' which the recreation of a version of the original conditions of performance will somehow naturally release. Aside from the allegedly terse comments of the spokesperson for the roadsweepers whom Shakespeare will displace, the only local voices to have been heard have been those of the North Southwark Community Development Group. Their appearance in the proceedings reported in 'This Wooden O' was brief: they were silenced, subjected to police control, accused by Wanamaker of 'madness', and dismissed as 'left-wing actionaries' – standing in the way, we may presume, of that most contradictory of all cultural impulses, a sentimentalised, reactionary progress.

What is at stake here is, quite obviously, the representation of 'Shakespeare' in our own diverse culture, and it is perhaps not surprising that the media presentation of a project such as this should throw up a montage of contradictions. In fact, the project is, in some ways, an alarming, multi-national capitalist parody of the politico-financial economy of the original Globe Theatre, deploying an impressive array of those ideological State apparatuses whose function is to legitimise the power, and smooth over the contradictions, of the Establishment. The range of examples chosen focuses for us two large problems. On the one hand there is the re-presentation of 'Shakespeare' as the bearer of an allegedly permanent cultural value, in which what Janet Wolff has called 'the political economy of cultural production'[24] remains masked, and which, even when it does surface, takes the form of 'art' versus 'economics' and 'politics', or 'high culture' versus an axiomatically debased 'mass culture'. The difficulty with this series of oppositions is that the avowed intention of 'giving Shakespeare back to the people' involves, in reality, a further transcoding of an already extant mythological entity which, as ideology, reproduces a particular set of social relations. The myth is presented in terms of the spontaneous desire of a patrician elite to replace 'mass culture' – itself an undesirable product of industrial capitalism – with what is called 'popular civilization'. But contradictorily, this removal of the detritus, human and inert, of a post-industrial society, and its replacement with a 'dream', serves merely to re-inscribe the 'popular' within the very same structures of cultural production which generate the subjects and the processes of 'mass culture'. Here the assumption that 'Shakespeare' can be subsumed into an order within which it can function as 'a non-historical reality'[25] facilitates the construction of an 'imaginary' realm of experience, the means through which social relations can be thought as a natural hierarchy.

This manifest appropriation of 'Shakespeare' into the ideological practice of the Establishment should not, however, lead us to the false conclusion that his texts, and his charismatic omniscient presence are nothing but the expression of the domination of a ruling ideology. Rather, they are, to use the terms of Michel Pecheux, 'the site and the means of realization of that domination'.[26] In this context, Wanamaker's 'dream' is much more than an engagingly eccentric whim: indeed, it is that 'necessarily imaginary distortion' which, in its articulation, represents nothing less than 'the imaginary relationship of individuals to the relations of production and the relations that derive from them'.[27] Or, to put the matter another way, what is at issue here is a conflict between opposed 'histories'; a product of class antagonism, in which the ruling ideology is able ultimately to exert control over both the terms and the boundaries of discussion.

Secondly, what is often proposed is an 'historical' reconstruction of an 'original', in which the position of the investigator advertises itself as neutral and transparent – the means through which the subsequently re-constituted object of enquiry is persuaded to disclose itself, that 'choric elegy for lost presence' for which 'This Wooden O' may seem an apt title. But even this narrative, which, of necessity, selects, values, and arranges *available* 'evidence', cannot but be deeply implicated in ideological practice. An important constituent element of that 'choric elegy' is, of course, the long-standing assertion of the 'popular' appeal of the Elizabethan theatre. If, as Andrew Gurr has suggested, 'Shakespeare's London more than most conurbations had a many-headed public divided against itself',[28] and if those divisions extended to Shakespeare's audience, then Alfred Harbage's long-standing account requires radical overhauling in a manner that will seek to explain its sophisticated ideologically motivated reading of the available evidence. For example, Harbage subsumes a sociological appraisal of the population of London as being 'split into many class-conscious and often mutually antagonistic groups', into the notion of an Elizabethan theatre audience as both heterogeneous and capable of habitually sinking its class differences in 'the magical process of dropping pennies into a box'.[29] This argument rests upon a controversial premise: that the discernible aesthetic unity of a Shakespearean text was the direct and unproblematical representation of a deeply ingrained democratic impulse. In fact, what Harbage's own liberal humanism registers here is certain (but by no means all) of the rhetorical effects of these texts, the product of a *selective* reading which resolves, albeit imperfectly, the contradictions which the empirical evidence has actually thrown up. The silent shuffling between the ideological effects of these texts – which Harbage explicitly rejects as 'evidence' – and the demographic evidence concerning the social complexion of the audience, produces a resolution which is as 'magical' for the investigator as it is assumed to be for the audience. In this way a 'heterogeneous' group of mutually antagonistic subjects is transformed into a gathering of autonomous individuals able to submerge their class antagonisms in an activity which is presented as the spontaneous expression of a universal, essentialist 'democracy'. But even so, it would be quite misleading to argue that Harbage's presentation of the evidence accords with the politically quietist myths which demonstrably underpin the reactionary populism of Tillyard and certain of his contemporaries; rather, he directs our attention, almost inadvertently, to the *radical* potential of the material.

A symptomatic reading of Harbage's analysis reveals the problems inherent in any attempt to manufacture a homogeneous Elizabethan audience out of radically antagonistic social groups. But the potential for an analysis in terms of the opposition between the necessary constraints of ideology and the release from it afforded by theatrical performance, problematic though this formulation is, is there; and the notion of the Elizabethan theatre as the site of a clash of discourses determined by class affiliation, in which the 'popular' voice struggles to be heard, is taken up in Robert Weimann's *Shakespeare and the Popular Tradition in the Theater* (1978), arguably the most penetrating analysis of the problem to date.[30]

What I want to suggest is that what we have come to call 'Shakespeare's theatre' – and the use of the possessive case here is indeed significant – is inscribed at two distinct levels within what in another context Pierre Macherey has designated 'the everyday language, which is the language of ideology'.[31] Firstly, we need to consider it as an institution within whose boundaries the contradictory discourses of Elizabethan and Jacobean society were strategically positioned, perpetuated, and, perhaps, undermined. In this respect, what we have come to accept as the 'authority' of those texts gathered under Shakespeare's name, now requires a re-formulation as the locus of a distinct, politically dynamic sequence of intersecting discursive practices, replete with competing ideologies. I want firmly to resist at this stage the ascription of a post-structuralist radical indeterminacy for these texts, though I want to ascribe to them a pluralism which, necessarily implicated in their historical conditions of production, becomes a strategic means to demonstrate that they bear the traces of more than what Fredric Jameson calls, 'the single voice ... the voice of a hegemonic class'.[32] Secondly, and in addition to what may be described as 'first readings' – interventions in a discursive terrain – we need to remind ourselves of the competing ideological investments entailed in the representation and circulation of these texts, both as performance and as Literature, as the perpetuation of that 'voice of a hegemonic class'. Jameson puts the general point succinctly, I think, when he says that in re-writing the text 'in terms of the antagonistic dialogue of class voices', then 'the individual utterance or text is grasped as a symbolic move in an essentially polemic and strategic ideological confrontation between the classes'.[33]

The customary elision of 'Shakespeare' and Shakespearean texts as the signifiers of a mystified creativity, serves as the main channel through which their joint status as 'myth' is reinforced. It is only when we reconsider the theoretical question of 'authorship', along with the kinds of material reality that these texts propose, that it becomes possible to demythologise this influential domain of cultural production, and to return these artifacts to the domain of 'serious but questionable constructions made by people in determinate material conditions'.[34] At a formal, textual level – synchronically, so to speak – and diachronically at the level of the text's passage through history, it then becomes possible to subject the myth of 'Shakespeare' to radical interrogation as the product of a concrete historical process.

Etienne Balibar and Pierre Macherey have analysed in general terms those elements of the structure of a literary text which they call 'effects', the means whereby the text foregrounds a range of contradictions and their ideological resolution. Borrowing their formulation, we may say that neither the dominant ideology nor a plebeian counter-culture are reflected *directly* in a Shakespearean text or an Elizabethan theatre performance; rather, these only appear 'in a form which provides their imaginary solution, or better still, which displaces them by substituting imaginary contradictions soluble within the ideological practice of religion, politics, morality, aesthetics, and psychology'.[35] Such a view would have a very significant bearing upon any naive attempt to reconstruct *physically* an institution such as the Globe, inscribed at a deep structural level within the signifying practices of Elizabethan and Jacobean culture. If it is, as Balibar and Macherey argue, generally the case that Literature 'is not outside ideological struggles', so that 'Its relation to these struggles is not secondary but constitutive',[36] then the proposal to reconstruct the Globe Theatre cannot but result in a series of quite radical discontinuities. Arguments supporting 'innovation' have been advanced, based on the tacit assumption that, in curiously Pirandellian fashion, the presence of a building will, somehow, summon forth its essence, 'Shakespeare'. In reality the result is little more than a haphazard transcoding, the consequence of bringing two distinct and very different cultures into collision, thereby reducing historical analysis to little more than the production of kaleidoscopic patterns. Here the historical Shakespeare – whose location, interestingly enough cannot be *precisely* determined – is made to confront a mythologised 'Shakespeare' who has now become both the signifier and mirror image of personal as well as national histories.

It is only when we recall that material life is always produced under determinate conditions of difference, involving questions of dominance, subjection, and negotiation, that the full implications of such a project stand revealed. Jonathan Dollimore has put the historical case eloquently in directing our attention away from essentialist categories and towards an 'historical understanding of subjectivity',[37] as it is distributed throughout Shakespearean and other Elizabethan and Jacobean dramatic texts. In various ways they construct and interpellate their audiences in accordance with the determinate contradictions which Elizabethan and Jacobean ideology produced, and sought to efface. By contrast, the audience(s) which a reconstructed Globe Theatre would construct and interpellate are of a radically different kind. If, as Sam Wanamaker evidently believes, Shakespeare is part of a common, unified history, and the plays which bear his name part of a 'common culture', then he is doing little more than rehearsing that fundamentally hegemonic strategy of constructing a common language and imposing it upon all, 'whether cultured or not', to use Balibar and Macherey's phrase. Similarly, the academic claims made that 'the recovery of old conventions and languages of theatre will from time to time enable us to make fresh discoveries about the art and significance of the plays and about their ways of entertaining us',[38] seems disturbingly opportunistic in its tacit subscription to the kaleidoscopic theory of history.

Beneath the surface of the Globe reconstruction project lies an attempt to produce what in another, not entirely unrelated context Terry Eagleton has called 'an organic unity of body and language'.[39] That is to say, the quarry is some peculiar Shakespearean self-presence, an entity that under certain circumstances, it is claimed, may be glimpsed through the superstructure of language and theatre. Such a project presupposes also the existence of audiences who inhabit this same imaginary realm of self-presence as the condition of access to what are mediated as permanent human truths. But of course, a project dedicated to the location of a self-presence in what are, in reality, discursive practices, as well as to the recovery of the essence of a mythological entity whose very existence resides primarily in linguistic (and hence ideological) difference, is doomed to failure. At a very practical and pedagogic level, the problem is one of 'reading' Shakespearean texts, of rendering them pluralist as a means of staking out the boundaries of the contest for their meanings. This is not to say that linguistic difference is merely a mechanism designed to enable us to recover a larger, static structure. Fully historicised difference becomes the site where the contestation of meanings takes place, and where human subjectivities are produced. The re-constitution within capitalist relations of production of an *objet d'art*, the Globe Theatre, by 'the right people' for the incidental benefit of the local inhabitants of the third poorest borough in England, involves, surprisingly, the re-constitution of 'the people' of Southwark as subjects

operating within a history which has been mythologised and re-pre-
sented to them as their history. What is more, their failure to recognise it
as their history prompts the outrageous suggestion that they are 'insane'.
This is, in short, as subtle an example of the operation of a cultural
imperialism as one could wish to see, in which culture and a philanthro-
pic international capital combine to engage in an act of urban renewal
upon their own hegemonic terms.

This convergence of interests which is The Globe Reconstruction
Project elides in a manner which is presented as 'natural' a plan of urban
renewal of a very special kind, with the more difficult issue of the
experimentation with what are offered as historically-verifiable techniques of performance for the plays of Shakespeare and his contemporaries. The discovery of fresh ways to foreground the contradictions of
these texts in performance is, of course, a very different matter from the
practice of erecting monuments which never quite get close enough to
what they purport to commemorate.

Recovery of the precise physical dimensions of the original Globe
Theatre – itself a literally 'derivative' building – would unquestionably be
of value to the theatre historian. The erection of a monument, such as
that proposed by The Shakespeare Globe Trust, and now sanctioned by
the force of law, is, however, a different matter involving a history
constructed around bardolatrous practice. The issue resolves itself into
the question of how, in our own diversified culture, we use 'Shakespeare', and the ways in which such usages can be examined in order to
disclose particular ideological investments in what has become a myth.
To suggest that the reconstruction of an unfamiliar physical structure
whose meanings have already passed into the language which is myth
will lead to the revolutionising of current theatrical practice is to conduct
serious and difficult debate at the level of journalistic sloganising. In the
face of an enterprise which habitually misrecognises the roots of its own
populist rhetoric, and which can regard tourism, property speculation,
and trans-Atlantic philanthropy as innocent enabling strategies, the
words of Charlie Cox, a roadsweeper permitted to speak under carefully
controlled conditions, are worth recalling: 'If Shakespeare moves in 'ere,
I'm moving out'. Few enthusiastic supporters of the project to reconstruct the Globe Theatre have stopped to consider this attenuated
expression of the victim's necessity. With the seeming inevitability of
Fate, roadsweepers, like Shakespeare's chimneysweepers, must, it
would seem, 'come to dust' (Cymbeline IV.ii.263). In this modern context
'dust' is the stuff of myths, and myths are profitable commodities, to be

exchanged for money and cultural *cachet*. It is not recorded that the roadsweepers, ushered in 'stage left' by a *Sunday Times* reporter, were involved in any legal settlement, in-court or out-of-court, which would entitle them to compensation totalling £7.2 million. Nor was it nationally reported that in addition legal costs of £15,000 were awarded against the Borough of Southwark and for The Shakespeare Globe Trust.

Notes

1 Tony Harrison, 'National Trust', *Selected Poems* (Harmondsworth: Penguin, 1984).
2 G. A. Wilkes, ed., *Fulke Greville, Lord Brooke: the Remains being Poems of Monarchy and Religion* (Oxford: Oxford University Press, 1965), p. 85.
3 Ibid., p. 86.
4 Ibid., p. 86.
5 Graham Holderness, 'Radical potentiality and institutional closure: Shakespeare in film and television', in Jonathan Dollimore and Alan Sinfield, eds., *Political Shakespeare* (Manchester: Manchester University Press, 1985), p. 194.
6 Walter Benjamin, *Illuminations* (London, Fontana, 1973), pp. 258–9.
7 E. M. W. Tillyard, *The Elizabethan World Picture* (London: Chatto and Windus, 1943), p. 102.
8 Theodore Adorno and Max Horkheimer, *Dialectic of Enlightenment* (London: Verso, 1979), p. 127.
9 Ibid., p. 144.
10 'Shakespeare – a Southwark resident', *Southwark Globe*, (Newsletter of the International Shakespeare Globe Centre), no. 3 (summer 1986).
11 'A friend in need is a friend indeed', *Southwark Globe*, no. 1 (winter 1985).
12 'The door is opening', *Southwark Globe* (winter 1985).
13 John Drakakis, ed., *Alternative Shakespeares* (London: Methuen, 1985).
14 Ibid., p. 160.
15 *The Times* (16 June 1986).
16 Cf. Bryan Appleyard, 'The Globe cast as political football', *The Times* (26 September 1984), which represented the conflict as being between a Labour council following 'their ideological nose', and 'the American actor Sam Wanamaker' who had dedicated his efforts to establishing a 'decent memorial to Shakespeare on his home ground'. The assumption was, and continues to be, that 'politics' are wholly and exclusively the preserve of a radical 'left' opposition, and that supporters of the Globe Project are well-meaning non-political eccentrics, who are now out of their depth.
17 *The Sunday Times* (22 June 1986).
18 *The Standard* (14 January 1985). For a much larger, theoretically informed analysis of the demotic culture which 'the Shakespeare Industry' has occluded, see Terence Hawkes, *That Shakespearian Rag* (London: Methuen, 1986), pp. 1–26.
19 Adorno and Horkheimer, *Dialectic*, p. 161.
20 Broadcast on BBC TV (Tuesday 24 April 1984).
21 Ibid.
22 Ibid.
23 Ibid.
24 Janet Wolff, *The Social Production of Art* (London: Methuen, 1981), p. 48.
25 Louis Althusser, *Lenin and Philosophy* (London: New Left Books, 1971), p. 161.
26 Michel Pecheux, *Language, Semantics, Ideology* (London: Macmillan, 1982).
27 Althusser, *op. cit.*, p. 165.
28 Andrew Gurr, *The Shakespearean Stage: 1576–1642* (Cambridge: Cambridge University Press, 1970), p. 141.

29 Alfred Harbage, *Shakespeare's Audience* (New York and London: Columbia University Press, 1941), p. 12.
30 Robert Weimann, *Shakespeare and the Popular Tradition in the Theatre*, trans. Robert Schwarz, (Baltimore, Md.: Johns Hopkins University Press, 1978). See also Graham Holderness, *Shakespeare's History* (Dublin: Gill and Macmillan, 1985).
31 Piere Macherey, *A Theory of Literary Production* (London: Routledge, 1978), p. 59.
32 *Op. cit.*, p. 85.
33 *Ibid.*
34 Alan Sinfield, 'Four ways with a reactionary text', *LTP*, no. 2 (Brighton: LTP, 1983), p. 91.
35 Etienne Balibar and Pierre Macherey, 'On literature as an ideological form', *Untying the Text*, ed. Robert Young (London: Routledge, 1981), p. 88. See also in relation to Shakespeare, James Kavanagh, 'Shakespeare in ideology', in Drakakis, ed., *Alternative Shakespeares*.
36 *Ibid.*, p. 89.
37 Jonathan Dollimore, *Radical Tragedy* (Brighton: Harvester, 1984), p. 153.
38 Philip Brockbank, 'Planning prospect', ratified at the International Conference held at Northwestern University, Evanston, Illinois, 28–30 June 1984.
39 Terry Eagleton, *William Shakespeare* (Oxford: Blackwell, 1986), p. 97.

Teaching the handsaw to fly: Shakespeare as a hegemonic instrument
David Margolies

When Hamlet finds out that Rosencrantz and Guildenstern have been sent to spy on him, he tells them: 'I am but mad north-north-west. When the wind is southerly, I know a hawk from a handsaw' (II.ii. 374–5). The sense, as part of ordinary human interchange, is never really in doubt: Hamlet is saying he is not so mad as he appears. But examined closely, in the spirit of A level, the statement becomes unclear: what is a 'handsaw' anyway? Maybe there is a subtlety beyond the ordinary reader's grasp? So thank god for annotated editions! The small print at the bottom of the page can elucidate the mystery, usually to the effect that 'hawk' is a hawk and 'handsaw' is perhaps a peculiar rendering of 'heronshaw', a heron, so that Hamlet is saying he can distinguish between two birds.[1] This would be entirely consistent with his role of prince and with a princely interest in the aristocratic sport of falconry. Other authors of the time, after all, used hawking images to appeal to an aristocratic audience, and the assumption underlying the interpretation is that Shakespeare writes in an aristocratic frame of reference and draws genteel metaphors.

But if we use a 'common' frame of reference instead, that of the apprentices, craftsmen and small traders who made up the bulk of Shakespeare's audience,[2] then 'handsaw' is a carpenter's saw and 'hawk' is a plasterer's hawk, the board on which plasterers carry their plaster. Hamlet says, in the alliterative style of popular sayings, that he can distinguish one tool from another. In short, he is saying that he knows what is obvious, an analytical meaning (even if it requires a footnote) which is consistent with the human, experiential understanding of an audience today.

The point of this is not merely that one reading is preferable to another; Shakespeare, as a central component of British culture, has inevitably been incorporated into the dominant ideology and made an instrument of hegemony. The plays are used in a deeply ideological fashion, to propagate and 'naturalise' a whole social perspective. They are filtered, and sometimes quite transformed, to represent a class position that accords with an elitist notion of culture and a ruling-class view of the world.

Because of the circumstances in which Shakespeare is presented to most people, usually first through school, this upper-class bias pervades everything to do with Shakespeare. And the fact that Shakespeare is the keystone of the examination syllabus in English makes it more difficult to reach an independent judgement. Students are made to plough through set texts and harvest abstract truths. However much teachers may work to encourage individual response, students know that examinations require 'received wisdom'. This makes the subject of their study into something alien, not of themselves, and demands that they deal in 'truths' that are not subject to the verification of their own experience but exist independently, in the realms of intellectual history and disembodied logic where the 'heronshaw' is just as real as the handsaw. The plays become mystified into pure cultural excellence.

But there is no 'pure cultural excellence'; even aesthetic principles relate to social and class values, and the excellence perceived in the plays is, not surprisingly, consistent with upper-class attitudes. Interpreted within the dominant ideology, the plays are given meanings which confirm that ideology. Thus the first scene of *Julius Caesar*, in which the tribunes Flavius and Marullus try to prevent the citizens welcoming Caesar, usually has no particular importance attributed to it – it is regarded as an opening scene, giving some necessary elements of plot nicely embodied in a humorous interchange. Like most of Shakespeare's opening scenes, it sets the tone. But what tone? Marullus and Flavius control the scene. When Marullus, having asked the Second Citizen his trade, receives the reply: 'Truly, sir, in respect of a fine workman, I am but, as you would say, a cobbler,' he demands a second time: 'But what trade art thou? Answer me directly.' Indirection still characterises the cobbler's response:

Cobbler: A trade, sir, that I hope I may use with a safe conscience; which is indeed, sir, a mender of bad soles.
Mar: What trade, thou knave? thou naughty knave, what trade?
Cobbler: Nay, I beseech you, sir, be not out with me; yet if you be out, sir, I can mend you.

Mar: What meanest thou by that? Mend me, thou saucy fellow?
Cobbler: Why, sir, cobble you.
Flavius: Thou art a cobbler, art thou?
Cobbler: Truly, sir, all that I live by is with the awl: I meddle with no tradesman's matters, nor women's matters; but withal I am, indeed, sir, a surgeon to old shoes: when they are in great danger I recover them. As proper men as ever trod upon neat's leather have gone upon my handiwork.
Flavius: But wherefore art not in thy shop to-day? Why dost thou lead these men about the streets?
Cobbler: Truly, sir, to wear out their shoes, to get myself into more work. But indeed, sir, we make holiday to see Caesar, and to rejoice in his triumph.
(I.i.10–31)

The element significant for plot, the celebration of Caesar, has been revealed and the citizens are driven away. Flavius remarks: 'See where their basest mettle be not mov'd; / They vanish tongue-tied in their guiltiness' (I.i.61–2). A reading of the incident in terms of plot demonstrates the superiority of the tribunes – they chase away the 'base mettled' populace who, because they are 'guilty', are unable to articulate any justification for themselves. The tribunes are allowed the final comment, ending the scene with a ruling-class perspective of the incident.

If the tribunes appear to have 'won' from the standpoint of the action, in terms of style it is the cobbler who wins. His circumlocution is part of traditional popular humour. Like the clever stupidity of Brer Rabbit or the Arkansas Traveller, it expresses the ironic power of the politically powerless. Technically the cobbler loses but he demonstrates the superiority of his wit to that of the tribunes. The doubt this casts on the excellence of the governing class, though never developed into an articulate opposition, informs the rest of the play; the honour of the conspirators can no longer be taken for granted and thus is laid open to questioning. Only through insistence on the complete and general superiority of those who hold superior social position can these doubts be ignored, and without such questioning the play becomes merely a conflict of virtues abstracted from a social reality. Brutus's civic concern, selflessness and honour, for example, are then timeless and having nothing to do with cobblers. Abstraction allows the first scene to be reduced to mere plot function, in which the tribunes win. The upper-class assumption of right, with the play viewed from their perspective, is confirmed.

The acceptance of an upper-class bias also transforms the content of some plays, what they are understood to be about. This is seen perhaps most clearly in relation to the second history cycle. Traditionally, where examinations prevail, these plays are presented as treating the themes of kingship and the nature of good rule or, in plot terms, they are about the education of a good ruler. Thus the appearance of Prince Hal in different social environments – Cheapside and the Court – in the *Henry IV* plays is interpreted as Shakespeare providing him with the necessary personal background for good rule: he learns about commoners as well as the Court and can thus avoid the one-sidedness that Richard II suffered from. The various adventures are seen as occasions for Shakespeare to provide the prince with a life education, while tactfully leaving his integrity unsullied (he returns the spoils of the robbery at Gad's Hill, he remains critical of Falstaff and finally rejects him upon assuming his regal responsibilities). The cycle thus builds from the disorder of *Richard II*, through the education of a wayward prince in the *Henry IV* plays, to a wise and popular king in *Henry V* who, without his worldly experience, could not have achieved the culminating great victory of Agincourt, the zenith of national and populist greatness.

This royal-education approach stresses the values appropriate to national unity under intelligent rule. The plays are interpreted in terms of what is relevant to ruling-class interests – order and authority. At the same time they are assumed to be attractive to a popular audience of tradesmen and apprentices who, though they may be very much interested in order, are unlikely to be gripped by the education even of a king. As with *Julius Caesar*, the recognition of a popular element transforms the plays from abstract considerations of kingship to matters of concrete (although dramatically generalised) concern for the audience – the opportunism of rulers, let us say, or the undermining of traditional, collective values by the economic individualism of the bourgeoisie.

The plays of the second history cycle have a number of elements which, because they fit uneasily in the education-of-the-king approach, are therefore marginalised or ignored. Falstaff's selfish transformation of traditional values, for example, is treated at best as an alternative mode of being from which Hal learns but must reject on achieving the kingdom. The subversive quality can be avoided by abstracting the plot function. Thus when he defends himself to the King and says he will restore his tarnished reputation by defeating Percy, Hal can be presented as conforming to a chivalric pattern. But the language conflicts with the literal content:

> For the time will come
> That I shall make this northern youth exchange
> His glorious deeds for my indignities.

Percy is but my factor, good my lord,
To engross up glorious deeds on my behalf,
And I will call him to so strict account
That he shall render every glory up,
Yea, even the slightest worship of his time,
Or I will tear the reckoning from his heart.

(1 *Henry IV*, III.ii.144–52)

'Engross', 'account', 'reckoning', 'factor' are all commercial terms. Chivalry for Hal has been reduced, we could say under Falstaff's tutelage, to a saleable image, as in Falstaff's earlier remark to Hal, 'I would to God thou and I knew where a commodity of good names were to be bought' (I.ii.80–1). Once again tone completely alters significance. In plot terms Hal is the repentant son returned to honour; but the tone makes him a manipulator who has learned to hide a new meaning in a traditional image.

Hal's learning from Falstaff also appears in *Henry V* in his success in involving the people in a war not at all in their own interest. The contradiction between the interests of nobles and commoners, evident throughout, forms the substantial material of the play. Plot and dramatic tone again diverge, as has often been pointed out in regard to this play: bare event makes Hal the hero of Agincourt, whereas the juxtaposition of scenes, and the play's failure to realise the rhetoric of the Chorus, suggest he is a cynical, self-interested abuser of the commonweal.

The education-of-the-king argument sees rule as important from the standpoint of the rulers. Henry's rule is good because it is effectively maintained and the misgivings of the commoners in the play need not be regarded as important. The upper-class bias is self-fulfilling.

The élitist message of the second history cycle that follows from the education-of-the-king view is given more credibility by the customary division of Shakespeare's audience into groundlings and gentlemen. The groundlings (so the old argument runs), having left their trades for the afternoon, sweaty, smelling of garlic, uneducated and rude, are supposed to have gone to the theatre for crude entertainment, whereas the educated and refined gentlemen were supposed to share the same philosophical interests as the playwright himself. Thus, while the gross Falstaff may be regarded as suitable for groundlings, the gentlemen were interested in 'the specialty of rule'. For students studying Shakespeare this presents an awkward choice: either, consistent with the supposed character of the groundlings, they do not appreciate the subtlety of the plays and suffer from underdeveloped sensibility or, being sensitive to the art of the plays and interested in such things as the education of a king, they must associate themselves with the gentlemen and the élite. Recasting the play as philosophical discussion produces an élitist view. That is, if people do not comprehend the plays through the philosophical precepts of kingship and the interests of the elite, if they grasp the significance through the gross wit of Falstaff, then they must be as thick as the groundlings. Thus to avoid the scorn for vulgar tastes and for the uncultured refusal to accept time-tested critical notions, or simply to flatter self-esteem by holding 'better' ideas, personal experience of the plays is subordinated to abstract understanding – readers become the victims of the hegemonic power of Shakespeare criticism.

Of more immediate importance than propagation of upper-class attitudes, in a society by no means enjoying equality but subjected to a constant barrage of phony egalitarian rhetoric, is the instilling of the value of authority. Even while Shakespeare's eloquent attack on authority in *King Lear* is held up for admiration – 'The great image of Authority: / A dog's obey'd in office' (IV.vi.156–7) – the plays are made into instruments for justifying the principle of authority. And the way they are taught is often an exercise in accustoming students to authority.

Measure for Measure, a play dear to the hearts of academics and a frequent set text for A level, is probably the Shakespeare play most concerned with authority. The Duke of Vienna, who meddles with the lives of individuals and the execution of justice, is often presented as a god-like figure because he controls events unseen, and brings disorder to a conventional comic resolution. Although recent productions have shown recognition of the dubious harmony of the ending (for example showing Isabella not at all pleased by the Duke's proposal), the status of the Duke remains by and large intact. The plot seems to justify his authority and, as he is the interpreter of his own and everyone else's actions, his failings are hidden by his own self-esteem. Moreover, the fact that superior knowledge of events is shared only by Duke and audience encourages the audience to accept his authority.

Yet in terms of character and plot, *Measure* is full of gross inconsistencies – in development of the action and motivation but also in the whole setting. The reasons the Duke gives for the action, in the first and third scenes, are both contradictory and insufficient. Customarily this problem is resolved by attributing private purposes to the Duke which are not revealed to audience or readers. This gives him an authority that operates beyond the reach of the audience – it is not explainable in terms of the information we have – which serves to strengthen it. Authority is right because it is authority. It is mystified.

As with other mysteries, the Duke's authority involves our acceptance of the result without understanding the causation; it lies not in what we experience but in what we don't. Therefore an understanding of the play that accords with critical tradition is one that is alienated from our personal experience. Although we can judge piecemeal the elements of the play – for instance the sanctity of virginity voiced by Isabella and in effect supported by the Duke is now rejected by most students – that does not challenge the mysterious justification of the Duke in general.

The single element of Measure for Measure that most challenges the position of authority is the character Lucio. A whoremaster and liar, he has a warmth of friendship that is not elsewhere shown in the play – he sees things in human terms and responds loyally when his friend Claudio's life is legally but unjustly threatened. Of much greater importance than his limited plot function is the nature of his dramatic relationship to the Duke. He mocks the Duke directly. In their first encounter he says it was a 'mad, fantastical trick' of the Duke 'to steal from the state and usurp the beggary he was never born to' but goes on to praise him for the leniency which Angelo lacks, attributing it to the Duke's own sexual experience: 'He had some feeling of the sport; he knew the service; and that instructed him to mercy' (III.ii.115–17). The Duke (still disguised as a friar) protests, 'I never heard the absent Duke much detected for women; he was not inclined that way'. Lucio continues with seemingly irrelevant fabrication, accusing the Duke of drunkenness as well as lechery which he knows as an 'inward' of the Duke. The mockery intensifies and becomes more relevant:

Lucio: The greater file of the subject held the Duke to be wise.
Duke: Wise? Why, no question but he was.
Lucio: A very superficial, ignorant, unweighing fellow.

The Duke, obviously piqued, interrupts Lucio to expound at length on his own virtues.

This apparently gratuitous humiliation of a royal figure still in power, by a personage outside the power struggle, is in Shakespeare's plays unique. It goes sufficiently beyond the tact Shakespeare usually displays toward royalty to be risky, and it should then have a dramatic purpose worthy of the risk. It offers an alternative view of events: because Lucio 'exposes' him, there is no need to accept the Duke from his own perspective. Viewed without a bias toward authority the Duke is self-important, irresponsible and pompous; the audience, freed by Lucio from accepting him at his own evaluation, can question all the attitudes expressed in the play.

From the character–imagery–plot standpoint Lucio himself poses a problem: he is not only morally dubious – a whoremaster – but, more importantly, he gives us information for which there is no factual base in the play. He may speak what is *essentially* true (we see that the Duke *is* very much given to self-indulgence) but in conventional terms he is a liar. Does he, like the Duke, know more than the play reveals? Or must the conventional assumption of consistent character be rejected? Lucio poses a definitive obstacle to making the play into a coherent, character-based representation. The consistency that such a representation demands is strained by the stock figures of Elbow and Froth, by contradictions of realism and artificiality (e.g., in the final scene, the realism of Isabella's problem of pleading for Angelo is set in a contrived crisis that mocks her humanity), and is ultimately destroyed by Lucio.

But as a pantomime-type representation, the play works; for pantomime allows realistic characters among stock figures and psychologically-realised problems amidst stereotyped responses. A pantomimic (or carnival) sense of the play not only allows but positively encourages the destruction of the Duke's dignity and his pretensions to genuine authority. The old saws he utters – such as 'That life is better life, past fearing death, / Than that which lives to fear' (V.i.395–6) – are transformed from wisdom into foolishness by the dramatic context. Even the Duke's most balanced judgement – 'Like doth quit like, and Measure still for Measure' (V.i.409) – is seen in the context to be at best inappropriate. The reduction to foolishness of Adam Overdo in *Bartholomew Fair* may serve as a parallel that generates a less ambiguous response (Justice Overdo, setting out to discover the 'enormities' of the Fair, misjudges both villains and victims and in his meddling demonstrates a ridiculous incompatibility between abstract notions of justice and complex reality). The theme of justice that attracts scholarly attention in *Measure for Measure* is travestied; without denying the real danger of miscarriage of justice, the whole serious image of justice is given a send-up in the play. The mockery subverts authority.

The play's subversive character is countered by presenting it in a way that effectively denies the contradictory quality of the representations. Along with the similarly contradictory *All's Well that Ends Well* and also *Troilus and Cressida*, *Measure* is given a special classification: it is a 'problem play'. By this sleight-of-hand critics can isolate plays which pose special difficulties for incorporation into the dominant ideology. The chief characteristic attributed to them is philosophic interest: they treat questions that are in themselves worthy of philosophical attention. Thus they need not be unified dramatic representations such as *As You Like It* or *Macbeth*; we can forget the contradictions because the plays are vehicles for ideas. Tillyard's treatment of *Troilus and Cressida* is perhaps the clearest example: in *The Elizabethan World Picture* he suggests Ulysses' famous speech on order ('Take but degree away, untune that string, / And hark, what discord follows') as the model of order of the period, ignoring the dramatic context of corruption and that Ulysses is cynically using the rhetoric of public good to further private ends.

The category of 'problem play' immediately gives superior status to consideration of abstractions. By prejudicing the play and its content, examination of concrete behaviour and dramatic context are devalued and the play, rather than material for personal response, becomes a collection of ideas simply carried along by a melodramatic plot. Authority deriving from the context of critic or classroom is transferred to the reading and events of the play have too little impact to call it into question. Students are directed to the abstract–philosophical level – 'Discuss the question of justice in *Measure for Measure*'. The definition justifies the treatment and the treatment confirms the definition.

All's Well that Ends Well also displays the irreconcilable contradictions between narrative form and human content that characterise 'problem plays' but it is less specifically concerned with authority than *Measure*. The appealing and highly individualised Helena, having had a fairy-tale success and won a husband whom she immediately loses, then proceeds on a second fairy-tale venture and recovers the worthless husband. In terms of the fairy-tale plots (curing the king and the fulfilment of tasks), she is a winner; but in terms of the specifics of human relationships, she is lumbered with a reprobate and her victory is her loss. All is well that ends well only if it really does end well. The proverbial title of the play may have been used by Shakespeare with as much irony as he uses in overturning the commonplaces of classical values in *Troilus and Cressida*. Generalised form and specific content – victory and pyrrhic victory – are in contradiction; what 'should' happen does, but only in a formal way, in such a way that the result essentially defeats the intention.

The subversive quality of *All's Well*, the general undermining of the notion of 'what should be', is avoided through invoking plot–character–imagery. As with *Measure*, concentration on the progress to 'happily-ever-after' without reference to the qualities of the marriage (let alone to the stylistic devices such as fairy-tale language Shakespeare uses to show the action to be artificial, to 'alienate' events), suppresses the contradictory elements. This is aided by naturalistic interpretation of character – the consideration (i.e. creation) of personal motives beyond what the play shows us. Thus Helena (like Cordelia) is presented as having character flaws that produce the initial rupture and Bertram is imagined to have undergone a genuine reformation, discovered a hidden goodness, that makes all end well.

Refusal to recognise the dramatic context not only makes *Measure*, *All's Well* and *Troilus and Cressida* difficult to grasp; it makes the plays 'timeless' and 'universal'. The qualities of specific human interchange are made into eternal elements of human behaviour and made irrelevant to the lives of ordinary people. In those plays where character is especially emphasised, the tragedies, this 'universality' is stressed even more strongly – Macbeth's ambition, Antony's flawed nobility, Hamlet's melancholy are treated as parts of an unchanging human essence, unrelated to the conditions that generate them and in which they are realised. This again makes it difficult to interpret the plays through personal response.

The 'timelessness' attributed to Shakespeare is thus neither a mark of excellence of the dramatist nor a neutral principle of interpretation; it is part of the ideological use of the plays. The plays are treated as models of behaviour, the acceptance of which is implied to be part of becoming a 'cultured' person, but the selection of material and construction of the model are part of the dominant culture. Thus whereas other authors such as Donne or Milton are recognised as belonging to a particular time and therefore to be subject to changing taste, Shakespeare is elevated above history; to challenge the timelessness of the plays is at once to call into question the whole ideology in which they are so deeply embedded.

The hegemonic use of Shakespeare does not consist simply in the enumeration of anti-popular attitudes or explicit statements of reactionary sentiment in the plays, such as the bitter scorn the noble Coriolanus displays toward the populace or the comic disdain with which the early comedies treat servants (e.g. *The Comedy of Errors*) or commoners (e.g. *Love's Labour's Lost* and the play of the nine worthies). Counter-instances of Shakespeare's concern for the populace are cited with equal irrelevance to the question of hegemony – the poverty of the apothecary in *Romeo and Juliet* that, Shakespeare points out, forces him to sell poison to Romeo, or

Bates's and Williams's doubts about the King's military adventurism in
Henry V, or even the political oppression that makes the scrivener a tool of
injustice in Richard III. The force of hegemony lies not in isolated incidents
that can be used in support of a particular position; it is in the use of the
plays as a whole, in how they have been 'naturalised' into the dominant
ideology. That is, the ruling-class views seem to arise from the plays
themselves rather than to be imposed on them. The material that is
presented to the audience as the play – what is made 'evident' – is
explained in a way that re-characterises it while still seeming only to
describe what is seen: the tribunes win, the Duke creates order, all's well
that ends well. The tone of the action, by which definitions of virtue,
respect, goodness, etc. might be seen to be inadequate, is subordinated
to bald narrative. Immediate personal response is thus alienated, subjected to an authority which the experience of the plays can no longer be
used to challenge.

Thus traditional character–imagery–plot is reactionary in more than a
technical way: denying social context, denying contradiction and
denying the multiplicity of ways the drama, even in reading, has of
creating meaning and significance, it allows only those interpretations
naturalised in a ruling-class perspective and thereby helps preserve the
status quo.

Why would anyone submit to such authority and let themselves be
robbed of their pleasure of immediate dramatic experience of Shakespeare? The Shakespeare they receive in school, on television, in the
theatre, is not the plays full of the vitality of contradiction and the
complexity of life; what they get is already defined and packaged by the
culture: serious, good for them, studiable, with heavy ideas meant for
analysis, in a language that must be read through footnotes because the
footnotes deliver the heavy ideas that then seem the stuff of which the
plays are made. As Costard recognises in Love's Labour's Lost, linguistic
power involves more than just control of language: 'To sell a bargain well
is as cunning as fast and loose' (III.i.100). Audiences and readers, sold not
Costard's goose but a heronshaw, have bought much more than a word –
they have brought home the hegemonic power of Shakespeare.

Notes

1 Although scholars have recognised other meanings, what is important is that this reading
  has become the one generally accepted. See: the Warwick Shakespeare series published
  by Blackie & Son; The New Clarendon Shakespeare (1947); Blackie's New Warwick Shakespeare,
  ed. Kenneth Grose (1969); the Collins Educational edition, edited by B. Davies; the revised

edition of *World Masterpieces* anthology (W. W. Norton & Co., 1965); A. L Rowse, in the Orbis
edition (1984); the Collins four-volume edition; The New Shakespeare (Cambridge, 1st ed.
1934); the old Penguin edition (first published 1937); the new Penguin (1980).

2 Ann Jennalie Cook's *The Privileged Playgoers of Shakespeare's London, 1576–1642* (Princeton, N.J.:
Princeton University Press, 1981) attempts to establish the composition of Shakespeare's
audience as an élite. Although she amasses considerable material, she uses it illogically,
anachronistically, insensitively and either naively or disingenuously. Martin Butler, in a
fourteen-page appendix to his scholarly *Theatre and Crisis, 1632–1642* (Cambridge: Cambridge University Press, 1984), provides a concise, forceful and thorough demolition of
Cook's thesis.

The popular perspective of Shakespeare's audience attacked by Cook was most
influentially advanced by Alfred Harbage in *Shakespeare's Audience* (New York and London:
Columbia University Press, 1941). Harbage's view might be seen as influenced by democratic sentiments prominent in the war against fascism. Cook's attempt to turn Shakespeare into a playwright addressing himself to gentlemen and aristocrats might be seen as
the spirit of Reaganomics in theatre criticism, justifying increasing economic inequality by
projecting it backwards to make it a 'natural' and inescapable condition of culture.

John Peter
interviewed by Graham Holderness

In a Sunday Times article arguing against cuts in theatre subsidy, you wrote: 'The arts are a great equaliser; and they make people equal by raising them rather than lowering them. Irrespective of age, class or income, whoever is excited by a good production of a good play is my equal. This is the source of that true and beneficial elitism which should be the aim of every civilised goverment: it consists in offering the highest spiritual and intellectual benefits to every one who can profit from them'.[1] Could you explain how the arts perform this democratic function?

I think the arts are a great equaliser: the problematic aspect of this subject appears when we start to talk about 'high art'. I have been present at a performance of *Hamlet* in front of a semi-literate public consisting mostly of Hungarian peasants; it was a good production, and they were talking very excitedly in the interval about what was going to happen next. Now if *Hamlet* isn't high art I don't what is. Do we call Henry Moore high art? I certainly think Henry Moore's drawings of wartime shelters would, if shown to large numbers of people who knew what they were about, act as a great equaliser, because these are experiences that a lot of people have shared, irrespective of background and education. I think you have a strong and legitimate query if you allude to the kind of high art represented by, say, the French structuralist novel, or to some of the more esoteric and difficult modern plays – it is quite clear that there will be a number of people who wouldn't understand what they were about.

I sense behind the question more than a suspicion that I'm talking very much *de haut en bas*: that behind what I say there is a strong sense of élitism, taking élitism in a derogatory sense. You are partly right about that: if élitism means that some people are more intelligent than others, then I'm an élitist all the way; if élitism means that the experience of any art, high or low, should only be available to one section of society then I'm not an élitist. I think the whole idea is a dangerous red herring: because what we are talking about is not people coming from different classes, but people coming to the artistic experience with different emotional and intellectual equipment. A thick-witted upper-class person can be just as hopeless watching a serious play as a thick-witted working-class person; and when I say that the arts should be available to everybody I would hope that audiences of all classes would come, and that the theatre would do something to change their assumptions.

In the same article you compared this shared theatrical excitement to the political concept of 'one nation': 'Everything Mrs Thatcher's government does in the name of free enterprise speaks of a desire to create One Nation as dreamed of by Disraeli. How well these intentions are working out economically is not for me to say; but starving the arts of adequate funds completely contradicts them. It leads to less being available to fewer people at a higher price'. How are these things related?

I don't think political reconciliation is one of the theatre's jobs – in fact I think one of the theatre's jobs is political trouble-making. It is one of the most unusual features of British drama that Shakespeare, who was a political pragmatist and definitely the opposite of a political trouble-maker, was able, despite these facts, to write plays that were extremely powerful and penetrating analyses of political action. This is partly because he lived in an age when the social and political unification of the nation was a much more important matter even than it is now: the Wars of the Roses, of which the Tudor era was the aftermath, were far more violent and more far-reaching in their social and political and religious implications than anything (including unemployment) that has taken place in the Thatcher years. What happened in the decades before the Tudor Age, and during the Tudor age itself, fundamentally shook (and reflected) the assumptions of people about the country they lived in, about the world they lived in, and about the God under whose direction they were supposed to be living. Shakespeare is therefore a very special case.

I don't see the theatre as a tool for uniting the nation. The theatrical experience is not there in order that the nation should be united: it is there in order to send people out thinking about what is wrong with the world. It follows from this that I don't take the hierarchical view of culture that you attribute to me: except in so far as I think a good playwright is one who has something of importance to say to his contemporaries about the way we live now. It's not really very important for a play to come out and say how wonderful everything is, even if things are wonderful: it's much more important to confront people with their problems. It's much more important to write a play for instance about the Campaign for Nuclear Disarmament – whether you agree or disagree with it – than to write a play about what a wonderful thing NATO is – whether you are pro- or anti-NATO. NATO is establishment, NATO exists, NATO is fact, NATO is power – whether for good or ill is, for the purposes of this argument, beside the point. I regard the theatre as basically a subversive art. Hence it is important that we all understand the language it speaks: and therefore the theatre should be open to everybody. I see the theatre as an art form which speaks *de haut en bas*, but with the purpose of raising those *en bas* to its own height. I don't think it's either élitist or undemocratic or hierarchical: if we accept that some people are more intelligent than others, and that some people are specialists in the thing that they do, I think this is an acceptable view of what the theatre is and does.

Aren't you describing a social process which goes on within a cultural minority? What proportion of the population ever visits the National Theatre or the RSC?

Everybody who runs subsidised theatre, from Sir Peter Hall to those running Monstrous Regiment and Foco Novo, wants an audience that can afford the price of their wares. This is a far larger problem, to my mind, than 'how many people ever visit the National theatre'. I think that some of us are still living in a cloud-cuckoo land about what popular culture is and what it is for. You have to accept, for better or for worse, that high culture and popular culture are different things. This is not necessarily a value judgement: it is a question of identifying a difference of technique and a difference of content. To be able to produce the *Andy Capp* cartoons is extremely difficult and not something that I could do: that's an example of popular culture. *Hamlet* and *Ulysses* are examples of high art, and become less and less accessible according to how well educated you are. Again this has nothing to do with class: you and I have met plenty of upper-class people who are as thick as a piece of wood, and would not be able to understand what *Ulysses* was all about. The problem is that people with social and financial advantages, unlike the bricklayer or the miner, have always been more able to find free time to sit down and understand *Ulysses*. But that doesn't really alter the position that there is such a thing as high art, and numerically more people are interested in the former than the latter. Numerically far more people would go to the Palladium to see Tommy Steele than would go to the National Theatre to see Albert Finney play Hamlet. This is not because *Hamlet* is very difficult – it isn't, there are more difficult plays; nor is it because Albert Finney is less accessible than Tommy Steele – he is actually among the most accessible of classical actors. It is simply that Shakespeare is conducting an argument about life, about morality, about decision-making, which is on an intellectual level that is beyond large numbers of people. They would understand what it's about if you put it in simpler terms, but

Shakespeare did not put it in simpler terms: Shakespeare assumed that there would be a certain amount of intellectual density in his arguments. He had every right to expect this. We simply have to accept the fact that in the end there will always be large numbers of people who will not be interested in seeing Hamlet but will be interested in seeing Tommy Steele. The important thing is to make the prices of the tickets to Hamlet within the reach of as many people as possible if they want something more demanding than Tommy Steele. I am not belittling Tommy Steele: I am simply saying that in terms of cerebral activity more is expected of you when you sit through a performance of Hamlet than when you sit through Half a Sixpence.

Would you then disagree with the long-standing tradition that holds Shakespeare's theatre to have been a popular theatre in itself?

On a certain level Shakespeare can appeal to an uncultured audience, by virtue of his ability to tell a story extremely well. He is a most exceptional case. It's not true of all of his plays. I don't think that Measure for Measure or Coriolanus or Love's Labour's Lost would ever be popular successes because in these plays the argument is being conducted on a rather more cerebral level. A Midsummer Night's Dream will always be more accessible than Love's Labour's Lost, because it is a more immediately popular and less intellectually-conceived play. I don't think we are in a position to say how many of Shakespeare's audience necessarily understood some of his more complex remarks about the operations of the law and politics, and so forth. I suspect that quite often the dramatic action, the confrontations between characters is what the plays meant for the popular section of the audience: they understood who was up and who down, who was in and who was out; and they were able to understand this because of Shakespeare's strength as a dramatic story-teller. It didn't matter that they lacked the intellectual equipment to absorb the more rarified economic and political arguments.

Finally how do you see your role as theatre critic of a quality newspaper? Are you occupied in protecting the values of high culture, or in mediating them to a popular audience?

I can only mediate them properly by protecting them. If I watered down what I believe to be true values I wouldn't be protecting them; and I wouldn't then be mediating what they are, but selling something else. I think that working in a 'quality' newspaper, as you call it, we have the luxury of knowing that the people who read us read us because they are interested in what we have to say, and the luxury of knowing that the people who read us will be willing and able to do a certain amount of work themselves. This is a luxury not available to some other news-papers, whose writers have to assume that they need to explain every-thing. I find this a difficult tightrope to tread; but one thing I am sure of is that vested interests do not enter into my arguments at all, and do not form any part of my concern or interests, whether political, sociological, psychological or cultural. What interests me is what playwright said what and why and how. And if I think that a play I believe to be very important is misunderstood, and I can identify how and why it is misunderstood, I would like to explain how that play works and why it's important. I recently read a review of Ibsen's *Ghosts* which argued that its concerns are irrelevant to the present day. I would ideally like to be able to explain what it is in *Ghosts* that ought to appeal to people now. This is a play about asking questions of the culture you live in: what rights do I have, what does my society have a right to demand of me, what can we expect from each other; at what point can I stand up and say no, I don't want any part of this. I think this is directly relevant to a historical period such as ours, in which a lot of people are very intensely questioning the nature and purpose of politics. I would like to think of my work as consisting in making clear to myself what a play is about, and then making it clear to my readers; trying to communicate what I have to say, so that I don't appear to be talking to them from a great height, but without hiding the fact that I do actually have the knowledge from which to pontificate.

Note

1 John Peter, 'Let the theatre play to one nation', *Sunday Times* (5 May 1985), p. 41.

'You base football-player!':
Shakespeare in contemporary
popular culture
Derek Longhurst

On our arrival in Denmark, we found the king and queen of that country elevated in two arm-chairs on a kitchen table, holding a Court. . . . My gifted townsman stood gloomily apart, with folded arms, and I could have wished that his curls and forehead had been more probable. . . . Whenever that undecided Prince had to ask a question or state a doubt, the public helped him out with it. As for example; on the question whether 'twas nobler in the mind to suffer, some roared yes, and some no, and some inclining to both opinions said 'toss up for it;' and quite a Debating Society arose.

Charles Dickens, Great Expectations, chapter 31

Within Dickens's comic representation of the more bizarre aspects of nineteenth-century theatrical performance it is arguable that the fault-lines of cultural difference play a crucial role. On the one hand, the novelistic mode of Dickens's own writing is predominantly associated with the domestic culture of the Victorian middle-class family while on the other, *embourgeoisement* of the London theatres is well under way by 1861. In one case literacy is frequently registered as a signifier of an educated, cultured subjectivity, constituted as a 'private' counter to the social world of competitive capitalism while the other, more public performance, excluding the presence of the lower orders both physically by economic means and culturally by a variety of stereotypical representations, manifests collective engagement with the 'spiritual' conflicts of love, honour and duty in 'high' melodrama, French adaptations and – of course – Shakespeare's 'classical' dramas.

History, then, is against Mr Wopsle. He is in the wrong theatre performing the wrong play at precisely the wrong time. Isolated in his private world of heroic pretensions to grandeur and cultural authority, he collides with a social world inimical to transcendence in the audience's ribald, participatory and communal traditions of popular culture –

of fairground and penny gaff Shakespeare, farce, melodrama and the newly-emergent music hall. It would, of course, be absurd to oppose 'high' and popular culture in the period too crudely. Fortunately, such simplistic dichotomies are now under increasing attack as theoretically sterile for the analysis of culture as, in any sense, 'a whole way of life'. Nor do I wish to suggest that literacy and the consumption of 'high' class-cultural artefacts are the sole determining factors in understanding the differences between élitist culture and popular culture. For one thing, there is evidence to suggest that Shakespeare along with the Bible and Bunyan retained considerable significance for working-class autodidacts, writers and political pamphleteers as well as for audiences who could afford the prices charged at Sadlers Wells. Tag-lines could be appropriated in the interests of radical politics in support of a specifically English democracy and in opposition to class oppression while the desire to read, see, hear and understand Shakespeare is often seen as a positive objective, an aspiration towards the possession of 'cultural capital'.[1]

> Now Toole he was a-playing Hamlet
> And Phelps he was a clown;
> Buckstone he was an acrobat,
> As the world turned upside down.[2]

Here, the counterpointing reversal of theatrical identities is blended with a sense of class-cultural change resultant from radical social change ('I dreamt there were no workhouses / And there were no starving poor'). However one regards this, it is certainly tenable that Shakespeare maintained a 'presence' within and around popular culture largely through the performing arts. There was, in other words, a hegemonic struggle over the body of Shakespeare in the relations between bourgeois culture and nineteenth-century popular culture.

No such struggle exists within contemporary popular culture. It is not possible to chart, in the scope of this essay, every step of this transition but clearly the canonisation/professionalisation of Shakespeare within the discourses shaped through national institutions of education is crucial as is the impact of the mass media industries especially as they have developed in the post-war era. It is, surely, undeniable that the dominant figuration of Shakespeare within the institutions committed to the reproduction of the values of 'high' culture is articulated around his texts as embodiments of literary genius constituted in a coalescence of the 'flowering' of the English language and the (consequent?)

'universal' truths of human experience.[3]

Now, it is certainly the case that a struggle for possession of Shakespeare is taking place within the institutions of higher education and that it is a cultural struggle with considerable political tentacles into other dimensions of social practice. There are also numerous indications that this contestation for meanings has assisted in the transformation of theatrical representation of Shakespeare since the 1960s. But beyond that we should not go. Whatever claims can be made for past cultural formations, it is quite clear that there is a wider gap than ever between the institutions and producers of Shakespeare and anything that could be described as a popular audience. The comic potential for exploiting this sense of disparity is, of course, huge. In a recent situation comedy (*Help*, BBC 1, 2 September 1986) centred on three Liverpudlian lads, for instance, the literary pretensions of Lennie are met by the dumb naiveté of Dava's inversion of historical origins in the discussion of joblessness in a bus shelter. Citing Shakespeare as an example of aspiration provokes

Dava: No, he didn't write *Wind in the Willows* on a bench in Renshaw Street Bus Station.
Lennie: No – he didn't come from round here.
Dava: No? How come he called himself after a pub on the Dock Road?

The cultural codes associated with the national poet are here brought into sharp confrontation with a comic representation of the social experience of working-class Liverpudlian youth (the Scouse 'voices' are crucial). It is this disjunction which has haunted a generation of actors, directors and academic critics who, yearning nostalgically for a common culture inclusive of Shakespeare, have sought ever more desperately for ways to bridge what they perceive as the cultural divide. Time and again, the question reverberates around the echoing theatres and classrooms – 'How is this text (do we make this text) relevant?' – either for voluntary or largely coerced audiences. Hence, everything becomes grist to the Shakespeare mill – fascism, Stalinism, Macbeth as Richard Nixon and *vice versa* – while popular culture and sub-cultural styles can be produced to construct 'contemporary' meanings for audiences which are drawn from anything but sub-cultural social groups. Never was this more clearly demonstrated than in Michael Bogdanov's wrestle with his audiences, in the televised series of 'rehearsals', over whether 'the text' should be *made* or somehow 'made itself' relevant through contemporary 'political'/ 'popular' analogy or whether this had a limiting effect as the texts were *already* abundantly full of 'human' meaning.[4] Clearly we are not here dealing with 'popular' responses but with shifts in a hegemonic dominant culture, a contestation for 'meanings' around and amongst the specific readership constituted dominantly from a fraction of the professional middle-class intelligentsia. That 'audience' is not, by and large, to be found outside Roker football ground in Sunderland where a massive advertisement appeared for the RSC's annual visit to Newcastle in which it was asserted, in north-east dialect ('pet'), that the RSC's performances at the Theatre Royal and the Newcastle Playhouse, located on the periphery of the University campus, would rival the attraction of staying at home to watch *Coronation Street*. At best, such naïvetë can be regarded as alarming in those involved in the public relations industry reproducing Shakespeare.

Let me be quite clear. One of the intentions of this chapter is to avoid some of the wilder manifestations of the polarisation of high–low culture – the 'either-or' analytical modes which can lead to a reflexive populist endorsement of popular cultural artefacts and practices versus the mystified sanctity of critique buried in the often astonishing simplicity of critical discourse concerning the 'texts' of literary culture. Some may argue that these broad strands of contemporary cultural debate represent an adolescence and senility respectively or perhaps less pejoratively, emergent and dominant/residual tendencies. In any case, approaches constructed from the assumptions intrinsic to unselfconscious élitism or populism are both tinged with the kind of myopic nostalgia which precludes thoroughgoing analysis directed towards revealing and debating the grounds upon which *all* cultural practices are inevitably being *interpreted*. The fact that the notions of 'discrimination' and 'value' have been so contaminated by *Scrutiny* discourse is no longer sufficient reason to prevent their redefinition and rearticulation within the analytical discourses applied to the interpretation of culture. *King Lear* and *Coronation Street* are not, in any sense but the most simplistic, similar 'texts' nor can they be satisfactorily analysed/valued through reference to each other regardless of which 'narrative' the critic wishes to back. Nor can their respective 'pleasures', audience responses and the cultural formations in which they have been (re)produced be 'read off' textually. It is precisely the epistemological status of texts themselves which is in question through contemporary cultural, interpretative strategies. My interest here, then, is to isolate, temporarily, those cultural forms and codes deriving out of 'Shakespeare' as a national, English monument upon which a broad range of 'texts' have drawn as a point of reference.

So far I have somewhat ignored the significant preposition in my title in order to investigate certain aspects of the Shakespeare industry *and* contemporary popular culture. I would like now to trace something of the iconologic presences of Shakespeare *within* contemporary popular culture. The 1960s ushered in the worst fears of cultural pessimists of both left and right in that Britain attained a new identity as the international capital of popular culture, certainly in terms of urban youth culture, rock music and associated sub-cultural styles. To this newly affluent and – in terms of dominant representations – self-confidently aggressive generation, Shakespeare and a literary education in general is no longer experienced as a passport to a socially-mobile cultured subjectivity but as identified with establishment and 'school' culture and often therefore the target of subversion and rebellion.[5] This may seem like an absurdly broad generalisation (of course, there are exceptions and qualifications especially in those regions of the country where the grammar school system was, to all intents and purposes, maintained in the face of the comprehensive movement) but the empirical evidence for the emergence of a hugely heterogeneous popular culture, dynamically disturbing gender and class boundaries *and* systematically multi-cultural, manifests the ever-increasing chasm between the hegemonic locations of Shakespeare within dominant institutions of English culture and the social experience of popular cultural forms. It is thus that within contemporary popular culture the most famous tag-lines are commonly represented as subject to irony ('Shall I compare thee to a summer's day?') or bawdy interpretation as in the birthday card 'How do I love thee? Let me count the ways . . . On the kitchen table / under the stairs . . .' and so on. There is, of course, a long tradition of popular burlesque of Shakespeare, not to mention seaside postcards, within which such 'texts' may be located: but what are the defining categories which articulate the contemporary popular discourses?

It seems clear that social class is always, in one way or another, a primary determinant in constructing perspectives from which such cultural referentiality may be read. One persistent strand, for instance, is the exploitation of the radical inapplicability of the 'text' of Shakespeare to the 'texts' of social experience. The underlay is, of course, the sense of Shakespeare as exemplar of universal genius and truth and the encapsulation of such truths in a particular set of linguistic codes. This is a model to be sustained or inverted and in the process language itself becomes the code either of identity or of a failure to achieve that identity despite aspiration. For instance, in the development of the television sit-com format which allowed the transposition of the persona of 'Hancock' across the media, one of the main sources of comedy in the Galton/Simpson scripts is the ideological gap exposed between that persona and social institutions – a hospital or library system – and at least one dominant characteristic is the satire of petit-bourgeois pretension in a period characterised by the upward mobility of precisely that class. Thus, Anthony Aloysius St John Hancock's audience 'knows better' when he (mis)quotes Shakespeare – 'As Portion said to Shylock Holmes who had stolen a pound of meat, "The quality of mercy is not strained" . . .' while Sid James's 'working-class' response provokes Hancock into 'I don't know why Shakespeare bothered with blokes like you around'. Here, the comedy of cultural and class conflict is clear-cut – the subversion of pretentious quotation of birthday-book tag-lines is met by Sid's 'earthy' realism. In fact the evolution of the Hancock persona is particularly interesting as one dimension of the character was constituted as a 'failed Shakespearean' forced to play the reps and halls, protesting that Olivier and Gielgud are where they are purely by chance. In the early days of television a comedian like Hancock could not afford to appear on the medium as the fees offered by the BBC were too low to compensate for loss of earnings in the halls; fees for radio shows were higher and they could also be recorded in an afternoon. Not until ITV started, offering higher fees from 1955–6 onwards and forcing the BBC to compete, could music-hall artists make the transition from radio and stage to television. The Hancock script which makes most extensive use of this strand of the persona is 'The Bowmans' from the 1961 television series. Hancock is killed off as a grotesque and disruptive Walter Gabriel-like character in a radio soap-opera heavily reminiscent of *The Archers*. Auditioning for the part of Hamlet for a 'British Arts Council tour of Tanganyika' he begins by confusing lines from different plays –

Tony: . . . Hush, what light from yonder window breaks? 'Tis Juliet, and the sun is in the West . . .
Voice: Mr Hancock, the play is *Hamlet*.
Tony: Hamlet? Is it? I was distinctly told *The Merchant of Venice*. I'm terribly sorry. *Hamlet* is a different cup of tea, of course.

– and proceeds to render *Hamlet* in his radio soap-opera character's Norfolk–Somerset–Robert Newton accent – 'To be or not to be, that be the question . . .' Rejected by the 'voice' of the producer, he characteristically protests: 'I warn you, the Tanganyikans aren't going to like this. I am very highly thought of in Dar-Es-Salaam. This is no way to keep the

Commonwealth together. You will be playing to empty mud huts, my man . . . I shall offer my services to those who appreciate the talents of a true artiste.' In fact his next artistic role is to appear in a series of TV adverts for 'Grimsby Pilchards' until the campaign causes sales to plummet. Owing to public outcry, however, Hancock is brought back to the radio soap-opera as brother of his original character, blackmailing the producers into having the whole Bowman family 'killed off' in one go, down a mine shaft, so that his character of Ben Merryweather can become the central star of the show. The interesting feature of the episode, then, is how in 1961 is has become possible to clash playfully and self-consciously the performance media, genres and cultural forms as a context through which the absurdly pretentious persona of Hancock tumbles.[6]

This featured powerfully in the successful transition to television of those other music-hall stars, Morecambe and Wise. Perhaps their best-known parody of classical, 'Shakespearean' performance was the 'Anthony and Cleopatra' sketch in the Christmas show with Glenda Jackson. Earlier, however, was the 'classic' *Death of Caesar* sketch, celebrating the 'quadrocentenary' (sic) in 1964, with Eric as Mark Anthony and Ernie as 'Caesar's body'. The former enters on to a stage with Roman pillars, bearing Ernie in his arms and begins the 'Friends, Romans . . .' speech. Gradually the speech disintegrates as the body gets heavier and a great deal of visual comedy is generated by the pair clutching at each other's cloaks and togas, Ernie being hoisted into a fireman's lift exposing his underpants beneath the toga. Eric begins to 'forget' the lines – 'He was my friend – an' all that', 'the good men do lives after 'em – I'll tell you that' – and he has to be 'prompted' in comically loud stage whispers by 'the body' ('the slings and arrows of outrageous fortune' / – Ernie (hissed): 'That's Henry V'). Finally, 'the body' carries off Mark Anthony in a fireman's lift exposing his shoes and socks under the Roman costume. Here the comedy is both culturally based and gender-based in that the 'failure' of Eric and Ernie's performance of the classic scene is one which punctures its rhetorical effects and any heroic pretensions with all the connotations of masculinity with which heroism is imbued.

In the 1970s and 1980s the case of Barry Humphreys is arguably more complex. The character of Dame Edna is, like Hancock, constructed around satire of petit-bourgeois aspirations and mores but this is of course rendered more ambivalent by issues of gender (cross-dressing) and ethnicity – Dame Edna's Australian identity is a central feature of the character's comic 'otherness' for English audiences. For the present purposes, however, I wish to concentrate only on the projection of Dame Edna's 'megastar' status rooted in a 'popular knowledge' which the character consistently counterpoises against the efforts of other 'Dames' to achieve popular success in the classics. In 'Housewife Superstar' for instance, the audience is asked 'Why is this show the most successful in the history of the English speaking world?' the answer being that 'people are sick of the theatre . . . they just like a little chat, a little chat like this'. Originally Dame Edna had been at the Apollo, 'before we came up to the Globe to accommodate the extra crowds', and next door 'Dame Joan, little Laurence Oliver's (sic) gorgeous little wife', 'struggling on' with her show, 'used to listen with her toothbrush mug' from her dressing room 'just to hear what a real audience sounds like'. To celebrate her success Dame Edna invited Dame Joan, Peggy Ashcroft, 'who's in a wonderful state of preservation' and Margot Fonteyn to 'a hen's party', reflecting 'I felt jealous of those women – jealous. I thought if only I was an ordinary star like you and not a superstar'. Here the comedy is rooted in the self-confidently patronising inversion of commonly-accepted value systems with the target of demystifying theatrical and associated social manners:

This is the Globe, darlings. Isn't it wonderful, the Globe! It's oozing, ravaged, riddled with pageantry and pomp. The history here! Little Shakespeare himself used to jump around on this stage, dressed up as a woman most of the time, not that that proves a thing these days.
The thing is – I've got a lot of time for Shakespeare, a lot of time. I love his shows – To Be or Not to Be, Lend Me Your Ear, Paint Your Wagon.

The claim to cultured authority – knowledge-of/'time'-for Shakespeare – is undercut by the ironic self-referentiality associated with transvestism/ homosexuality/the theatre, allied to the casual attitude to even the titles of his 'shows'. Indeed, a crucial strand of Humphreys' performance is an acute sense of the cultural signifiers of the English class system which 'the character' of Dame Edna both exposes and tramples through with the blissful 'ignorance' of the (colonial) 'nouveau'.[7]

The association of Shakespeare with an older generation of 'great English actors' and with a particular kind of theatricality is currently a central reference point within popular culture. Best known, perhaps, is the Spitting Image competition between Olivier and Gielgud for the title of 'greatest living Shakespearean actor', playing on their stylised and mannered vocal deliveries as well as caricature of their physical appearances. The overwhelming sense is of outmoded performance, a decrepit culture with its contrast between aged irascibility and a pseudo-genteel emotionalism. This representation of the 'knights of the Theatre' has stimulated a series of such references. The Steve Wright Show (Radio One, 3.00 p.m.), for instance, has a daily phone call from 'Malcolm of the Arts Council', plum-accented and usually threatening, in this time of Thatcherist economies of public spending, to withdraw the programme's grant unless the cultural tone is raised to a level acceptable to Sir John who is frequently 'moved to tears', like Malcom himself 'in the third act' of whatever classical play he has just seen. At the time of writing, Malcolm was 'at Edinburgh' appearing in *A Midsummer Night's Dream* ('You should have seen my Bottom' – 11 September 1986).

Classical performance, then, of Shakespeare is a frequent source of comic inversion within popular culture from Peter Sellers or Morecambe and Wise to Lenny Henry and Frank Bruno as Romeo and Juliet.[8] In the latter case, the balcony scene was rendered with all the stilted delivery of the school play, thus emphasising the grotesquely spectacular distance between the black, working-class personae and the institutionally constructed 'experience' of Shakespeare's lyrical verse. Recently, too, the Carling Black Label adverts have also exploited the contrast between theatrical-cultural manners and working-class 'expertise'. As Hamlet begins his 'Alas, poor Yorick' the actor drops the skull, catching it like a football on his toe. A sequence follows, familiar from sports programmes demonstrating the skilful ball-control of professional stars, with the skull bouncing from foot, head and shoulders to the excited 'oos' and 'aahs' of the theatre audience.[9] Another actor enters with 'My noble Lord Hamlet –' but immediately reverts to 'Over 'ere, son, on me 'ead'. Finally, 'Hamlet' overhead kicks the skull into the crotch of the evening-suited drinker of Black Label seated in one of the boxes, who smiles at his companions in some painful embarrassment.[10] The advertisement concludes with the skull as a ventriloquist's dummy in a parody of the voice of Sir John pronouncing 'I bet he drinks Carling Black Label'. An earlier textual variant had the same line delivered by a bust of Shakespeare draped with a football scarf. Clearly the targeted market is essentially male working or lower middle class and the identity of the product is created by disrupting and supplanting 'alien' cultural practices with a comic *spectacle* of the performance of expert skills in a 'familiar' cultural activity, an association of the popular leisure pursuits of football and beer-drinking. The pleasures of the body displace those of linguistic reflection. The images construct a polarity between a middle class culture of constraint and inhibition overturned by the freedom, power and vitality of popular culture – and of the products consumed, supposedly, by its most distinctively skilful exponents. (The companion advertisement in the Black Label campaign clashes the 'disruptive' genre of the spaghetti western and a variety of 'familiar' contexts – the supermarket etc.)

Satire of 'classical' *performance* of Shakespeare is, then, one key element in popular cultural representation. It is clearly central to the situation comedy format of *Blackadder II* for instance, significantly more successful than the first series through the shift to the Elizabethan period and its exploitation of the comic potential in the anachronistic disjunction between historical frame and grotesquely contemporary socio-linguistic manners. This extended from stylistic parody ('You are in good fooling, today, my Lord') to deliberate perversion of well-known lines from Shakespeare – 'As private parts are we to the Gods, they play with us for their sport'. In some cases, however, this can be extended to parody of 'experimental' production techniques as in *Robbins* (ITV, 27 August 1986) in which the 'Trampoline Theatre Company' performance of *Julius Caesar* was introduced by a be-suited trampolinist, followed by actors in Roman dress bouncing up into and out of screen as they delivered tag-lines from the play ('Speak hands for me' etc.). Appropriation or distortion of tag-lines, then, is a constant feature as in Les Dawson's 'Torpedo or not torpedo' to a *Blankety Blank* contestant from the Navy; so, too, is travesty of the figure of the 'bard of Avon' in, say, Roland Rat's self-designation, 'the Shakespeare of the sewer'.

It is important to stress that all these examples, a heterogeneous selection from the past two decades, were differentiated by medium, representational conventions and conditions of production; they were/are open to a plurality of readings. They are not in themselves 'progressive' or 'subversive' but what they have in common is an appeal to what I would describe as 'the popular grotesque' constituted through the displacement of the cultural identity and 'texts' of Shakespeare into disruptive and even anarchic performance contexts.[11] There is, of course, a great deal of pleasure to be generated in certain acts of liberation. They can be seen, in the post-1960s, as anti-élitist/pretension/ authority/establishment – in short, as progressively subversive because they appeal to 'genuine' popular pleasures as opposed to the 'educated' and, therefore, artificial pleasures of a complacent bourgeois culture. Acceptance of such binary dichotomies, as I suggested earlier, is to fall into the trap besetting much contemporary critical debate surrounding media and cultural studies – namely, either/orism rather than both-andism. Clearly, the current trend to jettison political-economy approaches or ideological analysis of cultural forms, texts and practices in favour of enthusiastic engagement with popular 'pleasures' has been gathered by the crisis, within a fraction of the academic intelligentsia, centred on the shift in political discourse associated with the authoritarian populism of Thatcherism. In the efforts to recapture the ground lost since 1979, it is arguable that the agenda has become polarised in a way which is evading discrimination within both popular and minority cultural processes. Hence, the strand of earthy satire directed, as we have seen, against the worst manifestations of Shakespearean 'foyerism' becomes politically ambivalent when extended to blanket, populist dismissal of the radical potential which can be generated within the cultural institutions and discourses through which 'Shakespeare' is constituted. In November 1985, for her sixtieth birthday, Jack Woolley offered to take Peggy for 'a nice evening out' at the RSC and dinner. Not much that is inherently objectionable or, for that matter, pretentious here. Indeed, Peggy was represented as regarding the 'treat' as an unusual and kind thought, but it is hard to escape a vision of many contemporary Dallasty 'fans' gathered around their tuners cheering wildly when Walter Gabriel pronounced Shakespeare as long on 'words' with too little 'action'.

The point to make is that cultured subjectivities, as Willy Russell suggests throughout *Educating Rita*, are not inherently 'a bad thing', always contaminated by privileged entrée into necessarily repressive regimes of power and authority. Like Walter Gabriel, Rita expects *Macbeth* to be 'dead borin' ' but her knowledge of the thriller converges with the immediacy of theatrical performance to construct an experience of liberation and excitement which then enters into negotiation with Frank's academic knowledge of definitions of tragedy (Act One, Scene Six). Indeed, negotiation is the key word in Russell's representation of a 'Romeo and Juliet' love affair across class-cultural difference posed in terms of a vitalistic immediacy awakening the bored, self-negation of educated cynicism – and, in the process, disturbing nostalgic or naive, received notions of cultural experience.[12] It is interesting that the popular success of the film version drew on actors – Michael Caine and Julie Walters – who are strongly identified with the electronic media and the spaces opened up by them since the 1960s for 'stars' with lower-middle or working-class identities. David Bowie is another such figure as the popular 'star' in the 'serious' film, *Merry Christmas, Mr Lawrence* (based on

Laurens van der Post's novel) in which the quotation of Shakespeare is constituted again as a cultural talisman, this time in the attempts of the Japanese Officer to construct some point of contact and sense between Eastern and Western cultures under the militaristic conditions imposed by war. Bowie's ironic 'Heroes' album bears interesting relation to this Anglo-Japanese production which was selected, along with *Educating Rita*, amongst the twenty-one films to represent the 'revival years' during 'British Film Year'.

One of the most eccentrically popular roles played on the political stage in recent years was that constituted by the media for Ian McDonald, Ministry of Defence spokesman during the Falklands/Malvinas war. In some contrast to the Thatcherist jingoism, built around often grotesque nostalgia for past 'glories' (*The Sun*'s 'blitz'), McDonald emerged as a complementary figure of the gentleman-classicist, always ready with the apt quotation. Asked about Argentinian military claims, for example, he referred the press to *Hamlet* (III.iv.52–4): 'Look here, upon this picture, and on this, / The counterfeit presentment of two brothers.' McDonald continued in this vein to the last, closing the Emergency Press Centre at the end of the war with Prospero's valediction:

> Now my charms are all o'erthrown,
> And what strength I have's mine own,
> Which is most faint . . .

It would be tempting to argue that Shakespeare is more appropriate for a right-wing nationalist political discourse[13] but thankfully Bill Jordan at the 1986 TUC Conference revealed alternative possibilities. Describing the despair of industry as akin to that of Macbeth, he was able to suggest that even the CBI could identify with

> I pull in resolution, and begin
> To doubt the equivocation of the fiend
> That lies like truth (V.v.42–4)

– the 'fiend' being resident, of course, in No. 10 Downing Street.

   Perhaps the dichotomies which enshroud Shakespeare, then, were most recently captured, at their most basic level, in Alan Plater's telescript of Hilda Bernstein's political thriller, *Death is Part of the Process*. Transposing 'a charity performance of a new play' into a production of *Henry V* in the context of South African racial and material inequality, Plater had Pila object to her mother's admiration for Shakespeare's 'poetry' on the grounds of the 'politics' the 'poetry' represents – to which Mrs Norval could only exclaim in disbelieving astonishment: 'Politics in Shake-speare!?'[14]

I have chosen these final examples from 'political' discourse deliberately as, in many ways, they typify my argument that 'Shakespeare', although largely appropriated in the present century by national institutions of education and interlocking cultural institutions, is not *essentially* and transhistorically the blockbuster of bourgeois culture and dominant ideology. Nor, on the other hand, can popular culture be adequately understood as either 'mass' culture or the 'authentic' voice of the people. In this chapter it would have been possible to subordinate the illustra-tions to a more 'theoretical' statement but I have chosen not to do so in the attempt to register the rich heterogeneity and tensions of what I would define, precisely in theoretical terms, as the negotiations and accommodations within and between hegemonic and oppositional cultural forms and practices. It is the mobility and dynamism of these adjustments which needs to be accentuated in the interests of clarifying the interactive processes of the cultural formation as a whole.

Further, these processes are conjunctural. 'Shakespeare' yesterday is not Shakespeare today or tomorrow necessarily – as Bill Jordan demon-strated. The cultural practices articulated around Shakespeare are depen-dent on a whole network of social and ideological practices which are open to change. Indeed, it is part of my argument that the construction of Shakespeare within English culture has become more complex since the war as a result of fragmentation within the structures and codes of the English class system, the loss of Empire, American cultural imperialism and British responses, displacement of cultural identities surrounding heavy manufacturing industries by those of the service industries, ero-sion of altruistic traditions of the middle-class landed 'gentleman' ethos, greater awareness of the complex of 'public' and 'private' practices in relation to patriarchal power, the development of the electronic media and the evolution of a heterogeneous, multicultural and primarily urban, popular culture.[15] Into the 1960s, for example, it was possible to locate Shakespeare as a figuration of cultural aspiration and a pivot upon which could be hung a discourse of 'land' and 'people' imbricated across social-democratic consensus politics. That sense of the nation-State, of an 'island race', has been severely disrupted in the postwar world of international political and economic relations (the IMF, EEC, multi-national corporate capitalism) and communication systems. Although residually available, that discourse was largely displaced, in the narrowly political sphere at least, by Wilsonian pragmatic populism on the one hand and the no less pragmatic, populist appeal of Thatcherist 'philistinism' on the other, the polarisation of the 'needs' of industry against the tendency in the 'broad liberal tradition' to 'reject' materialism.[16]

That tradition has also become subject, of course, to radical critique from both the women's movement and the left to the extent that it articulates the discourses of both patriarchal and capitalist social relations. One result is that the dead hand of cultural élitism has, in many ways, been more thoroughly undermined in Britain than elsewhere and the study of popular culture is now well established with its own methodologies, challenging theoretical models and fields of enquiry. Thankfully, here at least, the ghost of Leavis has been – largely – laid to rest.[17]

Notes

1 Since the nineteenth century, of course, the British State has evolved in such a way as to intervene strategically in cultural reproduction, most significantly in the case of 'Shakespeare' in the definition and transmission of 'knowledge' and 'values' through a national system of education. Hence, Bourdieu's concept of 'cultural capital' is particularly relevant here.

2 Roy Palmer (ed.), *A Touch of the Times* (Harmondsworth: Penguin, 1974), pp. 321–2.

3 See for example the cover of the *Radio Times* (20–6 September 1986). Headlined 'From Will to the World', a portrait of Shakespeare, with a map of the world implanted on his high (bald) brow is presented against a painted backdrop of (crucially) the English countryside. The sub-heading announces 'The great adventure that transformed the island speech of Shakespeare into the world English of 1,000 million – that's "The Story of English" '. For children, the Ladybird series includes, under the rubric of 'History', a similar narrative of 'Shakespeare' which constitutes the comedies as representing the English countryside while the tragedies are seen as dealing with universal themes.

4 See Graham Holderness, Chapter 16, and Michael Bogdanov, Chapter 8, pp. 92–3.

5 E.g. Gary Davies's Radio One 'Bit in the Middle Show' (11 September 1986), in which at least one listener described the return to school as typified by 'Shakespeare' relieved only by lunchtime communal listening to the programme.

6 Ray Galton and Alan Simpson, *Hancock's Half Hour* (London: Woburn, 1974), pp. 78–98. First Broadcast on Friday 2 June 1961.

7 *Housewife Superstar*. A live recording available on Charisma CAS1123, 1976.

8 These characters have often been figured as the archetypal paradigm of love relationship in pop music (e.g. B. A. Robertson, Dire Straits).

9 'Nothing more radically distinguishes popular spectacles – the football match, Punch and Judy, the circus, wrestling or even in some cases the cinema – from bourgeois spectacles, than the form of the participation of the public.' Pierre Bourdieu, *La Distinction* (Paris: Editions de Minuit, 1979), p. 569.

10 As Colin Mercer argues, 'it is generally true that in the body politic popular culture and its modes of reception have been located somewhere below the belt'. Tony Bennett *et al.*, *Popular Culture and Social Relations* (Milton Keynes: Open University Press, 1986), p. 60.

11 Clearly Bakhtin's conceptualisation of the carnivalesque is helpful here but in a way which needs to be clearly qualified. It is arguable that there is more than a hint of

appropriation in the current vogue for Bakhtin's work in much literary-critical discourse as it can be articulated around a very generalised notion of 'the people' with the carnivalesque constituted as *essentially* subversive through the 'radical' ironies played over 'high' or bourgeois culture. Once again, such dichotomies are – currently – politically appealing to many academics, especially on the left.

12 Willy Russell, *Educating Rita* (London: Longman, 1985).

13 See, for instance, Simon Barker, 'Images of the sixteenth and seventeenth centuries as a history of the present' in *Confronting the Crisis*, ed. F. Barker *et al.* (Essex Sociology of Literature Conference: University of Essex, 1984), pp. 15–26.

14 Hilda Bernstein, *Death is Part of the Process* (London: Grafton, 1986), pp. 141–4. Alan Plater's dramatization of the novel was first broadcast on BBC1 (Sunday 28 September 1986).

15 The urban-suburban-rural complex of cultural practices is not, of course, peculiar to the contemporary formation. Since the nineteenth century the dominant location of the popular has been largely identified with the inner city. The point to make here concerns the proliferation of electronic media of transmission since the 1960s and their relation to popular forms.

16 See Martin J. Wiener, *English Culture and the Decline of the Industrial Spirit 1850–1980* (Cambridge; Cambridge University Press, 1981).

17 The recent chest-thumping machismo of Tony Dunn on behalf of élitist culture in *The Guardian* and *New Socialist* manifests both culpable ignorance and an array of insecurities seeking a resting place in authoritarian discourse.

I would like to thank Dee Dine whose wide-ranging knowledge of popular culture greatly supported the research involved in the preparation of this chapter. I should also like to thank Lorraine Dykes whose patience and good humour were sustained throughout the typing of the manuscript.

'The warrant of womanhood':
Shakespeare and feminist
criticism

Ann Thompson

May we, with the Warrant of Womanhood and the witness of a good conscience,
pursue him with any further revenge?

The Merry Wives of Windsor, IV.ii.206–8

There has been an explosion of feminist criticism of Shakespeare during
the 1980s. It is arguable that the feminist approach will turn out to have
been one of the most lively, productive and influential aspects of Shakespeare criticism in this decade. My aim in this essay will be to investigate
this phenonomen: to relate feminist criticism of Shakespeare to the
wider context of feminist literary criticism, to provide a survey of what
has been done and is currently being done in this field, and to raise some
questions about what might be done next.

It seems appropriate to begin in 1980 when three American women,
Carolyn Ruth Swift Lenz, Gayle Greene and Carol Thomas Neely, edited
The Woman's Part,[1] the first anthology of specifically feminist criticism of
Shakespeare. In the following year, Elizabeth Abel edited a special issue
of *Critical Inquiry* on more general issues of feminism and literature under
the title *Writing and Sexual Difference*.[2] Both these volumes contain not only
individual examples of feminist criticism but also manifestos and general
statements and proposals as to what feminist criticism can do, is doing
and should be doing. *The Woman's Part* also contains a useful bibliography
of what by 1980 had already been done, as far as Shakespeare studies
were concerned.

But when we look at these two books together, a discrepancy arises
which is in fact one of the fundamental and ongoing debates within
feminist criticism. The contributors to *The Woman's Part* not surprisingly
assume that Shakespeare's texts constitute an appropriate focus for
discussion, whereas several of the contributors to *Writing and Sexual*

Difference would see any such discussion as unimportant and marginal to feminist concerns. For Elizabeth Abel, for example, introducing the volume, feminist criticism has moved on as it were from the primitive stage of demonstrating the blind spots in male-authored texts and cataloguing the problems of male-created stereotypes of femininity to a more advanced and more radical focus on feminist readings of texts by female authors.[3] Elaine Showalter would agree: in both of her influential and recently reprinted manifesto essays on feminist criticism, 'Towards a feminist poetics' (1979)[4] and 'Feminist criticism in the wilderness' (1981, included in *Writing and Sexual Difference*),[5] she allows for the possibility of a 'feminist critique' of male authors ('the concern with woman as reader'), but is clearly more excited by and committed to what she terms 'gynocritics' – the construction of a feminist framework for the analysis of texts produced by women themselves ('the concern with woman as writer'): 'Gynocritics begins at the point when we free ourselves from the linear absolutes of male literary history, stop trying to fit women between the lines of the male tradition, and focus instead on the newly visible world of female culture'.[6] Many feminist critics have indeed chosen this focus, but some have argued that the feminist critique of male authors, especially of powerful canonical ones like Milton and Shakespeare, is equally important. An element of personal investment and careerism may be involved (I for one am reluctant to throw away my hard-won expertise in Shakespeare studies and retrain as a specialist in women's novels) but there are also stronger and more principled arguments.

In a controversial essay first published in *Signs* in 1981, Myra Jehlen expressed anxiety about the tendency towards isolationism in women's studies, claiming that feminist scholars 'rather than appending their findings to the existing literature [in a number of fields] . . . generate a new one altogether in which women are not just another focus but the center of an investigation whose categories and terms are derived from the world of female experience'.[7] Hence, while women's studies proliferate, 'there is little indication of feminist impact on the universe of male discourse'. In other words, feminist critics are tempted to spend all their time and energy on re-building their own ghetto and rendering it as cosy and unchallenging as possible (bland visions of women teachers talking about the women characters created by women writers to women students who agree with every word), while failing to 'engage the dominant intellectual systems directly'. This essay has been criticised by other feminists for its assumption that texts can be read 'objectively' and for its desire to distinguish between 'political' and 'aesthetic' readings,[8] but it raises the important and sometimes neglected question of how feminist readers of much of the traditional literary canon can deal with 'what we do not like but recognize as nonetheless valuable, serious, good'. The attempt should be made, since it would seem cowardly, perhaps even irresponsible, if feminist criticism were simply to turn its back on male writers whose work is 'valuable, serious, good' – or powerful, admired and long-lasting within a particular culture (which may be to say the same thing in less 'aesthetic' terms).

Other critics have continued to worry at these issues, both in general discussions of literary canons and in specific studies of canonical authors. In a recent essay, 'Notorious signs, feminist criticism and literary tradition',[9] Adrienne Munich mounts a robust attack on the assumption that feminist critics should limit themselves to female-authored texts, seeing it as reinforcing 'a primitive patriarchal taboo forbidding women to approach sacred objects'. Since in modern patriarchal societies, women are in fact encouraged to participate in the reception of masculine discourse, Munich argues that we should make the most of our opportunity to reinterpret the traditional canon. She challenges over-simple notions of authorship itself – 'One cannot neatly equate a work with the sex of its author' – and argues that feminist criticism can and should consider 'the active role of women in the production [of male-authored texts] – how this two-sexed culture has produced gendered polarities which inform all its writings'. Rejecting the rigid dualism of sexual stereotyping, she claims that 'whether the text is male- or female-authored, the literary canon contains, not a uniform example of male as subject and female as object, but a valuable record of a conflict between sex, gender and common humanity'. The female viewpoint is not necessarily excluded just because the author is anatomically male. Discussing the Book of Genesis, Don Quixote and the Oresteia, she argues that the traditional canon 'may not be as masculinist as some feminist criticism has assumed' and that, moreover, 'Critical discourse has tended to be more misogynist than the texts it examines'. I shall be arguing below that this latter point is of particular interest for feminist critics of Shakespeare.

Perhaps, though, it is more difficult for us to reread Shakespeare. The very fact that he is less obviously and overtly misogynistic (than, say, Milton)[10] has turned out to be a source of confusion for some feminist critics who, understandably, have wanted to emphasise what they see as the more enlightened aspects of his works, the extent to which it can be claimed that he held more progressive views about women than his contemporaries, was able to see through the limitations of conventional gender definitions. At worst this can result in some rather sloppy criticism which focuses in a naïve and unproblematised way on female characters (the next best thing to female authors?) and does not go very far beyond old-fashioned character study. But this is not the case with most feminist studies which, even when they do restrict themselves to this area, tell us many things we did not already know.

'Apologist' critics who would like to claim Shakespeare as a proto-feminist have in fact often been able to demonstrate that his female characters are not the crude stereotypes we sometimes take them for. They point out that characters like Gertrude, Ophelia, Desdemona and Cordelia have an existence and importance beyond the limited perception of them experienced by Hamlet, Othello or Lear. Male critics have often encouraged us to see such women completely through the eyes of the hero, but feminist critics can reasonably counter that they often appear on stage without the hero, sometimes in relation to other women, and that it is frequently the case that the hero's view of them is shown to be shallow, simplistic or just wrong. Production studies in this area have revealed that it is not just critics who have given us a misleadingly misogynistic Shakespeare but male producers and adaptors of the plays in the theatre have often exaggerated the stereotyping and marginalising of women beyond what is required by the text. Irene G. Dash has shown in her study *Wooing, Wedding and Power: Women in Shakespeare's Plays*[11] that, through the use of cutting, rearrangement and rewriting as well as through editorial and critical comment, Shakespeare's female characters have often been converted into whatever was seen as properly 'womanly' at any given time.

Feminist critics have re-examined and stressed the importance of relations between women in the plays, the extent to which they confide in and support each other and create a female sub-culture separate from the male world, capable often of operating in terms of different values and attitudes. Women become friends in surprising circumstances, such as when the plot makes them rivals for the love of the same man (Julia's sympathy for Silvia in *The Two Gentlemen of Verona*, Viola's for Olivia in *Twelfth Night*), or when, as in *Measure for Measure* and *All's Well That End's Well*, they conspire together to outwit a man at just the moment that he thinks he is triumphing over one of them by forcing her into bed.

On the other hand, it is necessary for feminists to note how far Shakespeare's female characters are in the end restricted by the patriarchal structures that dominate their lives. It is regularly the case that female

friendship, though it may be strong, even passionate as in the declar-
ations of Helena in A Midsummer Night's Dream (III.ii), Celia in As You Like It
(I.iii) and Emilia in The Two Noble Kinsmen (I.iii), has to be supplanted by
marriage. Moreover, Helena and Hermia provide a counter-example of
women who do not develop a sisterly solidarity but instead behave
accordingly to the male stereotype which assumes that all women are
naturally rivals for the attention of men. They even fight: this is rare in
Shakespeare but when it does happen (in II.i of The Taming of the Shrew,
conceivably in II.i of King John) it is depressing how often directors resort
to the easy comic cliché of women ineffectively hitting each other with
their handbags. When women have intimate friendships with each other
it is assumed to be an adolescent phase that they must outgrow, whereas
men can continue to have strong ties with other men after they are
married.[12] Even when an important friendship between mature women
is supposed to exist, as in the case of Hermione and Paulina in The Winter's
Tale, it may not actually be dramatised: Paulina speaks to Hermione
through an intermediary in the prison scene (II.ii), and the two women
barely address each other in the final scene. Apparently powerful
women like Rosalind and Portia have to give up their power when they
become wives, Rosalind reducing herself to the status of a male possession ('To you I give myself, for I am yours; she says to both father and
husband in V.iv), and Portia describing herself quite untruthfully as 'an
unlesson'd girl' unworthy of Bassanio, in III.ii. An apologist feminist
critic like Marianne Novy makes the best of these situations, arguing for
the importance of 'mutuality' in Shakespeare's conception of marriage
which allows women, though technically or theoretically inferior to men
under patriarchy, to be accepted in practice as real partners.[13] Other
critics, including myself, are less sanguine.

It is however important to remember that this is an area where realisation in the theatre can make a major difference; a modern actress is
unlikely to deliver such lines in a solemn or portentous way. More likely
she will be affectionate and perhaps lightly ironic, indicating that her
self-deprecation is not meant to be taken too seriously. And of course we
have no right to assume that this is anything new: Elizabethan audiences
would not have awarded plays their unqualified ideological assent any
more than modern ones do. Both Rosalind and Portia have somewhat
more to say for themselves before the end of the play in any case: I shall
discuss the epilogue to As You Like It below.

At least feminist criticism registers these areas as 'problematic', and in
new ways. There have been many reassessments of characters who have

long been recognised as problems: Katherina in The Taming of the Shrew, Gertrude in Hamlet, Isabella in Measure for Measure, Helena in All's Well That Ends Well and of course Cressida and Cleopatra are favourite topics. At the same time we are putting the 'problem' label on more and more characters, plays or episodes (especially endings). I myself have tried to argue that The Taming of the Shrew has in fact always been a problem play and that modern feminist criticism is to be commended for recognising and addressing this in explicit ways.[14] It may, as Kathleen McLuskie says, be easier to challenge or deny the pleasure of comedy in this way since it is 'a pleasure many feminists have learned to struggle with as they withold their assent from the social approval of sexist humour', but it may be more difficult to deny the 'emotional, moral and aesthetic satisfaction afforded by tragedy'.[15]

The test-case here seems to be the ending of King Lear: as McLuskie says, when Lear enters with his daughter dead in his arms, 'the most stony-hearted feminist could not withhold her pity even though it is called forth at the expense of her resistance to the patriarchal relations which it endorses'. Peter Erickson equally makes the point that Lear at the end has got exactly what he wants from Cordelia: 'Upon her re-entry to the play, she obliges Lear in the role of the good, comforting mother, to which he had originally assigned her' (and in which she contrasts so strikingly with the 'bad mothers', Goneril and Regan). Her husband having been conveniently suppressed, she is both maternal and virginal, nurturing and non-threatening. However, 'This appropriation of Cordelia is not an act of love but a violation of it that echoes and repeats Lear's ritual possessiveness in the opening scene'.[16]

These readings lead us to what Wayne Booth calls the 'scandal' of the feminist critique whereby 'I find that my pleasure in some parts of [the] text has now been somewhat diminished by my critical act'.[17] Does feminist criticism have the right and/or the nerve to diminish or even downright destroy the sort of pleasure audiences and readers have traditionally taken in Shakespeare? Can we imagine feminist productions that take a similarly critical line? Kathleen McLuskie hypothesises such productions of Measure for Measure and King Lear only to reject them as impossible because they require too radical a revision of the texts, but it could be claimed that Michael Bogdanov's production of The Taming of the Shrew for the Royal Shakespeare Company in 1978 (discussed by the director elsewhere in this volume) took a feminist line which was hostile to the traditional reading of the play (especially at the end), and I have recently seen a production of A Midsummer Night's Dream at the Deutsches Theater in East Berlin (directed by Alexander Lang, 1986) which similarly played 'against the text' by refusing to treat love as a particularly positive or charming experience and by emphasising the victim-status of the women. Neither production was *enjoyable* in a straightforward way, something I could accept with *The Shrew*, believing as I do that audiences ought not to be encouraged to experience that text as simply rollicking good fun, but which I found more difficult in the case of *The Dream*.

Some people might immediately wish to object that feminist readings of this kind are 'anachronistic', imposing modern meanings on old texts. One response would be to say that we *can* only read Shakespeare (or anyone else) from our own modern perspective and that it is illusory to suppose that we can do anything else. This is not however to deny the importance of an historical approach: the better we can understand the original historical conditions of the production of the texts (both social and theatrical), the better we should be able to relate them to our own very different historical conditions. Of course this has to be done very carefully, remembering that 'history' is a complex and often contradictory discourse itself, not capable of providing us with simple 'explanations' of what we find in literature any more than literature can be seen as a simple illustration of history. However, several feminist critics (again preferring on the whole to see Shakespeare as a comparatively advanced or liberal thinker) have related the ideas about marriage and the role of women in the family found in the plays to a general shift in thinking in such matters which seems to have occurred in this period, mainly as a result of various waves of religious dissent.

The medieval Catholic church had of course been largely anti-feminist by modern standards, taking the line (reflected in the Elizabethan homily on marriage) that wives were to be strictly subjected to their husbands. But, beginning with humanists like Erasmus and continuing with Protestant and Puritan reformers, a number of writers were beginning to argue for a more equal view of marriage in which husband and wife were more like partners. Juliet Dusinberre makes much of this apparent advance in her pioneering study *Shakespeare and the Nature of Women*, published in 1975, claiming that 'The Puritans' gift to their world lay in the replacing of the legal union of the arranged marriage with a union born of the spirit'.[18] If women were to be men's spiritual partners, marriages must be freely chosen on both sides, leading to a validation of romantic love and a greater dignity and respect for women.

Writing ten years later, Catherine Belsey is less confident of wide-spread progress but still claims that there was 'a contest for the meaning of the family in the sixteenth and seventeenth centuries [which] momen-tarily unfixed the existing system of differences'.[19] This 'unfixing' pro-duced a 'gap' through which we are able to able to glimpse, represented in Shakespeare's plays, a disruption of the sexual stereotyping which had dominated perceptions previously and was to dominate them again subsequently.

Both Dusinberre and Belsey rely on investigations into social history conducted by scholars like Lawrence Stone who describes the rise of what he calls 'companionate marriage' in this period. (This concept also lies behind Marianne Novy's emphasis on 'mutuality' discussed above.) Yet Stone himself is rather less sanguine as to whether the influence of the dissenting tradition really aided in the liberation of women. He points out that in practice Protestantism gave husbands even more power than before as they took over some aspects of the role of the priest, and that the new emphasis on individual reading of the Bible further favoured men, who were much more likely to be literate than women.[20]

The theatrical conditions in which Shakespeare worked were of course overwhelmingly dominated by men. As Kathleen McLuskie says, the plays were 'the products of an entertainment industry which, as far as we know, had no women shareholders, actors, writers or stage hands'.[21] (We do however have good reason to believe that there were reasonable numbers of women in the audience.)[22] Not surprisingly, feminist critics have further explored the convention whereby male actors played female roles, a convention which in itself might be said to disrupt the system of sexual differences and make it possible to question overly simple notions of identity, including sexual identity.[23] Considering the epilogue to *As You Like It* from this perspective, Catherine Belsey asks 'Who is speaking?' at the point when the actor playing Rosalind comes forward to address the audience. She concludes that both 'a male actor *and* a female character is speaking' and that the conviction allows Shake-speare to hold the issue of sexuality open and unresolved.[24] Belsey's reading makes the point that the epilogue does not just 'reveal' the acting company but sets up a complex dialogue between actor and audience in which the sexes in the audience are explicitly named and foregrounded.

A different kind of historical approach is pioneered by Elaine Showal-ter in her essay 'Representing Ophelia: women, madness, and the res-ponsibilities of feminist criticism'.[25] She attempts to 'tell Ophelia's story' not so much from the minimal information offered by the text of *Hamlet* but from a study of her representation in painting, psychiatry and literature as well as on stage. She explores the ways in which Ophelia is seen as typifying female melancholy or madness (which 'must' be erotic in both origin and expression) and reveals the extraordinary consequences of her status as icon: women in mental institutions were encouraged to act the part of Ophelia while under hypnosis as a form of therapy; actresses playing Ophelia went mad in earnest. This then is a study of 'the Ophelia myth' since 'The representation of Ophelia changes independently of theories of the meaning of the play or the Prince, for it depends on attitudes towards women and madness'. This kind of feminist criticism, operating frankly at a certain remove from the text, or at least putting as much stress on the traditions that have accrued after and around the text, seems to me a particularly fruitful area. One could imagine equally interesting studies of 'the Cordelia myth', 'the Cleopatra myth' and so on.

Turning from approaches with an emphasis on history to those based more in psychoanalysis, a comparable model can be found in Jacqueline Rose's 'Sexuality in the reading of Shakespeare: *Hamlet* and *Measure for Measure*'.[26] As her title implies, she is concerned with the *reading* of the plays, from both a psychoanalytic and a literary perspective. She aims to show that 'psychoanalytic and literary criticism share with the literature they address a terrain of language, fantasy and sexuality – a terrain in which the woman occupies a crucial, but difficult, place'. Characters like Gertrude in *Hamlet* and Isabella in *Measure for Measure* have been required by both psychoanalytic and literary critics to bear the responsibility or blame for the 'disorder' perceived on both aesthetic and sexual levels: the 'problem' with these plays (from the point of view of the male reader) is identified as too much sexuality (in the case of Gertrude) or too little (in the case of Isabella): either way the woman is accused of failing in her duty to hold male sexual desire in place, and her failing leads to his crime. Rose sees T. S. Eliot's critique of *Hamlet* as exemplary of a peculiarly harsh and repressive kind of literary criticism in which 'what is felt as inscrutable, unmanageable or even horrible for an aesthetic theory which will only allow into its definition what can be controlled or managed by art, is nothing other than femininity itself'. She maintains that 'much recent literary theory can be seen as an attempt to undo the ferocious effects' of this tradition which 'siphons off or distracts attention from the difficulty of language itself' by concentrating too much on the woman.

Rose's essay is one of the most recent and to my mind valuable contributions to what is by now a considerable body of feminist criticism of Shakespeare from a psychoanalytic viewpoint. Such approaches can helpfully theorise or 'stiffen' the analysis of character as well as allow critics to consider the importance of gender to the author's motivation, the audience or reader's responses and to the latent structures of literary texts themselves. They have been more prevalent in North America than in Britain: some of the essays in *The Woman's Part* use psychoanalytical perspectives, as do books subsequently published by two of the contributors, Coppélia Kahn's *Man's Estate: Masculine Identity in Shakespeare*[27] and Carol Thomas Neely's *Broken Nuptials in Shakespeare's Plays.*[28] Coppélia Kahn has also edited, with Murray Schwartz, *Representing Shakespeare: New Psychoanalytic Essays,*[29] which contains several feminist contributions.

Paradoxically, a major advantage of the psychoanalytic approach is that it allows feminist critics to write about male characters and tragedy as well as about female characters and comedy. An influential essay by Janet Adelman shows how Coriolanus's masculine identity is based on his transformation of the 'feminine' qualities of dependency and vulnerability into phallic aggression,[30] and Coppélia Kahn has written interestingly on such topics as the passage from boyhood to manhood in *Romeo and Juliet* and the obsession with cuckoldry in the canon, particularly of course in *Othello.*[31] She worries about whether such a reading strategy is appropriate for a feminist critic: 'To read Shakespearean tragedy or any other patriarchal literature as the account of specifically masculine dilemmas of self-definition, it might seem, is to privilege male experience and allow its voice to speak for women as well, accepting just those assumptions which we as feminists are at pains to challenge.' However, this limitation can be turned into an advantage: 'The crucial difference . . . between the feminist reader in pursuit of the maternal subtext and Maynard Mack or A. C. Bradley is that they take it for granted that the male experience portrayed in Shakespearean tragegy is universal, while the feminist reader consciously notes the gender perspective of this genre, and tries to learn from it about the working myths of patriarchal culture.'[32] In practice, some definitions of both gender and genre have been over-simplistic. Marilyn French sees the plays straightforwardly and rather depressingly as debates between male and female principles with the male principle standing for violence, competitiveness and the power to kill while the female stands for the power to nurture and give birth.[33] And this is an area in which feminist critics have public disagreements: Lisa Jardine is scathingly dismissive of Marilyn French,[34] and

Kathleen McLuskie is dubious about the whole 'essentialist' tradition
typified by Kahn, French and Linda Bamber whose book *Comic Women,
Tragic Men: a Study of Gender and Genre in Shakespeare* has in my experience the
dubious distinction of representing the acceptable face of feminist
criticism for a number of male Shakespeareans.[35]

A more challenging and difficult mode of psychoanalytic criticism
draws on the work of Lacan and Derrida and their feminist counterparts,
Julia Kristeva, Hélène Cixous and Luce Irigaray.[36] Several essays in *Shakespeare and the Question of Theory* adopt this approach, including one in the
section called 'The woman's part', perhaps significantly one written by a
man, Joel Fineman's 'The turn of the Shrew'. Fineman seeks to establish
how what he terms the 'subversive discourse of woman' in *The Taming of
the Shrew* finally comes to endorse male authority, relating this to a wider
question of considerable interest for feminist critics: 'is it possible to
voice a language, whether of man or woman, that does not speak, sooner
or later, self-consciously or unconsciously, for the order and authority of
man?'[37] By placing the thematic oppositions of the play alongside the
theoretical debates within psychoanalysis – particularly the feminist
deconstructive approaches to Lacan – Fineman explores these questions
in a new way.

What then has feminist criticism achieved and what remains to be
done? Not one but many ways of discussing Shakespeare have been
discovered. It has proved possible not only to reread the texts themselves but, and this is equally important, to scrutinise the ways in which
the meanings of those texts have been determined by later generations of
critics, editors, adaptors, directors and teachers. Feminist critics have
challenged many of those meanings, pointing out both that the meanings
are different when women are reading the texts, and that the meanings
are in any case not 'timeless' or 'universal' as is sometimes glibly
supposed but historically and culturally constructed, both in Shakespeare's time and also in all subsequent times.

It is important for feminist critics to continue to intervene in every way
in the reading and interpretation of Shakespeare and to establish, even
more securely than they have already done, that their approach is not just
another choice amongst a plurality of modes of reading, not something
that can be relegated to an all-woman ghetto, but a major new perspective that must eventually inform *all* readings. It is encouraging to note that
I have been discussing the work of some male critics as well as that of
female critics in this chapter, and that in the case of a book like *Shakespeare*

and the Question of Theory it must have been difficult for the editors to divide the essays into the four sections they had labelled 'Language, rhetoric, deconstruction'; 'The woman's part'; 'politics, economy, history'; 'Hamlet'. The essays in 'The woman's part' (two out of four written by men) could have been allocated to different sections, while essays in all four sections assume a feminist perspective as part of their approach. This is no more surprising than to find that an anti-racialist perspective has by now become a normal part of most critical writing about black authors or the black characters in the works of white authors, regardless of the race of the critic.[38] Of course tokenism still exists (as witness my own role in this book) but 'something peculiar' has indeed been happening to this particular classic author and it is unlikely to stop.

Nevertheless, while feminist criticism has had a major impact on Shakespeare studies in the 1980s, there are still several challenges remaining. It is, for example, a little disappointing that feminist criticism has continued to follow traditional assumptions about the established hierarchy within the canon, privileging the tragedies above all, then the middle comedies and the problem plays. I am not suggesting that there should be a real revolution in these rankings, but I regret that feminist criticism has so far neglected the earliest plays (apart from the fairly inevitable promotion of The Taming of the Shrew) and the history plays. It would be fascinating to see what a feminist perspective would do for a reading of Henry V, for example,[39] and it seems particularly surprising that no one has studied the paradigms of female domination and male anxiety in Titus Andronicus or the Henry VI plays.

Close study of language can certainly be revealing. I myself recently discovered a strong ideological dimension to Shakespeare's use of printing metaphors in the context of a book which did not set out to be specifically feminist.[40] I observed that, while people in general are often seen as 'books' which can be 'read' by others, the contents of the book where a woman is concerned are more likely than not to be to do with her sexual innocence or guilt. Moreover, the sexual act itself is seen, from the male point of view, as being like printing in so far as the man is reproducing copies of himself with the woman as instrument or 'press'. The emphasis is on both the supposed passivity of women in sexual intercourse and on the dimension of authority and ownership: the printing metaphor is often used where questions of legitimacy are involved, implying that what happens in marriage is that the man acquires 'copyright' in the woman's body.[41]

But who has authority over Shakespeare's texts? It is disappointing that feminist criticism has had so little impact on the editing of the plays, despite the fact that it has been flourishing at a time when major new editions are in progress from both Oxford and Cambridge University Presses and when other standard editions like the Arden Shakespeare are undergoing revision. Few women (let alone feminists) are asked to edit plays, and male editors have not so far felt obliged to take much notice of feminist criticism. It is astonishing that two major new editions[42] of The Taming of the Shrew published in 1981 and 1982 did not so much as mention the recent explosion of feminist interest in the play, even in order to condemn it: this surely amounts to the editors neglecting their duty to provide an accurate overview of current critical opinion. No woman has ever edited a major tragedy; Anne Barton took over T. J. B. Spencer's work on Hamlet after he died but contributed only the Introduction to the final volume,[43] not the Commentary where the real power of the editor lies. The Introduction usually has to vie with all the other criticism a reader might encounter but the Notes and Commentary have a privileged authority since the editor is there, in an apparently objective spirit, explaining what the text is and what, word by word and sentence by sentence, it means.

This brings me to the important question of the impact of feminist criticism on the teaching of Shakespeare both in schools and in colleges and universities. It seems crucial that a feminist perspective should be beginning to 'filter down' through the system to inform all levels, and that it should not be seen as the preserve of advanced students. It is difficult to know if this is happening yet, but fortunately feminism as a political project is a much larger phenomenon than feminist criticism and it is possible that basic attitudes are changing in advance of or independently of academic research. In fact some changes are 'filtering up': many first-year students today, both male and female, notice and want to discuss sexist attitudes in texts by writers like Shakespeare and Milton in a way that simply did not happen ten years ago. This is more likely to be the result of a general shift in attitudes towards women than the consequence of selfconsciously feminist teaching. Nevertheless, academics have their part to play in supporting and strengthening these changes.

Notes

1 Urbana, Chicago and London: University of Illinois Press. Some of the contributors to this volume – Irene Dash, Coppélia Kahn, Carol Thomas Neely and Marianne Novy – have subsequently published books in this area: see notes 11, 27, 28 and 13 respectively below.

2 *Critical Inquiry*, vol. 8, no. 2 (winter 1981). This issue, with the addition of some critical responses, was reprinted in book form under the title *Writing and Sexual Difference*, ed. Elizabeth Abel (Brighton: Harvester, 1982). Page references below are to the book version.

3 Introduction, pp. 1–2.

4 This essay first appeared in Mary Jacobus, ed., *Women Writing and Writing about Women* (London: Croom Helm, 1979), pp. 22–41. It has been reprinted in Elaine Showalter, ed., *The New Feminist Criticism* (London: Virago, 1986), pp. 125–43. Page references are to the first publication.

5 This essay is also reprinted in *The New Feminist Criticism*; see footnote 4, pp. 243–70.

6 'Towards a feminist poetics', p. 28.

7 'Archimedes and the paradox of feminist criticism', *Signs*, vol. 6, no. 4 (summer 1981), 575–601. Reprinted in Nannerl O. Keohane, Michelle Z. Rosaldo and Barbara C. Gelpi, ed., *Feminist Theory: a Critique of Ideology* (Chicago and London: University of Chicago Press, 1982), pp. 189–215, and in Elizabeth Abel and Emily Abel, eds., *The Signs Reader* (Chicago and London: University of Chicago Press, 1983), pp. 69–95. The passages quoted are from pp. 70–2 and p. 79 in *The Signs Reader*.

8 *Signs* printed responses to Jehlen's article by Elaine Showalter and Patrocinio Schweickart in vol. 8, no. 1 (autumn 1982), 160–4 and 170–6. It is also discussed in detail by Toril Moi in *Sexual/Textual Politics* (London and New York: Methuen, 1985), pp. 80–6.

9 In Gayle Greene and Coppélia Kahn, eds., *Making a Difference: Feminist Literary Criticism* (London and New York: Methuen, 1985), pp. 238–59. The passages quoted are from pp. 243–4 and 251.

10 Virginia Woolf wrote that literate women must 'look past Milton's bogey, for no human being should shut out the view' in *A Room of One's Own* (London: Hogarth Press, 1929), p. 118. This brief and somewhat enigmatic reference is discussed by Sandra M. Gilbert in 'Patriarchal poetry and women readers: reflections on Milton's bogey', *PMLA*, 93 (1978), 368–82.

11 New York: Columbia University Press, 1981.

12 Peter Erickson explores this imbalance in *Patriarchal Structures in Shakespeare's Drama* (Berkeley and London: University of California Press, 1985).

13 See *Love's Argument: Gender Relations in Shakespeare* (Chapel Hill, Ind., and London: University of North Carolina Press, 1984), *passim*.

14 See the Introduction to my edition of *The Taming of the Shrew* (Cambridge: CUP, 1984), especially pp. 17–41.

15 'The patriarchal bard: feminist criticism and Shakespeare: *King Lear* and *Measure for Measure*' in Jonathan Dollimore and Alan Sinfield, eds., *Political Shakespeare*, (Manchester: 1985), pp. 88–108 (p. 98).

16 Erickson (see note 12), pp. 112–14.

17 Wayne Booth, 'Freedom of interpretation: Bakhtin and the challenge of feminist criticism', *Critical Inquiry*, vol. 9, no. 1 (September 1982), p. 68.

18 (London: Macmillan), p. 104.

19 'Disrupting sexual difference: meaning and gender in the comedies' in John Drakakis, ed., *Alternative Shakespeares*, (London and New York: Methuen, 1985), pp. 166–90 (p. 190).

20 Lawrence Stone, *The Family, Sex and Marriage in England 1500–1800* (London: Weidenfield and Nicolson, 1977), pp. 154–5. Keith Wrightson also discusses this controversy in *English Society 1580–1680* (London: Hutchinson, 1982), chapter 4.

21 McLuskie (see note 15), p. 92.

22 See Alfred Harbage, *Shakespeare's Audience* (New York and London: Columbia University Press, 1941) and Ann Jennalie Cook, *The Privileged Playgoers of Shakespeare's London: 1576–1642* (Princeton, N.J.: Princeton University Press, 1981).

23 See especially Lisa Jardine's chapter on this issue in *Still Harping on Daughters: Women and Drama in the Age of Shakespeare* (Brighton: Harvester, 1983), pp. 9–36.

24 Belsey (see note 19), p. 181.
25 In Patricia Parker and Geoffrey Hartman, eds., *Shakespeare and the Question of Theory* (New York and London: Methuen, 1985), pp. 77–94. The passage quoted is on pp. 91–2.
26 In John Drakakis, ed., *Alternative Shakespeares* (see note 19), pp. 95–118. The passages quoted are on p. 95, p. 101 and p. 102.
27 Berkeley, Cal. and London: University of California Press, 1981.
28 New Haven, Conn. and London: Yale University Press, 1985.
29 Baltimore, MD. and London: Johns Hopkins University Press, 1980. For a useful general survey of psychoanalytical feminist criticism, see Judith Kegan Gardiner, 'Mind mother: psychoanalysis and feminism' in Gayle Greene and Coppélia Kahn, eds., *Making a Difference* (see note 9), pp. 113–45.
30 ' "Anger's my meat": feeding, dependency, and aggression in *Coriolanus*' in David Bevington and Jay L. Halio, eds., *Shakespeare: Pattern of Excelling Nature* (Cranbury, N.J.: Associated University Presses, 1978), pp. 108–24. Reprinted in Murray M. Schwartz and Coppélia Kahn, eds., *Representing Shakespeare* (see note 29), pp. 129–49.
31 *Man's Estate* (see note 27), chapter 4 and 5.
32 'Excavating "those dim Minoan regions": maternal subtexts in patriarchal Literature', *Diacritics* (summer 1982), 32–41 (p. 41).
33 *Shakespeare's Division of Experience* (London: Jonathan Cape, 1982).
34 Jardine (see note 23), pp. 5–6 and 8.
35 McLuskie (see note 15), pp. 88–92. Bamber's book was published by Stanford University Press, Stanford, California, 1982.
36 A useful anthology of French feminist approaches has been edited by Elaine Marks and Isabelle de Courtivron under the title *New French Feminisms* (Brighton: Harvester, 1981). Introductory accounts can be found in Ann Rosalind Jones, 'Inscribing femininity. French theories of the feminine' in Gayle Greene and Coppélia Kahn, eds., *Making a Difference* (see note 9), pp. 80–112 and in Toril Moi (see note 8), pp. 89–173.
37 'The turn of the Shrew' in Patricia Parker and Geoffrey Hartman, eds., *Shakespeare and the Question of Theory* (see note 25), pp. 138–59 (p. 138). See also Madalan Gohlke, ' "I wooed thee with my sword": Shakespeare's tragic paradigms', in Carolyn Ruth Swift Lenz, Gayle Greene and Carol Thomas Neely, eds., *The Woman's Part* (see note 1), pp. 150–70. Reprinted in Murray M. Schwartz and Coppélia Kahn, eds., *Representing Shakespeare* (see note 29), pp. 170–87.
38 This too is of course a recent development; see the surveys of black feminist criticism by Barbara Smith and Deborah E. McDowell in Elaine Showalter, ed., *The New Feminist Criticism* (see note 4), pp. 168–85 and pp. 186–99.
39 The nearest thing yet that I know of is Peter Erickson's chapter in *Patriarchal Structures* (see note 12), pp. 39–65.
40 *Shakespeare, Meaning and Metaphor*, written in collaboration with John O. Thompson (Brighton: Harvester, 1987). See especially chapter 5.
41 For examples of printing as a metaphor for legitimacy, see *The Taming of the Shrew* IV.iv.92–3, *Measure for Measure* II.iv.42–9 and *The Winter's Tale* II.iii.98–103 and V.i.124–6, Riverside text, ed. G. Blakemore Evans (Boston, Mass.: Houghton Mifflin, 1974). The notion of women as 'blank pages' waiting to be inscribed by the male pen/penis is by no means exclusive to Shakespeare, as Susan Gubar has demonstrated in ' "The blank page" and the issues of female creativity' in Elizabeth Abel, ed., *Writing and Sexual Difference* (see note 2), pp. 73–93.
42 Brian Morris edited the play for the Arden Shakespeare (London and New York: Methuen, 1981); H. J. Oliver edited it for the Oxford Shakespeare (Oxford: Clarendon, 1982).
43 Published in the Penguin Shakespeare (Harmondsworth: 1980).

Michael Bogdanov
interviewed by Christopher J. McCullough

Your production of The Taming of the Shrew[1] changed the way many people now think about that play. Most post-war productions I know of seem to suggest that Kate is helped towards self-awareness and self-fulfilment through learning that Petruchio is her master. . . .

Quite an obscene idea – I don't believe Shakespeare thought that for one minute.

None the less, we cannot evade the fact that we (male director and male critic) are discussing feminist issues as they affect the work of a male playwright. What problems have you encountered in the response of women to your work: perhaps in particular that of radical feminists, who may well see your work (and our discussion) as yet another example of male-dominated discourse?

I don't see why they would do that, and it hasn't happened to me. I believe Shakespeare was a feminist, and all the plays I direct analyse that matter; analyse the roles of women from that ideological point of view. I think there is no question of it: he shows how women are ill-treated, abused, and how often they have to dress themselves up as men in order that they may be treated on an equal basis, if they are not at the seat of power. And, even if they are at the seat of power, they have to cling to it, or it's down the slippery pole – like Margaret in Richard III. Take the case of Gertrude in Hamlet, she has to marry two kings to stay at the top. Or look at Ophelia's position, the way her father and brother kick her around – no wonder the girl went mad, she must have been a depressed and repressed person before anything happened with Hamlet!

Shakespeare shows women totally abused – like animals – bartered to the highest bidder. He shows women used as commodities, not allowed to choose for themselves. In The Taming of the Shrew you get that extraordinary scene between Baptista, Grumio, and Tranio, where they are vying with each other to see who can offer most for Bianca, who is described as 'the prize'. It is a toss of the coin to see which way she will go: to the old man with a certain amount of money, or to the young man, who is boasting that he's got so many ships. She could end up with the old impotent fool, or the young 'eligible' man: what sort of life is that to look forward to? There is no question of it, his sympathy is with the women, and his purpose, to expose the cruelty of a society that allows these things to happen.

All the plays have an attitude to women that, for me, is very clear. The only criticism I suffer from some feminists is for doing Shakespeare at all; because there are so few parts for women.

Radical feminists might argue that a 'feminist' production of a play by Shakespeare does no good at all to the cause of female emancipation, and that it is necessary to establish alternative ideologies to those constructed by men.

I have long since given up apologising for not being a member of an oppressed, disadvantaged, or minority group: finally there will be no 'minorities' to belong to, because somebody, somewhere is criticising you for not having been born a certain colour or creed. It's like opening doors for people; I used to open doors for men and women, and with some women I got a tirade of abuse. What do I do now? I go through the door first and then hold it open; in the end everything is denied you. As somebody who works out my politics through theatre, I can't have that, because I have to reflect the world that I see around me through the plays that I direct. If I choose to direct Shakespeare, then Shakespeare is reflecting for me those views of other people who may well be described as oppressed or minority groups. The fact that I am none of these things myself, does not automatically exclude me from being able to discuss those affairs in public, through the medium of theatre; and that is, after all, the principal objective of theatre. It's meant to provoke debate: to explore issues that are carried on into debate with a passion and a commitment to change. That makes theatre worthwhile. Theatre, when it is doing its job properly, is a more effective medium than any other for provoking thought into action: unhappily, most of the time it doesn't do its job.

You have written that you believe Shakespeare to have produced in The Taming of the Shrew *a play that asks for 'an egalitarian society of equal rights and opportunity'.[2] Is that perhaps closer to your concept of feminism?*

I believe he set out to write a play about a wish-fulfilment dream of a male for revenge on a female. I think that emerges very clearly from the 'Induction', which is the key to the whole play. Sly, the drunken tinker, is thrown out of the pub by the hostess, falls asleep, and dreams a dream of revenge and power; not only power over women, but class power through wealth. The first image that comes to him in his dream is the huntsman who bets on the dog in exactly the same way, and with the same amounts of money, as the women are bet on at the end of the play. It is a cruel oppressive world where nothing will ever really change.

What of the historicist argument that a play like The Taming of the Shrew *is undeniably sexist in its attitudes, though it may be necessary to perform it in order that it might be exposed as such?*

You can only see it as a sexist play if you misunderstand what Shakespeare has actually written. Everybody is entitled to their own subjective view of the play, and in that sense, you could play it as a sexist drama. But you would have to cut something out; that is my point, you must distort some of the lines, or be called to account for what they mean. To play it as a sexist piece you would have to cut the 'Induction', for it is in that scene that the clues to the play's real nature are set down.

Many productions of the play do cut the 'Induction', whereas you foregrounded it.

The induction scene took the form of a drunk who wanders into the auditorium and starts to have a row with the front-of-house-manageress, who tries to throw him out. The drunk (Sly) clambers on to the stage and 'accidentally' destroys the pictorial Italianate setting; we are left, for the rest of the production, with the bare bones of the stage. It was a challenge to the audience as to what is illusion, and what is reality; the transfer of what appeared to be a live event in the auditorium, to the stage and the destruction of an obviously artificial setting.

Do you mean that the device of linking the 'real' event in the auditorium and the destruction of the set on stage, worked in the sense of Brecht's concept of 'alienation'?

Yes I suppose so – in a sense. But I don't really believe in Brecht's 'alienation'. I believe audiences are engaged emotionally in whatever you do. I don't believe you can objectify the theatrical experience in the way that Brecht intended. Therefore I do try to draw the audience into the experience emotionally, and then shock them. I suppose that is alienation in that respect; lulling them into that false sense of security, then disrupting it.

If the style of your 'Induction' scene, in the auditorium and on stage, drew attention to the contradictions between reality and theatre, then surely, by being self-reflexive, it was alienatory.

Yes, but it was a direct link to the Shakespearean 'Induction'; it wasn't in any way gratuitous. Everything was followed through with Shakespeare's induction being translated into a dialogue between the drunk and the front-of-house manageress. The act of theatre was self-reflexive, but leaving the nerve ends raw and tingling, ready for the violent experience to come. The violence of my production was meant to engage the audience on an emotional level, to the extent of asking the audience to stand up and be counted. To ask what you really believe, are you really sitting comfortably in your seats, or is there something else that theatre makes you do? Makes you angry, makes you fear, challenges you, and finally makes you want to do something to change the world. Catharsis has no meaning for me. I'm not interested in people purging their emotions in the theatre and then walking away without a care in the world. I am only interested in theatre that excites people enough to make them want to cheer, or be angry enough to walk out.

Could you develop your views on the 'relevance' of Shakespeare's plays today: what does your phrase 'Shakespeare Lives' mean?[3]

I don't see any point in directing Shakespeare for the stage unless you treat him, as Jan Kott[4] described him, as 'our contemporary'. There is no question of treating the plays as archaic anachronisms: you have to relate them to the society in which you live in order to make immediate contact with the audience. If that contact is made by presenting the plays in a particular way, then that is the way to do them. I work in modern dress all the time, because I find that method erects the least barriers between the audience and the language of the plays. There are other directors, of course, who are very successful in working in other ways. But I find that modern dress is the method I need to employ to highlight the contemporary parallel.

To claim a seventeenth-century playwright as 'our contemporary' may be understood as a claim for a Shakespeare whose work represents universal verities transcending history.

Some problems remain and some don't. Some things that Shakespeare wrote about were intensely parochial and local, and other themes, particularly his major themes – the nature of power and the territorial imperative – are things that pertain today, just as much as they did four hundred years ago. In what was a pre-capitalist era, he analysed that era in a way that is relevant to the capitalism of today. The nature of kingship and power is exactly the same now as it was then: the lust for power, greed, the thing that makes brother kill brother, mother betray son – all that scramble to the top for the crock of gold and then toppling off down the other side as somebody else slices off your legs from under you with a sword. All this, achieved in the context of what seemed to be the divine right of kings, was nothing other than sheer avarice and greed, the lust for power and the desire for power. These aren't claims made by me, they can only be revealed by the plays in production.

Very few of Shakespeare's plays are performed today without a certain amount of cutting, but the things that one tends to cut are the parochial areas: elements in the comedies that are too distant, or repetitive themes, where ideas are expounded again and again. If plays are cut, they are usually cut for the sake of clarity, to pare down an idea to its essential thought. What a play can take in cutting can only be determined when an actor speaks the lines on stage. The interpretation is, initially, a subjective process: the interpretation then has to be put to an audience to test its relevance.

Is this a matter of historical continuity, or rather the continual re-making of texts in different historical situations?

The plays are living organisms; they are malleable material. We re-create the plays every time a group of people perform them and re-interpret them, as Shakespeare did himself. Our problem is, that although once upon a time the practitioners outnumbered the academics, now the academics outnumber the practitioners, and Shakespeare's plays have become over-analysed by academics. The result is that it becomes harder and harder to produce Shakespeare in a fresh, living, and vital manner that attracts a new audience. We need a new, young, unsophisticated, open, and eager audience; an audience receptive to ideas that relate to the contemporary world. We suffer in this country from lack of experiment: most of the best exploratory work goes on in Europe where they are not so egg-bound in their ideas about Shakespeare. In Europe and America their productions are raw and rough, but with energy, enthusiasm, and new ideas permeating the texts. Europe has a history of art and politics being related, while in this country our art is apolitical.

Do you think this relates to the concept of Shakespeare embodying the spirit of England, and Shakespeare's language as a kind of national holy writ representing the highest manifestation of the English language?

He wasn't literature; he was theatre. His work became literature later on when people transcribed his plays on to paper. This dreadful tradition has standardised the plays of Shakespeare not only in the way they are set down on paper, but also in the way that they are spoken on stage. It is inconceivable to me that in a period when there was very little intercommunication between the provinces, that the actors who came from Dunfermlin or Devon didn't speak the words with those kinds of accents. They certainly didn't lose them when they got to London and speak with some quasi-standard BBC English. I am sure that the plays were delivered in a variety of extraordinary accents that gave the lines a richness and texture that we have now lost, because we intone and incant the lines, as if it were some kind of game.

In that respect do you think that the large subsidised companies, the 'national institutions', do Shakespeare a disservice?

I can't say they do Shakespeare a complete disservice; I think they mostly do him a disservice, often unintentionally. Most of the time in the theatre people are trying to open up the path to Shakespearean theatre in new and exciting ways. The thing that has done the greatest disservice to Shakespeare, in the last twenty-five years, is the BBC/Time–Life series. Those productions really did close it all down, and of course turned off yet another generation.

You've said that 'our theatre is apolitical and cerebral; Shakespeare is political and physical'.[5] *In what way do you see the plays of Shakespeare as 'political'?*

He is, all the time, analysing the nature of power and the way that it corrupts man. It is as if he were trying to find another society that could exist outside of this Elizabethan one of greed and avarice. The result is a paradigm of a status quo: you get a protagonist who pits her/himself against the status quo and either smashes her/himself against it, or momentarily brings down the structure; but always the establishment re-rights itself and lumbers on, protecting itself along the same path as before. I believe that Shakespeare implies that individual action is always doomed to failure, and that collective action is probably the only way to right the wrongs of this society.

People are fond of saying that Shakespeare was a humanist, which is a way of avoiding the idea that he was much more than a humanist. He was somebody who was looking at the evils of society and, laying the blame, not at the door of God, the Fates, the elements, or some abstract destiny, but fairly and squarely at the feet of men. He is saying we are responsible for our actions; we create this shit and we should be the ones who should sort it out. There is a terrific dichotomy in the plays between a 'man' of action who says, "that's what I want" – and does it: and the 'man' for whom everything happens in the head. In many of the plays we find an incredible tirade against the corrupting forces of 'man'. *Timon of Athens* is an extraordinary example of the bile that he suddenly unleashed about the power of gold. At the end of *Romeo and Juliet* there is a little scene between the Apothecary and Romeo, in which Romeo says that gold is the real poison in peoples' souls. Again, at the end of that play we see the Capulets and the Montagues vying with each other to see who can erect the biggest gold statue to the memory of their offspring.

As long as there is a society where fathers are allowed to barter their daughters to the highest bidder, then tragedies like *Romeo and Juliet* are going to occur. It's nothing to do with Fate or the stars; it's greed and avarice on the part of Capulet insisting that his daughter marries someone close to the seat of power: Escalus's nephew Paris. Other contributory elements such as the irresponsibility of the Church and the nurse toying with young people's lives, pale into insignificance beside the main cancer at the heart of society; the desire of Capulet to cement his position in society. Until you eradicate this power structure, then someone, somewhere, will marry their daughter against their will and the same tragic pattern will be re-enacted.

Notes

1 *The Taming of the Shrew*, directed by Michael Bogdanov, Royal Shakespeare Company, 1978.
2 Michael Bogdanov and Joss Buckley, *Shakespeare Lives!: The Taming of the Shrew* (Channel 4/Quintet Films, 1983), p. 5.
3 The title given to a series of televised workshops; see Chapter 16, pp. 181–3.
4 Jan Kott, *Shakespeare our Contemporary* (London: Methuen, 1965).
5 Bogdanov, *Shakespeare Lives!*, p. 5.

Shakespeare's private drawer: Shakespeare and homosexuality
Simon Shepherd

For many years the question has vexed them: was the Bard queer? Whatever the answer, we may be sure of one thing: that, being an English Bard, he didn't flaunt it. As the scholar tells us, 'Had Southampton seen all these sonnets, he might well have been amazed at the intensity of the feelings he had inspired. Probably Shakespeare put many of his sonnets away in some private drawer.'[1]

The Sonnets are the problem area. Earliest annotators tried to imply they were mainly written to a woman, but modern scholarship assumes the addressee to be male and offers as candidates a choice of Earls (of Pembroke or Southampton) or a boy actor. If the addressee is male, then the 'feeling' in the Sonnets is homosexual. A thin bent line of commentators, from Wilde onwards, has maintained so, against a majority who define this feeling as friendship or disinterested love, or anything not sexual.

More recently, the Sonnets relationship has been seen as a key to some of the plays. Homos have been spotted. There's Antonio in The Merchant and his namesake in Twelfth Night, both devoted to young men but abandoned; and their namesake in The Tempest, an unrepentant baddy. And if homosexuality can be used to explain mysterious melancholies, it can certainly sort out inexplicable villainies. Thus Iago's 'motiveless malignity' is frustrated by homosexual desire, and Leontes's rapidly rampant jealousy logically proceeds from his real desire for Polixenes. Of course. Queerness helpfully links things together. The foppish fairy Richard II, the sulky Achilles and that mummy's boy Coriolanus all make a muck of their countries.

Homosexuality in the plays has only been found in the last few years, and doesn't cause much worry. The Sonnets are different because, instead of showing a fictional world, they apparently depict Shakspere's real feelings. It might be expected that a great artist can deal with all manner of unsavoury topics, but can a great artist be homosexual? Especially if that artist is the national poet, who represents all that's best in English writing.

It is easier to concede that a supposedly lesser poet such as Marlowe may have been queer. In fact his homosexuality may be used to explain why he was a lesser poet: Wilbur Sanders[2] says Marlowe's works are distorted by an ill-disciplined homosexual passion, whereas Shakespier was a consummate artist. Discussion of homosexuality in Shakspeer seems to be motivated not by an interest in Renaissance sexuality but by Shakespaire's national status. Criticism's task is to discover a fitting sexuality for the National Bard. The task is specifically taken up by and shaped by literary criticism, for the literature is what is to be protected. The literature belongs to the nation.

Queen and country

The national importance of Shakespur's sexuality was explicitly stated in the 1950s and 1960s by those campaigning for reform of the law against homosexuality. They compiled lists of great men who were homosexuals in order to demonstrate that homosexuals were not failures and criminals, and were capable of producing publicly admired works of genius. In other words, their sexuality was entirely incidental to their social contribution and therefore it should not be criminalised. 'Douglas Plummer' invited his readers to 'Consider also some of the names of later times who are known to have had at least homosexual leanings; such outstanding military geniuses as Alexander the Great and Julius Caesar, already noted; the Greek philosophers Socrates and Plato; Sappho, the poetess; Pindar, whose odes inspired mankind; Marlowe and Shakespeare and Francis Bacon among many great Elizabethans; Leonardo da Vinci, Michelangelo, and Cellini among the giants of the Renaissance'.[3] Furthermore, homosexuals contributed to the nation, its culture and empire and should be treated as a respectable part of that nation. Thus the claim that Shagspeere was a homosexual specifically challenged contemporary thought about sexuality in post-war Britain. A more recent use of the same tactic is made in Larry Kramer's play about AIDS, The Normal Heart, which shares the law-reform mentality.[4]

Neither the academic debate about Shagspier's sexuality nor theatrical interpretations of homosexual scenes take place in a historical void. The cultural history of both may be explained by the history of sexuality in the social order in general. This essay will attempt to map these histories on to each other. It will focus centrally on the language of the critical texts since this language derives from and re-affirms dominant ideology, and its use within academic institutions helps to sustain in being a social status quo. If this language can be observed and understood in its process of relating the personal to the social, resistance may more readily be developed to the attitudes which it seeks to implement. The apparent intentions of the critical text, however, are rarely carried out smoothly. The positions adopted are often essentially contradictory, and sexual norms are only maintained at the cost of repressing what doesn't fit. But contradictions will declare themselves and the repressed will return where they are least looked for. Thus this essay also describes the insecurities in what is apparently dominant. To be alert to the potential instability of the dominant is, I hope, to be more optimistic about changing it.

The tidying-up of the National Bard's sexuality is one of the great services performed by Shackspaire scholarship for the national culture. A brief history of this activity is given by Joseph Pequigney's recent book on the Sonnets.[5] Not only have commentators denied the existence of homosexuality: editors have written notes and glossaries which keep silent about the possibility of homosexual meanings in texts. When the presence of homosexuality has to be conceded, the commentary works to remove the sex, creating the condition of homo-uality.

In his description of a conflict between hetero- and homosexual readings, Pequigney uses the word 'homosexuality' as if its definition was fixed. By contrast, most historians of sexuality argue that the terms – and the sense of sexuality itself – shift through history; and that the act of writing about homosexuality usually polices it by stating what aspects are sympathetic or disgusting. Such writing gains particular force when applied to the sex life of our Bard since it indicates what form of homo-sexuality is acceptable (if at all) to proper Englishness.

Scholars and squalors

The argument that follows is based on a small sample of books borrowed from my local university library, chosen because they are ones used by students. Most of the markings on the books show that ideas are being culled for literary essays. Assumptions about sexuality are not the main focus and hence they are presumably taken on board, uncritically; and thus the dominant reproduces itself.

My sample is agreed that homosexuality in general is 'squalid'. To this view the Bard is recruited: 'Shakespeare himself was aware of how sordid the whole affair must appear.'[6] Shagspair's personal life must be set apart, since it has become national cultural property and, as a biographical model, reinforces assumptions about sexuality. The life is frequently written about as if it is not a product of but transcends history, since it has to be recognisable to society now. Shackespieare has to be *seen* to be one of us. Not one of Them (deviants, criminals, homosexuals, hooligans). Therefore the sex life has to be kept tidy.

A brief chronological survey shows how the sample goes about its business of absorbing and replicating contemporary sexual politics. G. Wilson Knight's *The Mutual Flame*[7] (published in 1955) argues that Shackspeere's 'bisexuality', although conventionally 'abnormal', was a necessary precondition for the creation of great Art. A special footnote insists that 'homosexuality' does not 'signify physical vice', but is defined by the *Oxford English Dictionary* as 'having a sexual propensity for persons of one's own sex', where 'Propensity is defined as inclination' (p. 25); non-physicality is the essential mark of the Platonic 'higher integration' achieved by the Bard. These strictures against physical homosex derive from two specific homosexual polemics. The older one is a defence of boy-love which values the boy for his innocence and chastity, and for his elevating effect on the pederast: the boy is the poet's 'higher self' (p. 43). More closely contemporary was the argument for homosexual law-reform (the Wolfenden Committee was convened in 1954). These polemics stressed the respectability of serious homosexual relationships and upheld the value of love against irresponsible lust. On this model Knight constructs the 'Sonnets story': 'It appears to have been an exacting relationship on both sides, and when either of the partners indulged in loose behaviour in the outer world, there appears to have been trouble from the other' (p. 25). The law-reformers adopted a taxing sexual morality in order to make homos worthy of straight tolerance. When Knight says that homo love is abnormal, but allowable because it creates great – albeit tragic – Art, he, like the law-reformers, is accepting that homosex is basically guilty.

W. H. Auden's introduction to the Sonnets appeared in an American edition in 1964.[8] In it he chides the homosexual reader who wants to claim Shakespeare for the 'homintern'. His neologism, modelled on the Comintern (Communist International), constructs a picture of homosexual conspiracy analogous with the so-called Communist 'threat'. At precisely this date appeared the paperback edition of R.E.L. Masters' *The Homosexual Revolution*,[9] which used the idea of homosexuals as national security risks in order to oppose homosexual demands for civil rights. This book, like Auden's work, was a product of the McCarthyite witch-hunts of communists and homosexuals. Auden's 'literary' introduction acts simultaneously as a craven construction of homosexual guilt.

J. Winny's *The Master–Mistress* appeared in 1968,[10] the year after homosexual law-reform. It depicts the critic as a liberal in a new age of permissiveness, prepared to discuss those issues which earlier ages would have frowned on. In this version of the 'Sonnets story' Shagspier is 'manly' while the friend 'enjoys his unusual beauty at the expense of the sexual desire that characterises manhood'. The friend is not properly manly; his 'bisexuality' is 'an index of the friend's contradictory nature', which links with his 'duplicity' (p. 153). The negative terms cluster together around the sex object. Thus the anti-homosexual prejudice which Winny, as a self-confessed liberal, knows not to direct at the Bard is displaced on to the friend.

My sample gives pride of place to the Sonnets since they (apparently) raise the crucial question of the *Bard's* sexuality. But the 'discovery' of homosexuals in the plays, which tended to coincide with post-war permissiveness, is as instrumental in reinforcing received stereotypes. Graham Midgeley's 1960 essay on *The Merchant of Venice*[11] argues that the proper structure of the play depends on seeing Antonio as an outcast situated in parallel to the Jew. Antonio's homosexuality is established through his lack of interest in women, his loneliness and sense of guilt. These features are regularly attributed to homosexuals at this period: in *20th Century*, summer 1964, 'a middle-aged man in the professional classes describes . . . the lonely torments of a day in the hidden half of his life'. More politically, the law reformers Peter Wildeblood and 'Douglas Plummer' drew explicit connections (in 1955 and 1964) between homosexuals and Jews and blacks as persecuted minorities. Midgeley's essay is caught in a contradiction in that it enlists the aid of the Bard in a defence of minorities against gentile heterosexist Belmont/England, but it identifies the homosexual by the negative attributes which are themselves derived from heterosexist society.

To enlist the Bard for liberalism is part of the process of depicting him as a universal genius, who is able to write about all sorts of oddities with flair. Liberalism needs to employ an ahistorical definition of homosexual oddity before it extends its pity. To see homosexuality as a historical construct would be to examine the social and economic interests which need to victimise certain sexualities. This would progress beyond liberalism. Furthermore it might unsettle the idea of the Bard as universal liberal genius.

Renaissance homosexualities

'Homosexualities' might have been recognised by a Renaissance audience of Schakspeire's work in the forms of warrior camaraderie, male friendship, ruler's favourite and ladies' tailor. Let us look at the sort of depiction in each case.

Tullus Aufidius tells Coriolanus:

> But that I see thee here,
> Thou noble thing, more dances my rapt heart
> Than when I first my wedded mistress saw
> Bestride my threshold (IV.v.118–21)

The male-bonding is as sexual as marriage. Coriolanus has said that out of fighting Aufidius he gets a thrill which is *personal* and predominates over the 'higher' interests of nation: were he 'Upon my party, I'd revolt, to make / Only my wars with him' (I.i.231–3). When Montaigne described his relationship with another man, he said that form of 'friendship' came before all other bonds: 'A singular and principal friendship dissolveth all other duties, and freeth all other obligations'.[12] Coriolanus's relationship is both sexual and violent, and is certainly 'singular'. It is indicted by the narrative because it betrays the country and kills Coriolanus. The warrior camaraderie is attacked for its individualism and threat to national interest. In the England of 1607 this would relate to the tradition, and last desperate manifestation, of feudal warlords now seen as alien to a specific vision of an England nationally united under the monarch-in-Parliament, that unity being mirrored at the personal level by new egalitarian marriage. Both ideals connect in the outlook of the oppositional Puritan gentry. By contrast, Spenser – the epic poet of a desperate absolutism – celebrates the love between male heroes as the highest form of bonding.

Both Montaigne and Spenser speak of male 'friendship' as something specifically sexual. In Shackspere's work it may again be associated with a passing feudal order. Don Pedro, friend of the fatuously chivalric Claudio, woos Hero for Claudio. This leads to the disastrous story of slander and disavowal. By contrast with this 'old-fashioned' notion of marriage (based on negotiation and contract), Beatrice and Benedick form a relationship based on mutuality and debate. Don Pedro ends the play alone in a paired-up gathering, as do the Antonios in Merchant and Twelfth Night. All three are the residue of male–male bondings which have been associated with disaster, and then been replaced by male–female. In no case does Shaekespeare's text give them lines that call attention to themselves as casualties. Much Ado specifically seems an exercise in comparing forms of partnership and assessing their validity; Don Pedro is rejected from the theatrical plenitude and procreative promise of the hetero marriage.

The most well known homosexual type is that historically located in the figure of the favourite. Although Shakeyspear's Richard II tends to play down the role of the favourite more than do Thomas of Woodstock and Edward II, the stereotype in it is still recognisable. A Knack to Know a Knave defines the favourite Philarchus as 'more than wanton, / Because thou hast disobeyed the laws both of God and nature'. The threat of the favourite is as much economic as political, in so far as the monarch's desire cannot be accommodated within the marital and kinship systems which guarantee the security of the state. Such systems stabilise property ownership within individual hands; but, in a logical reversal, the favourite who is personally desired thus gains a power base which did not come from inheritance. Hence James I's public indulgence of favourites was a perhaps not unconscious display of the power of the absolute monarch, from whom come all benefits, however fanciful. The display was noted most keenly when the power of the wealth-generating gentry had developed to the extent that it could, materially, challenge the myth of absolutism. In their economic terms, the favourite is attached to the non-wealth-generating, non-productive monarchy. Hence it is wasteful, and, because weak, decadent.

The last case of Renaissance homosexuality is the stereotype of male effeminacy associated with the profession of ladies' tailor. It's equivalent to the 1960s male hairdresser, interior decorator or dress designer. Thus (in order of ascent through masculinity): 'I have turned myself into a tailor, a man, a gentleman, a nobleman, a worthy man' (Chapman). The Roaring Girl has a comic scene of complementary deviant types between the manly woman and her tailor. The Bard's handling of the type in 2 Henry IV explicitly undercuts mockery of effeminacy in that the type-named Feeble is shifted from joke status into a pathetic dignity: 'we owe God a death. I'll ne'er bear a base mind' (III.ii.230).

This last case presents the Bard performing correctly in role: his liberal humanitarian understanding refuses stereotypes. But there is also, precisely, no economic or class affiliation under pressure here. (The ladies' tailor exemplifies a private and narrowly decorative application of a specific craft within a guild whose increase in social power took the form of a move away from specific craft interests into larger mercantile and financial projects.) In the other three cases it is clear that Shackspeere's depiction of homosexualities is very much in line with the attitudes of an increasingly powerful gentry, a class he was publicly to align himself with. The unsympathetic portrayals are motivated by class interest. Thus is called into question the notion of Shakespeer the great liberal. His liberalism, like that of his critics, does not question social structure.

The secret of the drawer

The attitude of the scholars may best be summarised by returning to the title of this essay. What does the phrase 'Shakespeare's private drawer' imply? That homosexuality is a private matter, because it is embarrassing/illegitimate; that it is recognised as such by the national Bard, who thus confirms that there is a sex life proper to a public national career (and this excludes homosex); that in having shame, and a desk with private drawers the Bard is readily constructed and recognised as a modern bourgeois subject. And, finally, that the critic is in a privileged position in that s/he may have a knowledge of the contents of that otherwise private drawer.

Although the declared intention is to keep that drawer firmly closed, the homosexuality is in fact the force which generates the critical texts. It is seen as a horror which requires copious explaining away. Since it is a horror, the arguments which tidy it up or redefine it acquire a positive charge. The values carried by those arguments demand acquiescence since they provide an alternative to the negativity and shame contained in the drawer. Some examples may show how this works.

The favoured account of the Sonnets story has Sheikspeare as tragic central figure, frustrated in his desire for the youth and creating great poetry out of his frustration. This relationship is constantly rewritten in the plays. Thus great Art is seen to come out of very personal suffering. It's a definition of Art which obliterates politics but which feels comfortable and familiar in our age of liberal individualism, where full expression of the self is the highest good. This Art transcends any grubby human emotion, such as homosex, which produced it, and thus conveniently facilitates an evasion of the matter of homosexuality.

Furthermore, the Art involves *creation*. Winny says that Shakespeare's creations 'outlive the poet and their time' while the friend 'who only makes lifeless shadows of himself, displays the characteristics of a bad poet' (p. 158). The friend here is modelled on a 1960s queer stereotype – the non-productive narcissus. Shakspair, on the other hand, is seen as a creator, committed to procreation and permanence, indeed a father. The image of creator invites the reader's approval since it provides a commendable alternative to the distasteful prospect of sterile homosexuality. Simultaneously it valorises the patriarchal cluster of fathering, product and permanence.

The critical discussion transmutes the potential embarrassment of the private drawer into virtue and respectability. Behind the concept of great Art created out of suffering is a bourgeois model of alienated work; suffering is necessary to ensure the best product; that product might not ameliorate the personal life of its maker, but he can be valued in so far as he has produced the product; it is the critic who consumes the product and also earns her/his living by evaluating it.

A second characteristic of the Sonnet story is the portrayal of Sheikspeer as tragic individual, centrally caught between threatening Woman and inspiring Boy (Winny), between 'love and lust, light and darkness' (Knight). Shakespier comes through, says Knight, to a 'higher integration', which is not bisexuality but a feeling of 'love-as-power, love virile and victorious . . . royal power felt magically, almost . . . erotically'; the sun imagery 'fits any strong conviction of power or sexual virility fused with virtue' (p. 65). Already Woman has been described as dark and lustful, producing sin-*impregnated* sonnets. The poet transcends Woman and Boy through a chaste masculine individualism which eroticises power and competition. This is to be celebrated. . . .

In more 'ordinary' terminology, Winny presents Shaggspier as the virile creator. The friend, by contrast, enjoys his beauty only 'at the expense of the sexual drive that characterises manhood' (p. 153); he is 'spending fruitlessly the energy which marriage would put to creative purposes', indeed self-love will call 'the reality of his true being into question' (p. 149). So we learn that the true being of manliness depends on being able to procreate, to *spend*. When Angelo has sex with Mariana he 'wastes his sexual potential upon an imposter' (p. 148). The model of masculinity here debases women's desire and mimics the economic of commodity capitalism, where power is measured by the ability to spend productively, not to waste but invest. Both Knight and Winny offer their models of masculinity as transmutations into respectability of the otherwise embarrassing private drawer. We are to prefer, it seems, the Bard masculinised to the queer Bard.

Coming out of the drawers

The contents of the private drawer are not, however, easily tidied and transmuted. They continue to reappear in the texts which seek to repress them. The commentaries on the Sonnets are fascinated by the very spectre which they are trying to exorcise. The reason for this is, I think, not simply to do with the instability of straight masculinity nor with the alienations of a bourgeois gender system, but with the production of literary criticism itself.

In writing a connected prose account of the Sonnets story, the critic describes apparently real-life characters, emotions and situations. Thus the commentary becomes a narrative work in its own right, offering the reader a *novelistic* pleasure in a developing human situation, which is an attractive alternative to the 'difficult' narrative shape of the poem-sequence. The new narrative tells of an older man who is tragically frustrated in his love for a boy, whose favours are taken by another man, the rival poet. This story is not *automatically* suggested by the Sonnets. Indeed, the durability of the biographical approach, with its stock characters (fair youth, rival poet), may be explained not by its value as historical enquiry but by its own similarity to another narrative model, that of homosexual fiction. For example, Middleton Murray (quoted by Akrigg) says:

Probably each was captivated by the other. The young aristocrat was as yet sufficiently unspoiled to respond to Shakespeare's natural charm and genius; . . . The position of his patron-friend would merely add intensity to Shakespeare's love. It would appear to him as evidence of his friend's regard for him that it made light of the vast difference in rank. . . . The very reluctance with which he had turned to patronage inclined him to invest the particular relation into which he entered with a dignity that was illusory. (p. 238)

Murry's account, published in 1936, draws on an image of 'Uranian' homosexuality popular in the earliest years of this century. There the 'unspoiled' boys were usually *lower*-class, but the important element is the conjunction of love and class. The love is intense because it can temporarily transcend class barriers, but tragic because economic structures are eventually immovable. The story appeals not only to homosexuals, since the image of personal emotion contesting with social structure is fetching for anyone well-trained in bourgeois individualism, with the added attraction for straights that the male–male bonding is confirmed to be fragile.

The Sonnets stories offer the reader the 'poet' as a figure for identification, for a vicarious sharing of his 'tragedy'. But Winny's text also unwittingly suggests identification with the *sexuality*. He claims that, in a particular sonnet, 'the issues of man's sexuality are faced with something akin to masochistic frankness' (p. 14): why is it masochistic to face male sexuality, unless it involves facing something the presence of which it torments us to recognise? Later the text says 'the charming masculine guise adopted by Viola collapses under pressure, to reveal an equivocal being who lacks the characteristic vigour and drive of a man' (p. 160) – why is Viola's guise charming? The whole text invites admiration of Sheikspare's virility, but, through a metaphoric pairing of poetic creation and procreation, allows the reader a supposed pleasure in Art which conceals a pleasure in a virility which fucks well.

Many of the commentaries on the Sonnets have a repressed double-life as fantasies that eroticise the male. It was an overt homosexual who clarified the presence of desire in commentary. Oscar Wilde's *The Portrait of Mr W. H.*[13] frames its theory of the Sonnets with a short story. Although Alfred Douglas later said that the theory was too good for this treatment, it is, I think, precisely by presenting it as a *story* that Wilde's account is so radical and overtly homosexual.

The fictional originator of the theory of Cyril Graham – good-looking, sporty, effeminate – a classic sex object, who is desirable but absent, remembered but dead by the time the story begins. He spends time on his theory when he should be studying for the diplomatic corps: so the theorising is private, indulgent, non-masculine. The theory not only puts the sex into the Sonnets but sees them as of 'tragic' import, written out of the bitterness of Shakespieere's heart. This theory in its turn exerts a fascination on the two other men in the story. The recognition of homosexuality in the national Bard is an activity which expresses and develops the homoerotic desires of others and, additionally, undermines the duties of masculinity and empire.

Critic and author are linked by sexual fantasy. The sexy theory of the Sonnets is fictionally invented by a sexy person. In that he 'invents' Wilde's theory Graham is a version of Wilde, but he is also an overt creation of fantasy since he is a sex object who is never 'alive' in the text. Graham is said to be a fine actor of Shackespere's female characters, just as is Willie Hughes, the boy invented by 'his' theory. The boy who is discovered to be the addressee of the Sonnets is an extension of Graham. The relationship with the boy is said to be the key to an understanding of all Shackespeire's work. Thus the critic Graham, through the historical cloning of himself as Mr W. H., enters a *personal* relationship with the great author who can then be personally understood through a structure of shared and thus recognisable desires.

For the other two men in the story the adoption of Graham's theory takes them not only closer to the identity of Mr W. H. but to the tantalisingly absent sex object, Graham. Although the grip of the theory is strong, Wilde's story insists that it is always fantasy. The crucial evidence for W. H.'s existence has to be forged; the fantasy-theory cannot invent reality. The revelation of the forgery leads to the death of the theory's begetter. Real history thus ends a homoerotic fantasy. . . . In part this narrative delineates the social existence of homosexuality in the 1880s. For students of the 'Sonnets story', in particular, Wilde's text foregrounds the place of sexuality in the creation of textual commentary.

Private drawers, public jockstraps

The contents of the embarrassing private drawer reappear even where the aim is to repress them. Indeed, it might be that their very presence, continually fended off, itself makes Shagspear study fascinating. Certainly the most conspicuously money-making branch of the Shagspaire industry uses illicit sexuality in order to sell products to audiences.

This essay has to end with the theatre since here the Bard's works are in their most public, most capital intensive, showcase; yet any single performance of one of those works necessarily relies on the input of many more ideas than those of Shakspear alone. Study of performance shows again the policing of homosexuality; and in addition the exploitation of erotic masculinity. My texts here are the production photographs and reviews of Royal Shakespeare Company productions of Troilus and Cressida and Coriolanus from 1959 to 1981. The choice of company has to do with its culturally 'authoritative', hence influential, status; the choice of plays because they include male bonding and allow costuming which exposes the male body.

Scandal about homosexuality was occasioned by John Barton's 1969 Troilus. As part of a revaluation of masculine honour, Achilles became a sulky drag queen. Reviewers shrieked their hatred of homosex, and defended militarism, the nation and the Bard. B. A. Young asked if Barton imagined that 'brave and respected soldiers who have homosexual lapses while they are away from their womenfolk turn spontaneously into pansies? What does he think Kitchener was like?' (Kitchener, by the way, was a notorious queer.) The Ipswich Evening Star muttered about 'debauchery, sodomy and lechery that infiltrated the Greek nation'

– shades of homosexual conspiracy again. In a queerly bitchy homophobic review, Milton Shulman spoke of 'an atmosphere of homosexual corruption which almost smothers the Bard's original intention' and W. A. Darlington produced a special thinking piece, in addition to his review, to defend the Bard against homosexual intentions: he called it 'A queer twist to Shakespeare'.

Although the scandal was new, the homosex wasn't. The 1960 *Troilus* may have taken its grape-eating Achilles from a Greek vase, but Patroclus with his glistening blond hair comes from a homo physique mag (the homo ghetto regularly used 'high art' to make legitimate its illicit sex objects).[14] The Greek army scene suggests how Achilles' 'personal' indiscipline threatens the interests of the nation. This reinforces dominant notions of homosexuality. But the fact that homosexuality was only publicly 'noticed' in the 1969 production may have two causes.

First, in 1969 Gay Liberation began in America, and in Britain it was the year after law-reform. Drag was used as a political challenge to straight masculinity. This gives a gay political meaning to what in Barton's production was an essentially heterosexist association of drag with unhealthy self-indulgence. Homosexuality was on the public agenda.

Second, the homosexual costume labelling was explicit here (whereas it may have been possible to miss the stereotype behind the 1960 Patroclus). The labelling makes for the first time inadmissable and unpleasurable what had before been acceptable and indeed pleasurable, namely the eroticised male body. A double response is noticeable: the reviewer of the *Warwick Advertiser* noted 'many striking moments in the production – not least the balletic encounters of the bronzed, half-naked warriors beneath a pitiless sun. But there is also much that is sensual, erotic and disturbing'. For as long as the interest in bronzed warriors is not *defined* as erotic, it is allowed. B. A. Young's hatred for homosex does not prevent him noticing that 'the Trojans go into battle naked except for their helmets and their pants, their armpits tidily shaved'.

The inexplicitly eroticised male body is clearly a feature and a source of enjoyment in these productions, and it's a feature that the RSC production teams add to the words of the Bard (which are always so short on stage directions). In productions of *Coriolanus* much care is given to a comparatively minor element in the narrative, the Volscian soldiers. Whereas publicity photos tend to concentrate on stars and spectacular scenes, for this play it is deemed appropriate to give space to anonymous Volscian lieutenants, presumably because their costume might appeal to an audience.

The costuming does two things. It eroticises by drawing attention to genitals and thighs, and by using the leather, chains and fur associated with fetishistic sex. Secondly, it makes foreign: the 1959 Volsces in long hair and fur contrasted with white clothed Romans and clean-shaven Coriolanus, like (at that period) beatniks; in 1972 they were 'Mongolian in aspect but having . . . a look of the Amerindians', at that period the oriental combined with the Latin American evokes both Vietcong and Che Guevara. The eroticised men are also national or class enemies.

The male body can be safely erotic for as long as homosexuality is damned. The enemy can be made decorative by making him into a theatrical image, which can be bought and consumed by the theatregoer. Thus the class power of the Stratford audience can be titillated because the enemy is erotic, and reinforced because it never has to confront the implications of the titillation, the homosexuality or politics.

When the Volsces kill Coriolanus, his fatal attraction to Aufidius meets its doom, but at the hands of males the audience might find sexy. An exploitative double-standard towards homosexuality is encouraged. Indeed the Volsces remain erotic for *as long as* the text remains silent about masculine eroticism. Furthermore, the relationship between eroticism, masculinity and violence is never explicitly explored. The commercially motivated design makes of the viewer a voyeur, and the high art becomes as sexually exploitative as pornography.

The theatre makes explicit what has been implied. The shocking contents of Shagspur's private drawer play a major part in our culture's fascination with its Bard. In ensuring that he was not a queer, we can use his works for our secret national homoerotic fantasies.

Notes

1 G. P. V. Akrigg, *Shakespeare and the Earl of Southampton* (London: Hamish Hamilton, 1968).
2 Wilbur Sanders, *The Dramatist and the Received Idea* (Cambridge: CUP, 1968).
3 D. Plummer, *Queer People* (London: W. H. Allen, 1963), p. 36.
4 L. Kramer, *The Normal Heart* (London: Methuen, 1986).
5 J. Pequigny, *Such is my Love* (Chicago, Ill.: Chicago University Press, 1985).
6 Akrigg, *Shakespeare and Southampton*, p. 237.
7 G. Wilson Knight, *The Mutual Flame* (London: Methuen, 1955).
8 W. H. Auden, 'Introduction' to *Shakespeare's Sonnets* (New York: New American Library, 1964).
9 R. E. L. Masters, *The Homosexual Revolution* (Belmont Books, 1964).
10 J. Winny, *The Master-Mistress* (London: Chatto, 1968).
11 G. Midgely, 'The Merchant of Venice: a reconsideration', *Essays in Criticism*, 10 (1960); and see also M. M. Mahood, 'Love's confined doom', *Shakespeare Survey*, 15 (1962).
12 M. de Montaigne, *Essays* (1603), 1.27.
13 Oscar Wilde, 'The portrait of Mr W. H.', *The Works* (Spring Books, 1969), p. 205.

14 One issue of the 'physique' magazine *Body Beautiful* used Shakespeare's *Sonnet CIV* to accompany photos of a mainly naked young man (sometimes with candelabra) (undated: probably from the 1950s).

Shakespeare Tower, Barbican, London (photo Tristan Holderness)

A popular theatre? A Bankside Globe presentation at the George Inn Yard, 1974

As you like it?

'Here's Flowers for you . . .' Beermat from the Bard's local brewery

EXPERTS ON BITTER ALWAYS PICK FLOWERS

Shakespeare

'HERE'S FLOWERS FOR YOU'

A WINTERS TALE

Shakespeare was well known to enjoy the odd quart or two of fine ale. It is perhaps appropriate that Flowers ales established in Stratford in 1831 should have such strong links with the world's greatest poet and playwright. Edward Flower was Mayor of Stratford in 1864 and organized the town's tricentenary celebrations for its most famous son. The Royal Shakespeare Theatre was built under the Flowers family directions and the Bard became the brewery trade mark.

TRADE MARK

IT SEEMS THE BEST IN BOTH POETRY AND BEER HAVE THE KNACK OF LASTING THROUGH THE CENTURIES

Bardoloroso? By kind permission of Tesco

Distracted Globe? The Carling Black Label TV advertisement

Strip-cartoon Shakespeare (*Othello* illustrated by Oscar Zarate, Oval Projects, 1983)

Television Programmes

-4.15 WATCH WITH MOTHER
For the very young
Andy Pandy
ia Bird brings Andy to play with
- small children and invites them
oin in songs and games
Irey Atterbury and Molly Gibson
pull the strings
Hadys Whitred sings the songs
Script, music, and settings
by Maria Bird
(A BBC television film)

★   ★   ★

0   CRICKET
M.C.C. v. The Australians
from Lord's

Children's Television
- ' SEVEN
LITTLE AUSTRALIANS '
from the books
' Seven Little Australians '
nd ' The Family at Misrule '
by Ethel S. Turner
4—' Nell moves in Society '
er.................Sheila Shand Gibbs
y.........................Pixie Murphy
.........................Adele Long
ny.........................Barry Knight
.................Margaret Anderson
ain Woolcot.............Gerald Case
pet.........................Gillian Gale
.........................Barry Macgregor
el Fitzroy-Brown.Susanna Hogan
rice Fitzroy-Brown
Susan Kennaway
Fitzroy-Brown......Enid Lorimer
action takes place in the Wool-
home, just outside Sydney, in
1890s
ssistant producer, Shaun Sutton
Adapted and produced
by Pamela Brown

0-6.30   CRICKET
M.C.C. v. The Australians
from Lord's

★   ★   ★

0   NEWSREEL

**5   ' KINGDOM
IN THE NORTH '**
- ancient kingdom of Bernicia
s established by the Vikings in
-th-East England between the
enines and the sea
BBC television film shows the
ole of this land today—their music
their country, moorland, mining
n, and industrial city
film, which is introduced by the
Rev. the Lord Bishop of Durham,
been made to celebrate the open-
of Pontop Pike television trans-
er
Produced by John Elliot

**5 The Elizabethan Theatre
Company in
' KING HENRY V '**
by William Shakespeare
See columns 3 and 4
d ' Television Diary ' on page 15

The Elizabethan Theatre Company

'King Henry V'

BY WILLIAM SHAKESPEARE

at 8.45

'Into a thousand parts divide one man . . .'

COLIN GEORGE
King Henry V of England

TOBY ROBERTSON
Chorus
The Bishop of Ely
Captain Gower
The Duke of York
The Duke of Burgundy

MICHAEL DAVID
The Archbishop of Canterbury
Lewis, the Dauphin
The Earl of Warwick

CLIFFORD ROSE
The French Ambassador
The Governor of Harfleur
The Earl of Salisbury
Sir Thomas Erpingham

GORDON GOSTELOW
The Earl of Westmoreland
Captain Fluellen

JOHN SOUTHWORTH
King Charles VI of France
Montjoy, a French Herald

TRENOR STANLEY
The Duke of Bedford
The Duke of Bourbon
Lord Grandpré

JAMES ROUGHEAD
The Duke of Exeter

FRANK WINDSOR
Ancient Pistol
Williams

WILLIAM LAWFORD
Bardolph
The Duke of Orleans
The Duke of Gloucester

ROGER MILNER
Captain Macmorris
Bates
French Soldier
English Herald

PETER JEFFREY
Captain Jamy
The Constable of France

REGINALD SELOUS
Corporal Nym
Lord Rambures

KEITH FAULKNER
Boy

JOCELYNE PAGE
Mistress Quickly
Queen Isabel of France

BERNADETTE SOREL
Princess Katharine of France

YVONNE BONNAMY
Alice

The scene: England and France

★

The play produced for the theatre by
JOHN BARTON

Presented for television by
MICHAEL MACOWAN

Setting and costumes designed by REECE PEMBERTON

WITH very little money, and using the barest minimum of setting and the most elementary Elizabethan costumes, a dozen to a score of young men and women, mostly from Oxford and Cambridge, set out last summer to play Shakespeare wherever they could find an audience and a place to play in. Sometimes it was an inn yard, sometimes a college garden or the hall of an ancient house (the kind of conditions which Shakespeare's own company met on their tours), sometimes a Town Hall or an ordinary theatre. Despite many imperfections, the soundness of the principles on which they were working and their own vitality and talent created

minutes it is only possible to present a skeleton of the play, which lasts in the theatre for three hours, this appearance is a great opportunity for the Company. One of the great difficulties that pioneers in the field of Elizabethan production have to face is that it is so difficult to find any building in which the essential conditions of Elizabethan playing can be fulfilled. Perhaps the most important of these conditions, a close intimacy between audience and actor, television can certainly offer.

It is our hope, too, that we may find it possible on the screen to give some impression of the flowing movement in an open space on which an Elizabethan

---

Scene to screen: Shakespeare in the Radio times, 15 May 1953 [*facing*] 'Fair friend' from *Body beautiful*, a 1950s physique magazine

Troilus and Cressida at the Shakespeare Memorial Theatre, 1960 (Patroclus, Dinsdale Landen; Ulysses, Eric Porter; Achilles, Patrick Allen. Photo by Angus McBean, by permission of The Shakespeare Centre)

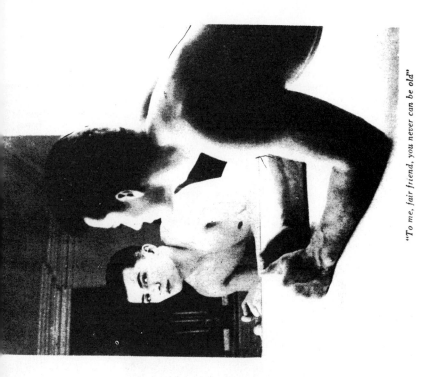

"To me, fair friend, you never can be old"

The pen of seventeenth century
SHAKESPEARE, and the camera of the twentieth
century VULCAN happily conspire to bring you
this photographic interpretation
by STEVE WENGRYN of the Bard's

SONNET CIV

To me, fair friend, you never can be old;
For as you were when first your eye I eyed,
Such seems your beauty still. Three Winters cold
Have from the forests shook three Summers' pride;
Three beauteous Springs to yellow Autumn turn'd
In process of the seasons have I seen,
Three April perfumes in three hot Junes burn'd,
Since first I saw you fresh, which yet are green,
Ah! yet doth beauty, like a dial-hand,
Steal from his figure, and no pace perceived;
So your sweet hue, which methinks still doth stand,
Hath motion, and mine eye may be deceived;
    For fear of which, hear this, thou age unbred;
    Ere you were born was beauty's summer dead.

Shakespeare boiled down

PART TWO

Cultural practices

The Cambridge connection: towards a materialist theatre practice

Christopher J. McCullough

I am a radical, and I could not work in the theatre if I were not. The theatre must question everything and disturb its audience.   (Peter Hall)[1]

Quite what Peter Hall meant by the term 'radical' in 1966 is open to a wide variety of interpretations, depending on how we now view the work of the Royal Shakespeare Company. The RSC has suffered, since its inception in 1959–60, criticism from all quarters: to many Fringe theatre workers of the 'left' it represents establishment, subsidised Shakespeare; to many on the 'right', it has the same regrettable left-wing and anarchistic tendencies as other British 'institutions', such as the BBC, taking public money and misusing it by failing to produce 'proper' Shakespeare, or by putting on 'dirty' (contemporary) plays, which ultimately degrade, by implied association, England's universal genius. The pattern of oppositions is by no means simple: questions of who is 'for' and who is 'against' are simply inadequate when attempting to analyse the complex interaction of seemingly subversive interventions into Establishment structures. What may appear to be subversive may, in fact, prove to be the paradoxical means by which a dominant order ensures its own continuance.[2]

RSC directors often justify what appears to be controversial work in Shakespearean theatre on the grounds of contemporary relevance. This has been, most notably, the position adopted by two of the main guiding energies of the RSC: Peter Hall and Trevor Nunn. Peter Hall, who in many ways has occupied the most influential role in the shaping of the RSC, in a talk to actors at the start of rehearsals for *Hamlet* in 1965, declared that '*Hamlet* is one of mankind's great images. It turns a new face to each century, even to each decade. It is a mirror which gives back the reflection of the age that is contemplating it. And the need to define these reflections produces, on average, a new appreciation of Hamlet every twelve years.'[3]

Hall's approach to Hamlet in 1964–5 displayed a symmetrical fusion of the elements identified in Alan Sinfield's formula: 'Shakespeare-plus-relevance'. Because of the play's 'greatness', its universality of meaning, it cannot be tied down to any particular time or place in history; or if it can, that history serves only as a background to illuminate the text's transcendence of context, which enables it to speak, in different ways, to all generations, since those generations ultimately share not only a consistent human nature, but a stable system of beliefs and values. Shakespeare's plays are assumed to transcend history: and are thus transformed into myth.

In addition, Hall's declared intention was to create a theatre for a wider audience of 'young people, poor people, working-class people' (a view that, in later life, he saw as 'curiously naive': 'anyone who wants to go to the theatre is today well able to afford to do so').[4] Hall's takeover of the RSC seemed to symbolise a new era that was based upon the ethic of equal opportunity for all: 'Hall seemed to be a perfect illustration of the early sixties myth: that swift tangible glamorous success was the prize of anyone, from any background, if they had the talent and the audacity to seek it; that a new social openness and freedom prevailed, and that the old barriers of age and class were tumbling.'[5]

Both Peter Hall and Trevor Nunn came from similar working-class, rural Suffolk backgrounds, by way of grammar school, to Cambridge University and the teaching and influence of F. R. Leavis. Hall and Nunn have specifically cited Leavis as one of the most important influences on their work as directors of Shakespearean theatre, both 'Cambridge educated and fervent Leavisites'.[6] Trevor Nunn in an interview described what it was like for him to be taught by Leavis at Cambridge:

He [Nunn] had read Leavis. The critic in person was even better. 'We literally sat at his feet, because he didn't have any furniture. He stalked around on coconut matting – sandals, khaki shorts, shirt open to the waist, flaring grey hair . . . He was wicked, magnetic, full of bitterness and bits of asides . . .' Nunn had been studying texts for style, wit, texture and tone. Now he heard a man who said: 'But what does it mean? And how did it change you? Hurt you? And if it didn't – you may as well throw it away.' It was like meeting an evangelist – you come out of the crowd and offer yourself. Here was a man who opened the gate and said: 'I don't mind where you run'.[7]

The tone is a peculiar and contradictory mix of pseudo-scientific language and evangelical desert mysticism: the description of Leavis would fit St John the Baptist (an analogy perhaps not inappropriate to Leavis's own conception of his relationship with Cambridge).

Leavis was a pre-eminently important influence on Peter Hall's directorial approach to Shakespeare's texts. Sally Beauman records that Hall regarded Leavis as having revolutionised the study of English literature by introducing a technique of cool scientific analysis amounting almost to dissection: 'for Hall the theatrical approach to a play, and to verse was similarly analytic, beginning always from the text and searching it for meaning, symbolism, structure, and ambiguity'.[8] Behind the flamboyant role of nineteenth-century actor/manager/impresario, Hall saw himself as scholar/director, bringing to the theatre the possibility of a new academic status, through the employment of the methodology of close textual scrutiny to search out the metaphors upon which performances might be built. In an interview with Roger Manvell, Hall revealed that 'The greatest influence on me, on my generation, was Leavis, who believed above everything in a critical examination of the text, the search for meaning and metaphor . . . Kott's understanding of the ambivalence of Shakespeare has been as useful to us as Leavis's insistence on scrutinising the text for its real meaning'[9] (my italics). This approach to constructing the theatrical text, centred on the employment of 'diligent scholarship and hard work', was calculated to bring to a modern audience Shakespeare's intentions in terms that they could understand.[10] Peter Hall exemplifies the ideological conflict between literary criticism and theatre, by his own seemingly contradictory position: 'radical' modern theatre practitioner; and advocate of the process of privileging the literary text as an absolute value, the latter belief implied by his view that there is one Shakespeare for all time, transcending, as culture, the historical-material forces of its own original production. At the centre of Hall's work in the 1960s we find hints of the immanent verity at the heart of the Shakespeare play: a cultural token that contains, no matter how many different interests may tamper with it, encoded, unchanging truths about human nature. Hall in 1966: 'Whatever our mistakes, a baby will succeed us to continue the story and make his own mistakes. This regenerative principle is the only concrete lesson that can be drawn from the plays, despite the efforts of Marxists, Christians, Royalists and Whigs to extract their own particular moral from the immortal Bard.'[11] Yet on the other hand Hall urges us, as he did with *Hamlet*, to seek our own meaning in the plays of Shakespeare. He repudiates any kind of substantial historicist approach by declaring that 'if we could see a Globe production, with

Burbage at his best, I am perfectly sure we should not understand it'.[12] His argument rests upon the notion that only the texts, encoded in a literary form, remain as the repository of man's highest genius; they are our only guide to the true meanings of the plays, which are recoverable through the labour of scholarly criticism. The whole, the totality, can never be perceived, only glimpsed in relation to our own lives. This view, far from urging a confidence in the potential plurality of the drama as theatrical performance, would seem to indicate that all we are capable of is a momentary flicking back of the velvet curtain in order that we might hold, as it were, our own mirror up to art.[13]

The Leavis connection can also be seen beyond the methodology of close textual scrutiny, in the broader ideological and cultural aspirations of the RSC as an instrument for the appropriation and reconstruction of Shakespeare's plays in performance. Hall, in the early 1960s, was faced with the task of deconstructing an old order in his ambition to build a new and relevant RSC. The Stratford Memorial Company – the predecessor of the RSC – with its summer festival seasons based on a 'star-system', was part of an old order of natural heritage. The ruling classes, whether they were the old landed gentry or the aspiring commercial bourgeoisie, by virtue of their privileged educational opportunities, would receive the Bard as part of their continuing membership of the hegemonic ideology. Hall saw his task as wresting Shakespeare from this 'aristocratic' group in order to make it available to those individuals in the masses willing to reach for the experience. A part of this building process was to be the restructuring of the acting company. It is usually assumed that Hall drew inspiration from Helene Weigel and the Berliner Ensemble and formed the RSC along those lines: but in practice that arrangement enabled Hall to establish an apparently collectivist form of theatre within what was in fact a privileged élite. This structure was analogous to the Cambridge English seminar, which similarly made little minority groups into representatives of a collective society.[14] Thus an apparently democratic educational or theatrical group was actually a training-ground for the vanguard of a petit-bourgeois cultural revolution, aimed at forming a new audience of petit-bourgeois intellectuals who would co-exist in a cultural relationship with the new 'collectivist' group of actors replacing the individual 'stars'.

Hall and his company sought to create a vehicle by which Shakespeare would function as a socially unifying factor in opening up opportunities for the acquisition of access to a *national culture*.

In a world of complex communications, the theatre is a most potent force on people's imaginations . . . In the heat of theatrical experience, the audiences are not simply passing time before returning to their jobs; they are enriching their future living . . . *a strong national culture not only relieves boredom and frustration, it makes passing our lives a positive rather than a negative experience.* Given low enough seat prices, the theatre could undergo a popular revolution. The masses who buy paperbacks would stream into it.[15] (my italics)

Hall's belief in the moral purpose and power of great art rests upon the idea that our society may be unified in the experience of Shakespeare's drama. For its continued success and stability, those individuals who have attained the true state of awareness (the use of terms reminiscent of a spiritual vocabulary is appropriate here) must defend the national culture by marginalising, or seeking to absorb to their own ends those 'sub-cultures' that would threaten to subvert and demystify the inherent conservatism of the national spirit.

Again this position can be traced back to Cambridge. *Scrutiny* and Leavis posed a particular view of history that rejected the modern industrial society, seeking the roots of a cohesive national culture in a rural agricultural past.[16] Paramount was the view that there was an organic past when there was no divide between popular and sophisticated culture.[17] The petit bourgeois intelligentsia were to seek a new unity through literature: 'We who collaborated in *Scrutiny* recognized, for all our diversity of creed and 'philosophy', that we belonged to a common civilization and a positive culture. That culture was for us pre-eminently represented by English Literature.'[18]

There is a fundamental irony in Hall looking to Leavis as a mentor in the search for a methodology to reproduce Shakespeare (theatrically) as a 'relevant' component of a national culture. The emphasis from Cambridge English and Leavis was that national culture was embodied in the 'constant' form of literature. Leavis possessed a strong antipathy to the idea of performance, never more strongly expressed than when the 'performance' entailed the appropriation of a literary text:

I cannot countenance in any way that Lawrence's *Women in Love* (or Eliot's *Four Quartets*) could be filmed, or that there could be any profit in arguing with 'transposers' (translators, adaptors?) who assumed otherwise . . . No one who has any inkling of the *thing* the novel is, or how the 'significance' of a great work of literature is conveyed, or what kind of thing the significance is, could lend himself to such an outrage. Great writers, even when they're dead, ought to be protected.[19]

This is an attitude which privileges the literary form, as alone possessing the potentiality to contain encoded moral values, only to be released through the application of scholarly criticism. Live performance – film, theatre etc. – is excluded from this role by virtue of its inherent iterability and necessary state of flux.

The Leavis connection performed a very important ideological service to Shakespearean theatre by naturalising theatrical performance within what was to become a dominant cultural practice. Theatre could then play its full role in unifying disparate social elements through its potentiality to appeal, in Peter Hall's words, to 'the masses who buy paperbacks'. Directors and actors began to use scholarly textual analysis, as an intrinsic part of their rehearsal procedure,[20] a critical practice which supported and reinforced the seemingly contradictory positions of tradition (universal verities) and social relevance. Jan Kott concludes his collection of essays on the subject of Shakespeare as our contemporary: 'Productions like this [Hall's *Hamlet*, 1965], in which relevance emerges so clearly from a play's timeless greatness, will make it thrilling.'[21]

For a materialist criticism the question 'what is to be done with Shakespeare's plays?' may be addressed on two grounds: that occupied by the various critical methodologies – deconstructionist, psychoanalytic, feminist, historicist – which continue to be preoccupied with *readings* of literary texts; and that which conceives the plays in terms of theatrical performance. In the former case much deconstructionist criticism is as actively engaged in the privileging of the literary object over theatrical production, as more reactionary modes of criticism. It is therefore all the more necessary to address 'theatrical' as well as 'literary' and 'cultural' reproductions of Shakespeare from a theoretical perspective which can provoke from the material its latent contradictions. Only in this way can Shakespeare's plays fully be recognised as forms of cultural practice capable of becoming, in Alan Sinfield's words, 'a site of cultural struggle and change'.[22] The dominant concern of Shakespearean production over the last twenty-five years has been the effort by various directors to make their productions 'relevant' through the process of seeing the poetic language of the plays as definitive of their entirety. The language in this sense, being the highest manifestation of a national culture, contains the encoding of unchangeable constants such as 'human nature', and the primary task of these theatre practitioners has been to seek the embodiment of these constants through the medium of their personal experience of contemporary society.

To produce a play by Shakespeare we must begin with a text of some description. This is not however, the simple operation that it may at first appear to be. If the play was, in its original form a pre-literary discourse, then it must be accepted that every literary–'textual' manifestation of the play is a new inscription, within a new ideological context, of that original theatrical event. Even in the familiar pattern of textual inscription up to the First Folio of 1623, there is with many of the plays enough discrepancy of evidence to make a nonsense of the concept of a 'true' text. The process of textual scholarship, aimed at establishing an exact copy of the author's intentions, involves certain value judgements: in the quest for literary excellence, a text that may be (as in the case of the 1603 version of Hamlet) the nearest we have to a record of a performed script, is inevitably marginalised as a 'bad' quarto. Such acts of exclusion are based on the acceptance of literature as a transcendent form, existing above the ideological context of production.

'Textual' history may be examined at another level: that of performance as text. As it is necessary to take account of all contexts of textual production, so it is necessary to take account of performances as the process by which the play as theatrical text is continually remade. The original performance pre-dated the first literary inscription, and by its lack of fixed textual structure, guaranteed the play's potential for iterability. This is not however, to deny the necessity for a clear understanding of the historical context of production: the undeniable plurality of the texts was inscribed into them by their historical–material conditions of production.[23]

The director attempting to construct a contemporary performance of a play by Shakespeare has, as a base, this complexity of textual (both dramatic and literary) apparatus from which to work. But for the socialist director there is also the problem of how the plays work as a challenge, both in terms of their ideological position within a given culture, and in terms of their ideological content. The question of iterability has to be handled with care, for as Brecht reminds us, 'What really matters is to play these old works [Shakespeare's plays] historically, which means setting them in powerful contrast to our own time. For it is only against the background of our time that their shape emerges as an old shape, and without this background I doubt if they could have any shape at all.'[24] Brecht's comment allows for contradiction, not only in terms of the elements juxtaposed within the content of the plays but also for the director to create contradictions in images of historical perspective: it is the 'background of our time' that may illuminate the historical context and form the particular dialectic of Shakespeare's plays in performance today.

The literary-critical 'reading' of Shakespeare by director, actor, and audience, is essentially an individualist practice that works antagonistically against the collectivist concept of theatre; theatre is not the product of an individual reading of the play, but the result of a collaborative effort in a continuous state of remaking.[25] An ideology that privileges lyric form over dramatic form could only work in an illusionistic theatre in which the audience's relationship with the events on stage is subjective and based upon empathy. From a historical–materialist perspective the complexity of Shakespearean theatre consists in certain historically-inscribed characteristics, such as the rapid movement of 'scenes' within a play (made possible by the open stage unencumbered by pictorial scenery), and the combination of juxtaposed levels of articulated ideas, moving effortlessly from the 'poetic' to the 'naturalistic'. This juxtaposition of forms of language, within the aural experience of the drama,[26] resists the development of a naturalistic (or Aristotelian) flow of experience and action: an inherent episodic disturbance is inscribed into the very nature of the dramatic form.

The language of theatre extends beyond the language of literature and contains within its definition the continual redefining of context: the production of a play must in its definition of language contain, as John McGrath outlines:

the text, mise-en-scène, lighting, performances, casting, music, effects . . . also the nature of the audience, the nature, social, geographical and physical, of the venue, the price of tickets, the availability of tickets, the nature and placing of the pre-publicity, where the nearest pub is, and the relationships between all these considerations themselves and of each with which is happening on stage.[26]

Gramsci in his *Prison Notebooks*,[27] indicates that a concept of art contextualised in this way has the potentiality to engage with audiences as a popular culture that challenges the position of the removed, transcendent form of high art that Shakespeare has become: a popular culture, which can be, in Gramsci's definition, the site of political struggle.

An old lady recently spoke to me outside the Stratford theatre. 'I am terribly interested', she said, 'in your attempts to make Shakespeare alive for our time, but don't you think you ought to do occasional productions for colleges and schools of what Shakespeare really meant?'. I said, 'What did Shakespeare really mean?'. She replied, 'We all know, don't we.' 'Well', I said, 'I'm trying to express Shakespeare as I honestly understand him . . . I must admit that I am a modern' . . . What the old lady meant, of course, was that if I departed from what she expected of a Shakespearean production, I was being un-*Shakespearean*. I subsequently learned that she yearned for a more pictorial Shakespeare, a taste which is assuredly more Edwardian than Elizabethan.[28]

Peter Hall's narration of this incident, subsequently retold many times by many different people, is intended to reinforce the need for a relevant contemporary appropriation of Shakespeare's plays. By insisting that Shakespeare 'is our contemporary', his Shakespeare is distanced from the genteel Shakespeare exemplified by a 'a taste assuredly more Edwardian than Elizabethan'. The first impression that we are likely to gain from Hall's unequivocal call for a contemporary Shakespeare, is to see his position as demystifying, progressive, radical, even socialist; he appears to be making a radical break with what he sees as a dead tradition: the pictorial staging of Irving and the nineteenth century theatre. By stating his position as a modern, only understanding Shakespeare in terms of the world of the 1960s, Hall seems to be claiming the role of myth-breaker. However, later on in the same essay he says: 'Yet in human terms, the plays are very near to us . . . our own chaotic thinking is very contrary to the world of the Elizabethans. So what man hopes he is like changes, but not, alas, what he is really like. Shakespeare deals in this constant.'[29] A historical origin, a historical point of production may be recognised, but must be reduced to a 'background', supporting role, in order to allow the literary text to transcend history and achieve universal mythic status. While making a claim to be a modern myth-breaker, Hall is in another sense, a myth-maker. His modern Shakespeare, in every way as much as the old lady's, emerges as another form of tradition that sees the plays of Shakespeare as autotelic: transcendent of history.

Notes

1 Peter Hall quoted in David Addenbroke, The Royal Shakespeare Company (London: Kimber, 1974), p. 66.
2 See Alan Sinfield, 'Royal Shakespeare', in Jonathan Dollimore and Alan Sinfield, eds., Political Shakespeare (Manchester: Manchester University Press, 1985), p. 159.
3 Charles Marowitz and Simon Trussler, Theatre at Work (London: Methuen, 1967), pp. 145–7.
4 J. Goodwin, ed., Peter Hall's Diaries: the Story of a Dramatic Battle: 'July 22, 1972' (London: Hamish Hamilton, 1983), p. 14.
5 See Sally Beauman, The Royal Shakespeare Company: a History of Ten Decades (Oxford: Oxford University Press, 1982), p. 238.
6 Janet Watts: 'The Nunn story', Observer Colour Supplement (2 May 1982), p. 39.
7 Ibid., p. 39.
8 See Beauman, Royal Shakespeare Company, p. 268. Sally Beauman's notes (p. 367) to this section reveal that the source was a conversation with Hall himself in 1979. The section concludes (p. 268) with a direct quote from Hall: 'Perhaps our ideal was to speak like Rylands, and to think like Leavis'. George Rylands, a contemporary (albeit an anatagonistic

one) of Leavis at Cambridge, was famous for his Cambridge productions of Elizabethan and Jacobean plays.

9 Roger Manvell, 'On the dank and dirty ground', Peter Hall in interview, *Shakespeare and the Film* (London: Dent, 1971), pp. 121–2, 123–4.

10 Peter Hall, 'Shakespeare and the modern director', *Royal Shakespeare Company 1960–63*, ed. John Goodwin (London: Max Reinhardt, 1964), p. 41.

11 *Ibid.*, p. 41.

12 See Beauman, p. 273. Also Terry Hands interviewed, Chapter 11.

13 John Barton, discussed elsewhere in this volume by Graham Holderness, is another important member of this Cambridge/Stratford axis. His case is interestingly disclosed by Michael L. Greenwald, 'The marriage of true minds: the Bartons and *Hamlet*, 1980–81', *Deutsche Shakespeare-Gesellschaft West* (Bochum: Jarbuch, 1983), p. 162.

14 See Francis Mulherne, *The Moment of 'Scrutiny'* (London: Verso, 1981), pp. 76–7, 100–15, and Graham Holderness, *Shakespeare's History* (Dublin: Gill and Macmillan, 1985), pp. 164–200. See also John Barton, *Playing Shakespeare* (London: Methuen, 1984), pp. 134–49.

15 See Hall, 'Shakespeare and the modern director', p. 48.

16 For a full discussion of *Scrutiny*'s 'organic past' see: Perry Anderson, 'Components of the national culture', *New Left Review*, 56 (1968), pp. 50–6; Terry Eagleton, *Criticism and Ideology* (London: Verso, 1976), pp. 12–16; Graham Holderness, *Shakespeare's History*, pp. 151 and 176; Derek Longhurst, 'Reproducing a national culture: Shakespeare in education', *Red Letters*, 11, pp. 3–14; Francis Mulhern, *Moment of 'Scrutiny'*, pp. 112–13.

17 The relevance of this aspect of Leavis's argument may be seen on close examination of the *Wars of the Roses* cycle of productions directed by Peter Hall and John Barton, 1963 (full records in The Birthplace Centre library, Stratford-upon Avon). See also for example E. M. W. Tillyard, *The Elizabethan World Picture*; also George Bourne: *Change in the Village*, quoted in Denys Thompson: 'A cure for amnesia' (*Scrutiny* vol. II no. I), p. 2; also F. R. Leavis, 'The organic community', *Letters in Criticism* (London: Chatto and Windus, 1974), pp. 100–1.

18 See F. R. Leavis: 'Scrutiny: a retrospect', *Scrutiny*, vol. XX (1963), p. 4 and p. 5.

19 F. R. Leavis: 'The filming of *Women in Love*', *Letters in Criticism*, p. 134.

20 See Barton, *Playing Shakespeare*.

21 Jan Kott, *Shakespeare our Contemporary* (London: Methuen, 1965), p. 300.

22 See Sinfield, 'Royal Shakespeare', p. 131; and David Hornbrook, Chapter 13.

23 See Holderness, *Shakespeare's History*, p. 13.

24 Bertolt Brecht, *The Messingkauf Dialogues*, trans. John Willett (London: Methuen, 1965), pp. 63–4.

25 Terry Eagleton: 'The author as producer', *Marxism and Literary Criticism* (London: Methuen, 1976), pp. 63–7.

26 John McGrath, *A Good Night Out – Popular Theatre: Audience, Class and Form* (London: Methuen, 1981), p. 5.

27 See Antonio Gramsci, 'The modern prince', *Selections from the Prison Notebooks*, ed and trans. Quintin Hoare and Geoffrey Nowell Smith (London: Lawrence and Wishart, 1971), pp. 130–5.

28 See Hall, 'Shakespeare and the modern director', p. 41.

29 *Ibid.*, p. 42. See also Terry Hands interviewed, Chapter 11.

I am grateful to my friend and colleague Graham Holderness whose keen editorial observations have brought order to this essay.

Terry Hands
interviewed by Christopher J. McCullough

You have worked with the Royal Shakespeare Company for twenty years, the years of Peter Hall and of Trevor Nunn, with whom you have latterly shared the joint artistic directorship. What is for you the justification of a national institution whose primary aim is the production of Shakespeare's plays?

I think that is a loaded question. The phrase 'national institution' is presumably intended critically: but let's just examine the RSC as a theatre. There is every justification for a theatre devoting itself to the works of Shakespeare, simply because he has, by his ability to focus on universal human problems, proved himself to be as relevant today as when he was first writing.

Shakespeare reminds us of how little we have evolved in the last five centuries in language, thinking, clothes or even physical behaviour. People forget that our evolution is very slow; though we can choose to be vegetarians, we are built and programmed as carnivores and no amount of yoghurt will dispel our canine teeth or our dog-like motivations. Whatever miracle or happy accident made Shakespeare the writer he is, there is every reason for him being the centre of any theatre's output.

How has the RSC grown to be a 'national institution'? That was by accident. In the 1960s, a group of young people gathered together who wanted to explore Shakespeare. They recognised that if, by such an exploration, they were to encounter all the difficult myriad layers of Shakespeare, they could never completely succeed. An important aspect of this process was a very English masochism that always celebrates defeats to a greater extent than victories, and which paradoxically draws support from the notion that Shakespeare will always remain unattainable. Gradually, stimulated by its association with modern drama, the RSC grew; but it grew through a period of general deterioration in the theatre in the rest of the country. When I was a young director the whole country was bubbling with various schools of Shakespeare: there was the Bristol Old Vic; the National Theatre; and the activities of Jack Neville and Frank Dunlop in Nottingham. The whole place was tremendously alive. Gradually subsequent governments have starved the regions leaving the RSC as a kind of provincial refugee centre.

The rigorous and relentless spirit that kept it growing was really that of the original artists who wanted to explore Shakespeare. The fact that the RSC has carried on growing must be the measure of the value, not just of the people who are here at Stratford but of that particular playwright.

To follow on from that, it does seem that the RSC has acquired, with various governments over the last twenty years, something of a reputation for radicalism: not only with the present Thatcher government but with previous Labour governments too. In 1966 Lord Goodman accused the company of being far left and of having an anti-establishment tone.[1] *Yet the company is based on a very traditional concept of culture, and its title bears the royal insignia. How do you feel the RSC manages to sustain these seemingly contradictory reputations?*

I agree that the RSC sustains those reputations: but they are contradictory only through your choice of words. The same applies to your use of the word radical. I think all theatres do, and should, question our way of life in an apolitical manner. I have no great personal interest in politics. Politics, like the swelling associated with dropsy, is a fat and watery exterior to the real problem: which is a disease of the heart. Shakespeare and the theatre in general should be concerned with the real sickness. If they are, they are bound to be questioning whatever political party is in power; and so no theatre can be 'establishment', no theatre can be a 'national institution' – though it may be a nationally recognised theatre. Our particular task must be to question, not to give answers; if we give answers, we become a political operation, which we are not.

I think that the problem for us in the RSC, in the twentieth century, is Shakespearean tragedy. It is much harder to do a Shakespeare tragedy, or any tragedy, than it is to do a comedy, mainly because I think – although both are equally rigorous – tragedy works off an accepted system of values shared by the (original) audience. If anybody went against those values, they knew they were doing wrong; wrong within whatever it was: a social or moral context. Therefore, the tragedy became the story of what happened when certain basic values, or principles, were denied. The problem today is that all the old systems have been devalued, so we have to set up a system in production before we can challenge it. Shakespeare simply had to challenge. The values were integral to his society. If we get the balance wrong, we may appear to be establishment or right-wing. Conversely, the process of breaking them down can look excessively radical. It's a question of balancing the basic humanity and passion at the centre of all the plays.

How far do you consider personal relationships should affect the nature and work of the RSC? I'm thinking of Sally Beauman's definition of your relationship with Trevor Nunn as 'an odd symbiotic relationship which became progressively central to the artistic development of the RSC'.[2]

Relationships inevitably do affect the work of the RSC; one hopes they affect it for the better. In the early days the name of the game was survival: so the relationship between Trevor and myself was developed out of an immediately recognisable kinship. When we joined the company (he a little ahead of me) we became friends immediately because we found ourselves thinking in the same way; as we were the only two young ones in the place we shared attitudes to what was going on. All of us in those early days were prepared to wait for, rather than shape, tomorrow. The RSC developed in the kind of way that rehearsals often do, with a mixture of inspiration and accident. In the early days we were able to look to other great theatres to see where we might go tomorrow. The Royal Dramatic Theatre Stockholm, the Comédie Française, the Berliner Ensemble and the Moscow Arts Theatre have all been important to us in inspiration: but we have outgrown them all in the size and strength of our ensemble. Tomorrow's inspiration is a mystery; today is a panic; yesterday was a form of despair.

Hidden in your question is the belief that the RSC is a publicly-subsidised organisation, and that personal relationships should not matter to something that is being run for the good of the people. My answer to that would be that only one-third of our income comes from the government, not as a subsidy but as an investment. We are more akin to a merchant bank or an underwriting firm; we are maverick, buccaneer, private. We are not the National Theatre and never will be. Our organisation is built on personal relationships, making the whole structure analogous to a family. As a family we have our problems and our tensions, but we work together with the common aim of providing a service to the public.

John Barton, Peter Hall and Trevor Nunn are all Cambridge University graduates. Peter Hall and Trevor Nunn have made a number of references to the importance of F. R. Leavis and the influence of 'Cambridge English' on both their theatrical work with Shakespeare and their general view of the functions of culture within our society.[3] *How important do you think this 'Cambridge link' has been in formulating the policies of the RSC?*

It was very important, and thank God it was there. Hall and Nunn were certainly under the influence of Leavis. They were also influenced by the Moscow Arts Theatre, which came over here in the 1950s and stunned everybody with an attention to detail which we were not using then. There was in both kinds of work a necessary terse, dry, cynical, rather rational, rather journalistic counterbalance to the prevalent theatrical over-indulgence.

The only element in your question with which I would take issue is the use of the word policies. The key, and in my opinion the only policy initiated was the application of university-trained men (and latterly women) to the study of Shakespeare – to living research, living academia, living literature.

There have been many attempts to bring Shakespeare 'to the people'. Peter Hall spoke of making Shakespeare a 'positive experience' that might make 'the masses who buy paperbacks stream into the theatre'.[4] *Buzz Goodbody set up the Other Place with the intention of bringing Shakespeare to the people, and in your early months with the RSC you were director of Theatreground.*[5] *Do you consider these initiatives authentic attempts to broaden the cultural basis of the RSC, and how successful have they been?*

Again I find the question loaded. Anybody who comes into a theatre is 'people'. We are all human beings under the skin and there have been at various times different schemes for bringing more people into the theatre. The reason why Shakespeare is the backbone of our policy is because he speaks to so many people over such a wide range. Our job in the theatre is twofold: to catch in performance the human being inside the external being that gets classified into a social group; and to get at school-children before they become streamed into middle-, working- or upper-class, when they are still open to what may stimulate them, or make them wish to involve themselves. Peter Hall talked about making theatre a positive experience, so he included a very strong rational way of directing Shakespeare.

Buzz Goodbody set up the Other Place with Trevor, myself and other directors. Her intention was not that of bringing Shakespeare to the people. It was simply an idea of making theatre more immediate in a circumstance which was, in terms of stage-craft, much easier to control. Working on a big proscenium arch stage involves areas of craft and technique that are totally unnecessary when working in a space like the Other Place. It was simply a way of allowing the audience to be right on top of a performance, while the actors could work in the kind of detail they would use in television and film. When they performed back on the big stage, we hoped they would be able to carry that experience with them. You can't talk about bringing Shakespeare to the people and then move into a 150 seat house; it is in the 1,500 seat house that you bring Shakespeare to the people.

What I think was radical about the Other Place, to us and to the public, was the possibility of doing classics which could be examined in a different way. In addition, out of an impulse which Trevor and I wished to maintain, we started a policy of new writing. We couldn't afford it in the main houses: the costs were enormous and the losses at the box-office titanic. We needed something smaller where we could build audiences, do a lot of new plays and encourage new writers. We found that by having a smaller theatre like the Other Place, and the Warehouse, we were able to put on the work, say, of half a dozen writers, for a tenth of the cost of one writer in the main house.

In Stratford itself there is a cultural industry apparently based on this concept of Shakespeare as cultural token and as embodiment of the English national spirit: you have described it as the 'curious factory' of the tourist and souvenir trade, in which the theatre functions as a kind of temple. It is common to find descriptions involving terms like 'devotion' applied to the playwright and the town; and it is difficult to avoid the analogy with medieval pilgrims. Where does the company's work stand, between your notion of 'living' theatre and the monumental productions proper to this devotional industry?

The Stratford industry is nothing to do with us. The Stratford industry is the town of Stratford, which is quite different from the theatre of Stratford. 'That curious factory'; it is a curious factory; we work longer hours, at less than factory rates, and never in factory conditions. We are not élitist, we cannot afford to be. We must have a full house in order to survive, therefore we are a popular theatre. Yes, of course there is tourism and souvenirs. So what? They exist in the same way that the great cathedrals used to have stalls and prostitutes, dice-players and three-card-tricks, going on all around the buttresses and even inside. So too the great theatre for Shakespeare – and I say it blatantly – is sur-rounded by money-grabbing vendors. And why not? It's like the oak tree which supports, we are told, a greater ecology than any other plant form. Hundreds of species of insect and grub life live on it; so too with Shakespeare, and so much the better. I am tired of finding descriptions involving words like devotion, that almost suggest it is a rather sad state of affairs, some kind of sin. I think that devotion is what you will find, unashamedly, at the centre of the RSC.

Notes

1 Sally Beauman, *The Royal Shakespeare Company: a History of Ten Decades* (Oxford: Oxford University Press, 1982), p. 284.

2 Ibid.
3 See Christopher J. McCullough, pp. 113–14 above.
4 Peter Hall: 'Shakespeare and the modern director', in *Royal Shakespeare Company 1960–63*, ed. John Goodwin (London: Max Reinhardt, 1964), p. 48.
5 See Colin Chambers, *Other Spaces* (London: Methuen, 1982), pp. 34–46.

Making space: appropriation and confrontation in recent British plays
Alan Sinfield

Myth and power

The space we usually think of the dramatist as requiring is physical space on a stage. But any writing needs, also, cultural space: a language, institutions to present it, and understanding audiences or readers. To make cultural space for writing, one must contrive some kind of adjustment with the prevailing languages, institutions and audiences.

For many dramatists, one factor to be negotiated is the Shakespeare myth. They must come to terms with the Shakespearean theatre language – this factor is manifest in the instances of Tennyson, Shaw, Eliot, Brecht, Arden and Bond. Some institutions are devoted to presenting Shakespearean texts, others feature them with unique frequency, so that they exercise influence over the whole repertoire and style. And audiences are accustomed to these arrangements. In 1955 J. B. Priestley elaborated the modern dramatist's 'Case against Shakespeare': 'we are asked to compete with a dramatist who starts with every advantage of prestige, who is sound culture personified, who can demand audiences of school children to eke out the matinées, and who does not even ask a royalty for his services'. Of course the playgoer chooses Shakespeare: 'The play is a masterpiece of its kind, which the whole family can enjoy; there is a wonderful cast, probably the best in town; the production is said to be magnificently lavish; the seats cost no more, perhaps rather less, than seats elsewhere. So once more it is Shakespeare, while round the corner the production of a new play totters towards bankruptcy, and the man who wrote it wonders whether he will ever again find a management brave enough to produce him.'[1]

The dramatist's bid for cultural space is (among other things) an attempt to take part in the making of culture. Raymond Williams defines 'culture' as the *signifying system* through which 'a social order is communicated, reproduced, experienced and explored'.[2] More simply, culture is an amalgam of the current stories about who we are, where we stand in relation to each other and the world, and, especially, about the power relations between us. These stories don't all come in the mode, manifestly, of narrative. Often they are directly experienced – being welcomed or refused entrance, for instance, announces your relationship to the establishment being approached. But many of them are transmitted through writing, theatre or other media. The survival and prevalence of particular stories depends finally upon the interaction of culture with economic and political conditions; yet these conditions may be changed by people, and the decision to attempt change depends, perhaps more than anything else, on people realising that the prevailing stories are not the only possible ones. That is why the ruling élite, in Shakespeare's time and ours, both promotes and controls education, preaching, printing and theatrical production; and that is why the process of analysing and changing stories is politically important. Shakespeare altered, often hugely, all the stories he dealt with. A conservative academic institution tends to represent those changes as technical improvements or advances in wisdom. But by altering stories of power relations and human possibilities, Shakespeare was working politically, making his culture. And our subsequent work with the idea of Shakespeare and with Shakepearean texts is the same kind of activity.

Often Shakespeare is perceived as having a role in processes such as I have described; but, at the same time, he is seen as rising superior to them. In other words, his name and the texts we associate with it have mythic status: they represent truths that transcend particular circumstances. That is the idealist conception of myth. But in a materialist analysis, meanings are *made*, continuously, by people in determine conditions, and they are intricately involved in the power relations that inform specific institutions and the society at large. To the materialist, Shakespearean texts are identified, understood and accorded status by us in our social structure; they are part of our story-making. Certainly, they are a powerful cultural token, but the mythic transcendence attributed to them is both an illusion and a strategy for claiming cultural authority (my story is better than yours because it is a myth). Moreover, the category of myth is usually conservative in tendency, for it implies that the profoundest stories are already known, and thereby discourage thoughts of change.[3] The materialist has two objections to myth, as it is conceived by the idealist: it engrosses cultural authority, and it implies the necessary permanence of current stories, and hence power relations.

That the apparently mythic eternal relevance of Shakespeare is secured in actuality by strenuous cultural work is the argument of the present book. In literary scholarship and criticism it is usually held that the critic is only establishing or interpreting the text; in fact, however, these practices are always active, producing certain meanings and disqualifying others; getting Shakespeare to mean in terms of a current academic discourse. On the stage, notoriously, directors develop the text and the action in ways not anticipated by audiences, for only thus, they find, can they make them 'work'. Yet directors, too, claim invariably that what they are producing is, after all, the real Shakespeare.[4] The power of the myth makes it discreditable to say otherwise. Here, I shall focus on recent dramatists who have sought to intervene in the processes of cultural production – in collusion with or defiance of all this work to sustain Shakespeare – by writing new plays manifestly related to Shakespearean texts. This is a very particular way of making space, but an illuminating one. The dramatist's need to negotiate the presence of Shakespeare, particularly on the stage, is apparent everywhere, in borrowings, quotations and allusions; I shall be concerned with wholesale reconstitutions of Shakespearean texts, since these offer the most provocative instances. Tom Stoppard, Charles Marowitz, Arnold Wesker and Edward Bond have produced different kinds of reconstitution, and with diverse political purposes. Through comparing the terms in which they appropriate and confront the Shakespeare myth, I shall develop a further analysis of the structures and politics of cultural production.

Touching the hem of the garment: Stoppard

'And when the men of that place had knowledge of him, they sent out into all that country round about, and brought unto him all that were diseased; And besought him that they might only touch the hem of his garment: and as many as touched were made perfectly whole.'[5] When the action of *Rosencrantz and Guildenstern Are Dead* runs into that of *Hamlet* as we recognise it from the Shakespearean play, the characters exit speaking, or the dialogue 'is overtaken by rising music and fading light' and it is the end of an act.[6] Stoppard's play is written, we might say, in the margins of *Hamlet*; it is performed in the wings; it is the not-said of *Hamlet*, its other, its unconscious. At the same time, there is endless play upon the theme of illusion-and-reality, with the action undermining, continually, any belief of the characters or the audience that they have a secure grasp of reality. It seems that the Shakespeare myth is challenged in two ways: formally, in that the 'natural' flow of the Shakespearean text is disrupted, and the familiar relationship between it and the experienced audience is broken; and thematically, in that the 'tragic hero' is displaced from the centre of his own play and the substitute protagonists (Rosencrantz and Guildenstern) achieve no heroic control of themselves or their destinies.

Formally, *Rosencrantz and Guildenstern Are Dead* may seem to offer the radical undermining of ideology that we associate with a Brechtian alienation-effect. In that effect, no discourse is allowed to become established as simply dominant, as the natural and self-evident way to think about the action. The audience is denied the secure relationship with the text that characterises the process through which ideology normally normalises itself; the *activity* of language and ideology, in making the world rather than reflecting it, comes into view. Stoppard's play seems to present a double alienation-effect, for it disrupts the experienced audience's relationship with the text of *Hamlet*, and disrupts also its own surface by playing incessantly with audience expectations of character and narrative.

However, *Rosencrantz and Guildenstern Are Dead* is actually a very conservative play. As the discourses of the text are reduced to the one set of notions (illusion, allusion, contrivance, acting, joke, logical play), a new meta-discourse emerges behind them, controlling them and reassuring the audience. It is the metadiscourse of metadiscourse. The disturbance of *Hamlet*, and of all other discourses in the play, becomes what the play *is about*; we have not a surface and a rupture, but a theme, almost a statement. Moreover, there was already, in 1966, a genre that familiarised such metadiscourse. Beckett's *Waiting For Godot* was presented in England with considerable critical attention in 1955, Eugene Ionesco disputed with Kenneth Tynan in the *Observer* in 1958, Pinter's *The Caretaker* was presented successfully in London in 1960, and Martin Esslin's book *The Theatre of the Absurd* explained what it is all about in 1961. Absurdist theatre plays with illusion and reality and suggests, like Stoppard's play, that although the final reality may be death, even that is 'the absence of presence, nothing more' (p. 93). When the audience locates *Rosencrantz and Guildenstern Are Dead* within this genre, it knows where it stands. While the characters are increasingly baffled and anxious, the audience becomes more confident in its knowledge. This is because its members understand about the absurd, and also about *Hamlet*. Turns of event which baffle Rosencrantz and Guildenstern – such as the contents of the two letters to England (pp. 81, 91) – offer for the audience a pleasant little surprise, as they pick up the cues from Hamlet. The audience is able to cope with it all – unlike the unfortunate characters – because they are cultured and know their Hamlet.

Certain egalitarian implications in Stoppard's reduction of discourses to the one level of (non)significance may be acknowledged. But because there is no analysis of the founding of discourses in power relations (including the cultural superiority that arises from knowing about Hamlet and the absurd), this has little impetus. The idea of Hamlet and the Shakespeare myth stands unchallenged, and is probably enhanced by this new evidence of their universal applicability.

Thematically, also, the absurdism of Stoppard's play was already being reconciled with Shakespearean texts. Stoppard's characters feel that they are scripted ('Give us this day our daily cue', p. 76), but Shakespeare's Hamlet declares, after all, 'there is a special providence in the fall of a sparrow . . . if it be not now, yet it will come – the readiness is all', and A. C. Bradley discovered 'fatalism' in Hamlet.[7] In the 1960s, absurdism seemed to make more sense than heroism and rational purpose, and the infinitely adaptable Shakespeare was reinterpreted in its terms. Esslin found the plays rich in 'precisely the same type of inverted logical reasoning, false syllogism, free association, and the poetry of real or feigned madness', and identified there 'a very strong sense of the futility and absurdity of the human condition'. Jan Kott suggested that King Lear has much in common with Beckett's Endgame, and in 1962 Peter Brook directed the play with this in mind. Peter Hall in his Hamlet of 1965 sought to disclose 'an apathy of the will so deep that commitment to politics, to religion or to life is impossible', that 'we need to discover and understand the universe in anguish'.[8]

People who believe themselves to be conservative, at least in relation to Shakespeare, often complain that 'the text' is being interfered with. But although absurdist productions of the plays and Rosencrantz and Guildenstern Are Dead were initially surprising, they were actually working to keep Shakespeare going. The hegemonic culture cannot afford to rest complacently: it must reproduce itself actively and continually, responding to changing economic and political conditions and meeting the specific challenges of subordinate cultures. It must strive to sustain the authority of its cultural tokens and to keep control of interpretation of them, and this may require large adjustments. The need to adjust myths is proportionate to their power, for they cannot be relinquished or surrendered to subordinate groups without prevailing power relations coming into question. It is a paradox of myth-strategies, that the more a phenomenon is proclaimed as universal, the more it must be adapted to changing conditions. The more a myth is consolidated, the more it must be interfered with. If Shakespearean texts are truly for all kinds and conditions of people at all times, then the pressure upon them to speak meaningfully to current society, or at least to that part of the society likely to be interested, becomes overwhelming, and the need for cunning adaptations becomes very great. In the 1960s, people believed they were experiencing particularly rapid social change. Young people especially (and they constituted the growth audience for theatre) distrusted conventional political forms but had difficulty discerning more radical possibilities, and therefore were ready to invest in the idea of absurdist futility. They suspected conventional cultural forms also, and were ready to delight in irreverent eclecticism. Esslin, Kott, Brook, Hall and Stoppard demonstrated that the Shakespeare myth was equal to these developments.

Stoppard and the Shakespeare myth serve each other, for even as Stoppard updates the myth, he makes space for his own writing. In adjusting the Shakespearean text, Stoppard does not aspire to dislodge it from its cultural space, but to alter the configuration so that there is space for him too, and for his kind of writing, alongside Shakespeare. Like the sick people with Jesus, *Rosencrantz and Guildenstern Are Dead* touches the hem of Shakespeare's garment, and some of his power is conducted into the new work. Most reconstitutions of Shakespearean plays are like that. Bernard Kops's *Hamlet of Stepney Green* (1958) uses *Hamlet* as a way of writing about the modern Jewish family; W. S. Gilbert's *Rosencrantz and Guildenstern* (1891) finds opportunity for characteristic Gilbertian humour; Barbara Garson's *MacBird* (1966) plays with *Macbeth* to satirise Lyndon Johnson and the Kennedies; Michael Innes's radio play, *The Hawk and the Handsaw* (1948) rewrites *Hamlet* so as to focus the possibility and the danger of a Freudian view of people; Gordon Bottomley designs *King Lear's Wife* (1915) and *Gruach* (1923) as manifest extensions of the stories of *King Lear* and *Macbeth*, in order to promote a 'poetic' drama of domestic situations; Steven Berkoff in *West* (1983) scatters Shakespearean quotations and motifs through his representation of lower-class life in Stamford Hill in the 1950s. These instances make diverse kinds of raids upon Shakespearean texts, but they all (even *West*, where the juxtapositions of register are very marked) aspire to share cultural space with the Shakespeare myth, and to appropriate significance from it.

All that is, in my view, legitimate and no more than characteristic of the way cultures are extended. Because Shakespeare is such an exalted cultural token, such appropriations strike some people as impertinent; but that is just one of the factors with which appropriators have to work. What I would positively celebrate, though, is attempts to confront the Shakespeare myth. I have two reasons for this: first, confrontation may help to disperse cultural authority, making it easier to open up cultural space (and I would wish authority of all kinds more dispersed than it is); second, the ideologies that Shakespearean texts are customarily read to produce are reactionary (in terms of class, gender, sexual orientation and race), and confrontational reconstitutions may oppose those ideologies. An alternative strategy, I grant, is to re-read Shakespearean texts so as to produce other, radical readings. Brecht, at times, proposed both re-reading and rewriting; in his *Coriolanus* he wanted to do both. But re-reading does not disperse cultural authority, on the contrary, it produces a radical Shakespeare alongside the others.

The progress of Marowitz

Charles Marowitz's *Collage Hamlet* started as a twenty-eight minute condensation in 1963 and was then reshuffled and expanded to eighty-five minutes. Marowitz himself describes it well: 'The play was spliced-up into a collage with lines juxtaposed, sequences rearranged, characters dropped or blended, and the entire thing played out in short, discontinuous fragments which appeared like subliminal flashes out of Hamlet's life and, in every case, used Shakespeare's words, though radically rearranged'. Despite the apparent disturbance of the received text, the enterprise depended on Marowitz's sense of the Shakespeare myth: he assumed explicitly that everyone knew enough for him to 'predicate a performance on that mythic memory'.[9] At the same time, he believed it was the myth that makes reconstitution necessary, since *Hamlet* has been so worked over that the question, in 1963, was whether 'it is possible, today, to sit through the play as Shakespeare wrote it and still respond to its story and structure'.[10] Yet Marowitz's intention was not to demystify but to rescue the Shakespearean play. He believed that 'once the narrative sequence is broken, one has direct access to the play's ambiances', and wanted to 'maintain contact with what is essential in *Hamlet*'; in 1978 he was still offering as a 'justification' for his 're-structuring' that it is 'an indirect way of making contact with that work's essence'.[11] And so it is that this reconstitution, like others we have considered, does not challenge the cultural authority of Shakespeare.

Marowitz had a theme as well as a technique. He wanted to expose the character Hamlet as the prototype of contemporary liberal intellectuals who, in his view, equate 'the taking of a position with the performance of an action' (*Marowitz Hamlet*, p. 22). So towards the end, for instance, the other characters deride Hamlet for just those attempts to explain his situation which have seemed to manifest his sensitivity:

Hamlet (*weakly*): To be or not to be that is the question.
  All laugh
(*weakly*)   The play's the thing wherein I'll catch the conscience of the King.
  All laugh again
(*vainly trying to find the right words*)   There is something rotten in the state of Denmark.

Fortinbras proclaims in response, sarcastically, 'What a piece of work is man' (*Marowitz Hamlet*, pp. 108–9). But this idea of Hamlet's weakness is not very different from orthodox readings of the Shakespearean play (it is related to the fatalism and nihilism already discussed). Indeed, in so far as Marowitz opposes Fortinbras to Hamlet, as the man who presents true resolution, he does not seek to displace even the concept of the hero, merely to deny that Hamlet is such a one. Marowitz's *Hamlet*, for all its formal disturbance, does not confront the liberal and conservative ideologies that usually dominate consideration of the Shakespearean text.

Marowitz experimented with *Macbeth* in 1969 and *The Taming of the Shrew* in 1973. *Measure for Measure*, performed in 1975 at the Open Space Theatre in London, was however a breakthrough: Marowitz concedes that his politically radical handling of the play is 'patently not what Shakespeare intended' (*Marowitz Shakespeare*, p. 20). Marowitz's version takes the action through briskly to the point of Isabella's blackmail by Angelo, cutting the Shakespearean text but appearing not to depart significantly from it (the lower-class characters are omitted). But instead of standing by her rejection of Angelo, Isabella finds herself assailed by a phantasmagoria of voices from the play, confusing her, demanding her submission, leaving her no way out; and she allows herself to be seduced. But Claudio is executed nevertheless. When the Duke returns Isabella appeals to him and, as in Shakespeare's play, he seems to disbelieve her. But here he maintains his public condemnation of Isabella and she is sent to prison. Angelo tells her he has 'a motion much imports your good' – the words through which the Duke proposes marriage in the Shakespearean play, but now manifestly only a further attempt at exploitation. Finally the Duke, Angelo and Escalus dine together privately and joke about it all: none of them is seriously surprised by Angelo's behaviour.

Marowitz had in mind Watergate and corruption in high places today: but he was also exposing the politics of the Shakespearean text. At each point where corruption in the power elite is likely to produce permanent damage, Shakespeare veers away – so explicitly, purposefully, and in defiance of his source, that the concomitant twists and turns of plots and characterisation are perennial topics in criticism. So blatant are these evasions that we might conclude that Shakespeare wants us to distrust them, to go straight forward when the text turns aside from the probabilities it has created, and hence to meditate upon the oppressive mode of government that has come into visibility, though not into full actualisation. Customarily, criticism does not do this. Instead it finds, in the awkward turns, signs that the Duke's State is blessed by a special dispensation, either divine or human, or limits its critique to the Duke's personality. Yet the most enthusiastic Christian or liberal may grant that Marowitz's text offers the more likely working out of the play's initial presuppositions.

This is why it is so important that Marowitz makes his version out of lines which, we recognise, derive from the Shakespearean text; his play is, precisely, a reconstitution. He enables us to see that the violence, injustice and oppression which he foregrounds *are* in the Shakespearean text, though there they are distributed so that we may feel reassured, overall, about how the ruling elite exercises power. Here is part of the dialogue from the concluding private dinner:

Duke (*Mimicking the lower-classes*): What news abroad i' the world?
Angelo (*Mock guiltily, also with put-on voice*): Sir, I have been an unlawful bawd time out of mind, but yet I will be content to be a lawful hangman. I would be glad to receive some instruction from me fellow partner.
Escalus (*Laughing at Angelo's imitation; mock-astonished*): A bawd, sir? (*To Duke*) Fie upon him, he will discredit our mystery.
Angelo   Faith, my lord, I spoke it but according to the trick. If you will hang me for it, you may. But I had rather it would please you I might be whipped. (*All fall about with laughter*)[12]

These lines are spoken in the Shakespearean play by the lower orders, who are shown exploiting each other, apparently justifying the repressive 'measures' of the State. This displacement of violence and oppression onto some of its victims[13] is reversed by Marowitz, and the lines are spoken by members of the power élite. In so speaking, they return the blame to its proper place; the joke, to them, is that the penalties mentioned are applied not to them but to the people they despise. The only danger is that Angelo has discredited the mystery of Statecraft – which is thoroughly implicated with killing people and the buying and selling of their bodies.

Marowitz's *Variations on The Merchant of Venice* (1977) begins with a news report of the bombing of the King David Hotel in Jerusalem by Zionist guerillas in 1946, and then presents Shylock lamenting a dead comrade. Marlowe's *Jew of Malta* is drawn upon to establish the suffering and resistance of Jewish people in British Palestine; the relationship between Jessica and Lorenzo, echoing that between Abigail and Don Lodowick and the convent in Marlowe's play, is a device to infiltrate the (British) enemy. The wooing of Portia as a way of restoring Bassanio's fortunes is briskly conducted. Brilliantly, Marowitz has Bassanio playing the first two suitors in disguise, to make sure that he gets the right casket; this is part of a general tendency to make the British unpleasant, so that Shylock's refusal to forgive becomes understandable. His violence, like that of guerilla fighters combatting an imperialist power, cannot simply be dismissed as lack of Christian love or forgiveness, or a personal failing, or arbitrary malignancy; but must rather be recognised as a response to a violent situation. Finally the court scene proceeds through to the attempt, as in the Shakespearean play, to humiliate and destroy Shylock: but the Jews attack, and disarm the British. Shylock's famous speech from Shakespeare's play, 'Hath not a Jew eyes?' is placed here with vivid political effect, for it concludes: 'The villainy you have taught me I will execute, and it shall go hard but I will better the instruction'. The scene blacks out as the first shots are fired, and the play ends with the continuing news story of the King David Hotel and the response of the occupying forces: 'all border posts have been shut, all street-corners are blocked with armoured cars and barricades, and a curfew is in force throughout Jerusalem'. Violence is continued, not concluded, by repression (*Marowitz Shakespeare*, pp. 282–3).

Marowitz's *Merchant* and *Measure for Measure* are, in my judgement, both radical and powerful. By reconstituting the Shakespearean text they raise the possibility that other stories might be told, both by it and alongside it, and they indicate the direction those other stories should take. Marowitz both unsettles the cultural authority of the Shakespeare myth and draws attention to the power relations that it is customarily made to endorse.

Wesker and the limits of humanism

In Wesker's *The Merchant* (1976–8), Shylock and Antonio are close friends; the bond is their protest against the oppressive laws of Venice and,

beyond that, against the whole, well-attested history of European perse-
cutions of Jews, occurring most viciously at the time of the play's action
in Portugal. The friends mock a barbaric law with a barbaric bond.[14]
When the bond cannot be repaid, both Shylock and Antonio believe that
the law must take its course because the safety of the Ghetto depends
upon it: 'Having bent the law for us, how often will they bend it for
themselves and then we'll live in even greater uncertainties than before'
(p. 243). In the manner of the Shakespearean play, Portia gets them all off
the hook, but at the expense of Shylock's property – his books; and, as he
leaves bitterly for Jerusalem, at the expense of his humanistic optimism
and the inter-racial, cross-cultural association with Antonio that has
expressed the humanistic optimism. Portia suffers a parallel oppression,
and protests against the view of her potentiality expressed in her father's
imposition of marriage through the casket riddles; the play ends with her
and Bassanio anticipating a power struggle. Jessica leaves her father
because she finds his expectations of her oppressive, but finds Lorenzo
worse.

Wesker's Shylock suffers because, in the terms of the present essay, he
mistakes the conditions upon which dissidents may win cultural space. It
would be anachronistic if he were impressed by the Shakespeare myth,
but he is comparably enthusiastic about the Renaissance rediscovery of
classical learning. He sees it not as a body of writing open to diverse
constructions in particular conditions, but as possessing mythic radical
power: 'When generals imagine their vain glory is all, and demagogues
smile with sweet benevolence as they tighten the screws of power – up!
Up bubbles the little spring . . . full of blinding questions and succulent
doubts. The word! Unsuspected! Written! Printed! Indestructible!' (p.
233). Shylock knows that the texts he admires have come into modern
circulation because of institutional developments – in trade, law,
government, education and printing (p. 232). But then they are imagined
to work by and of themselves, in the hearts and minds of individual
people. It is because of this idealism that Shylock believes his friendship
can transcend the political situation and they can mock the law with
impunity. The bond they draw up, for a pound of Antonio's flesh, is a
reconstituted text, a subversive rewriting of the kind of contract the State
expects. But such dissident writing is liable to suffer under the system it
challenges. Shylock is made to realise that the hegemonic discourse will
try to accommodate and control gestures like his: 'You will have us all
ways won't you? . . . If we are silent we must be scheming, if we talk we
are insolent. When we come we are strangers, when we go we are

traitors. In tolerating persecution we are despised, but were we to take up arms we'd be the world's marauders, for sure' (pp. 259–60). The reply we might make to Shylock is implicit in the present study: the conditions upon which cultural space may be won are indeed set against radical innovation, but understanding this is one step towards changing it. Shylock sees all the evidence but achieves only a bitter repudiation of humanity.

In the perspective of Wesker's work, The Merchant is one more story of the defeat by the system of the well-meaning individual believer in art and education. Brilliantly, the failure of humanism is focused by Wesker on the 'Hath not a Jew eyes?' speech, the one place in The Merchant where Shakespearean words are used. Wesker has it spoken by Lorenzo, who thinks he is doing Shylock a favour, to Shylock's outraged protests: 'I do not want apologies for my humanity. Plead for me no special pleas. I will not have my humanity mocked and apologised for. If I am exceptionally like any man then I need no exceptional portraiture. I merit no special pleas, no special cautions, no special gratitudes. My humanity is my right, not your bestowed and gracious privilege' (p. 259). In its context in The Merchant of Venice the speech has seemed to proponents of the Shakespeare myth to manifest the transcendent humanism which is otherwise hard to find in the play; by Wesker's Shylock, it is recognised as the ultimate insult. Yet Wesker finds himself in a blind alley, for, of course, the lines he has written to repudiate 'Hath he not eyes?' reassert Shylock's humanity. As a Jew, Wesker is entitled to do this, but it affords no political analysis or programme for action. Like Shylock, Wesker has believed in personal relations and the liberal idea of the naturally progressive influence of art and knowledge; he has expected them to transcend material conditions. The reasons for their failure are apparent in The Merchant, but Wesker offers no follow-up analysis or direction; only the mythical (for Wesker) Jerusalem. So it is in the sequence of quarrels about the way his plays have been produced and received.[15] Wesker complains as if there were some natural reason why good writing as he conceives it should be given space: not recognising that he is involved in a cultural struggle and that 'aesthetic' criteria are never separable from political values.

People sometimes say: 'But why tinker with Shakespeare? Why not write a totally new play?' I think The Merchant is sufficiently interesting, and its topic sufficiently important, to indicate the answer. The racism of The Merchant of Venice – for all that criticism can unearth qualifications, hesitations and complexities – must not be ignored. While we have a competitive economic and political system rooted in differentials of class, gender, sexual orientation and race, this will manifest itself at the level of culture. Subordinate and dissident groups make their culture in the space left by the hegemonic culture – there is nowhere else. Shakespeare is a powerful cultural token, and hence a place where meaning is established and where it must be contested.

Bond and the error of art

If there are grounds for disquiet about the project of Edward Bond, they concern his reluctance, comparable with Wesker's, to confront the conditions of cultural production. *Lear* (presented at the Royal Court in 1971) challenges the Shakespeare myth at its grandest by taking on the play which is commonly taken as the most profound insight into the sources of human suffering. Determinedly, Bond shows that the problem is not rooted in a general 'human condition' but in political systems. Constructive engagement with violence and oppression (which Bond presents as every bit as powerful in the twentieth century as in Shakespeare's time) cannot consist in lamentations about the supposed condition of 'Man', nor in hopes for individual changes of heart; it must involve theoretical analysis of the power structure and practical effort to change it. In Shakespeare's play Cordelia can find nothing to say in response to her father's tyranny: she feels herself confined by the bonds of duties and obligations as they are defined in the prevailing social organisation. When she decides that she must do something to resist the tyranny of her sisters (which reproduces the tyranny of Lear himself) she invades with an army of her own, offering to reproduce *once more* the cycle of violence and domination. Of course, she means to rule differently when she has won; and so does Bond's Cordelia, the leader of a 'revolutionary' insurgency. But Bond makes it manifest that, by taking over Lear's power system, Cordelia also sustains the pattern of his oppression; and that even Lear's band of outlaws is subject to the same temptation. Cordelia restarts work on the wall around the State:

Lear: Then nothing's changed! A revolution must at least reform!
Cordelia: Everything *else* is changed!
Lear: Not if you keep the wall! Pull it down!
Cordelia: We'd be attacked by our enemies!
Lear: The wall will destroy you. It's already doing it. How can I make you see?[16]

Lear tells her: 'Your Law always does more harm than crime, and your morality is a form of violence' (p. 85). Bond moves the Lear story into the realm of political debate, where the processes of power can be seen and assessed.

Much more could be said by way of interpretation of Lear, but this fact, in itself, points towards the disquiet I have indicated. The difficulty of Lear is part of its aspiration to be Art, to be High Culture, to be myth. The whole manner and style suggest this, the grandeur and density; Bond may wish to displace the authority of Shakespeare, but not the authority of myth, and this leaves half the battle unfought. There is, indeed, a second text of mythic authority in play, Sophocles' Oedipus at Colonus: it affords the structure for the third act, and carries the implication that Lear is, like the aged Oedipus, a figure of mythic potential.

If we suspect that Bond's idea is to replace conservative myths with some of his own, this is confirmed by what he himself says in his introduction to The Fool. To be sure, he is aware of the reactionary functions of myth: 'An irrational organization needs myths to maintain itself. . . . Obvious myths are, from the past, the dogma of original sin, and in our day the dogma of original violence. . . . Both these myths have been used to justify force to preserve social relationships.' Nevertheless, alongside this materialist awareness Bond carries an essentialised, idealised conception of 'art' and 'culture' as, by definition, expressive of positive human potential, and therefore able to use myths 'not for Plato's reasons, but as working hypotheses in matters not yet fully understood'.[17] The terms 'myth' and 'working hypothesis' emanate from different and antagonistic discourses. Bond is trying to reorient the terms 'art', 'culture' and 'myth', to wrest them from their current exploiters and use them for socialism. However, by retaining established connotations of 'myth' he risks sliding into an idealist conception of culture and a regressive conception of cultural authority.

Making space

In this paper I have considered the winning of cultural space mainly in terms of political commitment and writing strategies, since that is where one may aspire specifically to appropriate or confront the Shakespeare myth. But as I argued initially, cultural space is not separable from institutions and audiences: where and for whom one works is probably as important as how one tries to write and, indeed, influences hugely how one tries to write. This is why I have focused my account on a particular cultural situation. The suggestions I have made about how texts mean would not apply in other times or places, where formal expectations and the roles of Shakespeare were or are different. I have tried to assume the kind of audience or reader likely to come across these plays – in effect, the educated, youthful, left–Liberal audience that came into existence in conjunction with changes in theatre in the late 1950s,[18] with a conservative slippage through the 1970s. In fact, there are striking correspondences between the institutional positions of these plays and the textual and political analyses I have offered.

Rosencrantz and Guildenstern Are Dead was first presented on the 'fringe' of the Edinburgh Festival in 1966, but it reached the National Theatre (at the Old Vic) in the following year. The speed at which this apparently avant-garde play moved to a central position indicates its acceptability to the cultural establishment. It has long been a favourite text of GCE examiners.[19] Despite Wesker being an established playwright, it took him two years to get a British production of his more challenging appropriation, *The Merchant*; and then it was at the Birmingham Repertory Theatre – a historic and worthy venue, but not very prestigious. Of course, Wesker, like Shylock and Antonio with their bond, meant *The Merchant* to be an embarrassing text for British culture to handle; but like Shylock, he found that there is a penalty for such exploits. The play has not been set by the GCE boards (though Wesker's *Roots* is a familiar stand-by).

Lear was presented at the Royal Court – the site of the most persistent (though intermittent) attempts in post-war British theatre to bring together art and political commitment. It was revived by the Royal Shakespeare Company in 1982 (an acknowledgement, we may say, of its status as art), and is now (alone among Bond's plays) set at GCE. Since 1978, Bond has worked mainly at the National Theatre; this is the institutional equivalent of Bond's use of the concept and manner of myth, and involves the same danger that cultural authority will be relegitimated in the name of socialism. This danger is apparent once more in Bond's reply to a question about how far he considers his audience when writing: 'not at all'.[20] But all audiences are positioned by their cultural assumptions and the institutions they use: Bond, like Wesker, seems to imagine that writers simply communicate with people. No doubt he is imagining the universal 'human' audience of Art, but he is likely to find only the National Theatre audience and the higher-education readership that prefers to be in the presence of Art and myth.

Marowitz founded his own theatre, the Open Space, in 1968, to produce experimental writing by himself and others. This position slightly outside the main system (though with subsidies from the Arts Council and Camden Borough Council) has evident effects in his writing. His reconstitutions are impishly iconoclastic; they have a provisional, perhaps student air about them; are less than fully achieved. Among the plays considered here, they are least likely to be seen as Art or Literature, as having mythic resonances. They are not set at GCE. I think theatre and culture generally are better like that – more flexible and responsive, leaving more openings for artists and audiences, more space to move. Perhaps, even, that is how it was in Shakespeare's theatre, before the myth got hold of him.

Notes

1 In Ivor Brown, ed., *Theatre 1954–5* (London: Max Reinhardt, 1955), pp. 111–12.

2 Raymond Williams, *Culture* (Glasgow: Fontana, 1981), p. 13.

3 See Frank Kermode, *The Sense of an Ending* (London: Oxford University Press, 1966), p. 39.

4 See Alan Sinfield, 'Royal Shakespeare', in Jonathan Dollimore and Alan Sinfield, ed., *Political Shakespeare* (Manchester: Manchester University Press, 1985), especially pp. 173–9. See also Ralph Berry, *Changing Styles in Shakespeare* (London: Allen and Unwin, 1981).

5 Christian Bible, Authorised Version, Matthew, 14: 35–6.

6 Tom Stoppard, *Rosencrantz and Guildenstern Are Dead* (London: Faber, 1967), pp. 27, 38. Stoppard also played with Shakespeare in *Dogg's Hamlet and Cahoot's Macbeth*, 1979 (London: Faber and Faber, 1980).

7 See Alan Sinfield, 'Hamlet's special providence', *Shakespeare Survey*, 33 (1980), 89–98.

8 Martin Esslin, *The Theatre of the Absurd*, revised edn. (Harmondsworth: Penguin, 1968), pp. 322–3; Jan Kott, *Shakespeare Our Contemporary*, 2nd. edn. (London: Methuen, 1967); Peter Hall, in Charles Marowitz and Simon Trussler, eds., *Theatre at Work* (London: Methuen, 1967), p. 162. On the Absurd, see Alan Sinfield, ed., *Society and Literature 1945–1970* (London: Methuen, 1983), pp. 181–8. On Kott, see John Drakakis, ed., *Alternative Shakespeares* (London: Methuen, 1985), pp. 208–10, and *Political Shakespeare*, pp. 131–2, 161–4. On Hall, see *Political Shakespeare*, chapter 9. For numerous politically inert 'metafictions', see Patricia Waugh, *Metafiction* (London: Methuen, 1984); Linda Hutcheon, *Narcissistic Narrative* (New York and London: Methuen, 1984); Linda Hutcheon, *A Theory of Parody* (New York and London: Methuen, 1985).

9 In Marowitz and Trussler, ed., *Theatre at Work*, p. 170.

10 Charles Marowitz, *The Marowitz Hamlet* (London: Allen Lane, 1968), p. 16.

11 *Marowitz Hamlet*, pp. 16, 18; *Marowitz Shakespeare*, p. 12.

12 *Marowitz Shakespeare*, pp. 224–5.

13 See Jonathan Dollimore, 'Transgression and Surveillance in *Measure for Measure*', in Dollimore and Sinfield, ed., *Political Shakespeare*.

14 Arnold Wesker, *The Journalists/The Wedding Feast/The Merchant* (Harmondsworth: Penguin, 1980), pp. 204–5, 216.

15 See Glenda Leeming, *Wesker the Playwright* (London: Methuen, 1983), especially pp. 100–7, 130–6.

16 Edward Bond, *Lear* (London: Methuen, 1972), p. 84.

17 Edward Bond, *The Fool and We Come to the River* (London: Methuen, 1976), pp. x, xii. Cf. Terry Eagleton, 'Nature and Violence: the Prefaces of Edward Bond', *Critical Quarterly*, 26 (1984), 127–35.

18 See Sinfield, ed., *Society and Literature 1945–1970*, chapter 6, and Dollimore and Sinfield, ed.,

Political Shakespeare, chapter 9.
19 Arts Council of Great Britain, Set Plays and Books List, July 1986 (London, 1986).
20 Theatre Quarterly, 2, no. 5 (1972), 12.

I have benefited greatly in writing this paper from the knowledge and wisdom of Colin Counsell, Peter Holland and Mark Sinfield. While endorsing aspects of Marowitz's theatre practice, I do not endorse the sexist comments and implications that recur in his writing.

'Go play, boy, play': Shakespeare and educational drama

David Hornbrook

You taught me language; and my profit on't
Is, I know how to curse: the red plague rid you,
For learning me your language!   Caliban in *The Tempest*, I.ii

While it may be a common assumption among the educated classes that generations of our children continue in some rough and ready way to 'do' Shakespeare in school, the élite folk-memory which gives rise to this view with its impressionistic canvas of Quiller-Couch editions[1] and school theatricals bears little relationship to the realities of present-day State education. Today an educational anthropologist would have to penetrate deep into the backwoods of the private sector to observe the recitation and verse-cramming of that mythologised past or to find sufficient evidence to reconstruct the hard-chaired ritual of the Shakespearean School Play. The brightly-lit English departments of comprehensive education offer an altogether more up-to-date literary agenda and any attempt to chart the location and significance of Shakespeare on the contemporary curriculum is to embark upon an ethnography of absence.

At the same time it is undoubtedly the case that the determining structures of Shakespeare education, where it does exist, remain securely in place. The universities and their related boards still adjudicate examinable learning for the fifteen per cent or so motivated enough to seek academic enlightenment beyond the national school leaving age; and if, as we shall see, the new GCSE syllabuses are offering alternatives at sixteen plus, the GCE Advanced Level still mounts a strictly selective guard over matriculation.

In general the questions on the examination papers which lay out the parameters of most school Shakespeare teaching reveal a continuing commitment to well-established and familiar conceptions.[2] A post-Leavis consensus, inspired by an interrogative circularity, operates within a world assumed to share its metaphysical vocabulary. Teachers in schools, with whatever degree of reluctance, are necessarily in the position of having to prepare their classes within their ontological framework, and in sharing (as many undoubtedly do) Leavis's abhorrence of what he saw as the new barbarism of a media-fed commercialised culture, they subscribe to the powerful sense of humanity evinced by his defence of the canon. Commendable success in drawing young people to literature, and in particular to Shakespeare as the supreme paradigm of excellence, guarantees the continuation of a set of assumptions about our relationship to texts. These assumptions, it is true, have long been open to challenge,[3] but their almost mythical quality, the degree to which they have been absorbed into a general consciousness so that they effectively *define* literature for us, has made a determined assault on the presuppositions of the examination boards extremely difficult. Instead, there has been a steady withdrawal of support within the schools from the very idea of teaching Shakespeare at all: a rearguard action based less on literary theory than on the lived, untheorised politics of the classroom.

Tradition and relevance

Put simply, the special demands of old texts are increasingly considered by teachers to be quite marginal to the needs of contemporary children. For the Progressivists, conscripted by Newsom[4] and anxious to break down the cultural alienation of working-class pupils, the metaphorical linguistic tangle and complex metaphysical structure of the plays make them too inhibitive of the spontaneous response to writing which they seek to draw from their classes. The unavoidable identification of Shakespeare with the examination system is seen as in itself alienating and prohibitive of creative growth. Furthermore, Shakespeare for most children is inescapably associated with social snobbery. Perceived (accurately) as the property of a minority of 'academic' children at the top of the school, the literary A stream, the plays carry an elitist tag which excludes them from the legitimate business of a world defined by *Brookside* and *EastEnders*. For most children Shakespeare is likely to have been written off as an irrelevance at an early stage in their formal education. Meanwhile, outside the school, a routine dismissal of his plays as part of an inaccessible middle-class ritual of 'theatregoing' further strengthens this sense of alienation, and the most worthy attempts by 'socially aware' theatre groups to break it down by means of reduced prices and educational programmes have failed to shift this view in any significant way.[5]

Teacher response can be clearly seen in the English and Drama syllabuses for the new General Certificate of Secondary Education. Firstly, the monolithic structure of English which has stood for so long at the centre of the curriculum has been broken into three separate examinable components – English (approximating to the old English Language qualification), Oral Communication, and English Literature. Thus it is possible to acquire proficiency in two English examinations without any necessary contact with the canon. Of the Literature syllabuses offered by the five GCSE boards[6] three offer exclusively Coursework options with the choice of texts left to the teacher. Where texts are prescribed, as in the Southern Examining Group's Syllabus A, Shakespeare appears as an option against four or five other playwrights. Nowhere does there appear a compulsory Shakespeare question. For Drama the pattern is broadly similar, with no syllabus requiring the obligatory study of dramatic texts, and only two (the Southern Group and the Northern Examining Association) offering Shakespeare as an option within an option. The questions that *are* set require for Literature familiar O-level-type answers: on, for example, the relationship between Macbeth and Lady Macbeth or the qualities of kingship; and for Drama ideas for costumes or advice for actors.

The complete absence of compulsory Shakespeare questions is in marked contrast to the old GCE O-level English Literature examinations, and reflects the influence of the teacher-based CSEs.[7] While the new syllabuses have undoubtedly been victims of over-hasty preparation,[8] they nevertheless represent an acknowledgement of developing practice and concerns in English and Drama teaching which will be familiar to those used to CSE preparation. For teachers at home with more traditional pedagogy the mounting emphasis on practical work and continuous assessment is proving more problematic, and as it is in those institutions priding themselves on academic 'excellence' that such conditions are most likely to prevail, then it is certainly a desirable though doubtless unintentional achievement of the Secretary of State that teacher pressure has managed to shift the balance *away* from university dominated notions of scholastic success. While this must represent some kind of victory for the Progressivist wing of the teaching profession, it is nevertheless one viewed with some scepticism by many English teachers: and in particular by those involved in educational drama. For many of them the realignment is not radical enough, and in some cases is seen as actually retro-gressive;[9] for while the general public consciousness may still be of O levels as the final validation of five years of secondary education (as School Certificate was well after its demise in 1950),[10] these teachers have tended to work consistently among those eighty per cent struggling with CSEs or with no certificate aspirations at all.

The implications of these moves for the tradition of English – the humanising project of Arnold and Leavis – are profound. In one way, perhaps the most obvious, the gradual diminution of that great corpus which simply *was* English Literature in schools – who today studies Conrad or Milton or Tennyson at sixteen? – leaving Shakespeare the sole guardian of the 'universality of human experience'[11] has virtually emptied the stock cupboards of a generation of English teachers weaned on the crusading values of *Scrutiny*: who had gone out into schools 'to do battle there, nurturing through the study of literature the kind of rich, complex, mature, discriminating, morally serious responses which would equip individuals to survive in a mechanized society of trashy romances, alienated labour, banal advertisements and vulgarizing mass media'.[12]

From humanism to progressivism

If the dismembering of this consensus has been effected less by ideological confrontation than by the simple pragmatics of the classroom, it is clear on the other hand that most if not all of the underlying teleology of the Leavis revolution remains securely in place. It is certainly true that the reverberations of the post-1968 politicisation of letters and the post-structuralist invasion of university English departments have been felt by many young school teachers, but while the debate within the National Association of Teachers of English may be a fierce one,[13] classroom practice on the whole maintains the heritage and moral form of the humanising project if not its content and bibliography. The familiar emphasis on the 'creative response' to poetry, the primacy of words like 'sincerity' and 'authenticity' in assessing children's work, and the commitment to the superior value of 'felt experience' in relation to texts, creative writing or drama, are the systematic sub-structure of an intense and secular morality derived from the same 'timeless truths' that Leavis discerned in Donne and Shakespeare and the literary heirs he nominated for such drastic and upward revaluation.

Thus in turning Shakespeare away from their classrooms teachers are by no means rejecting the humanistic paradigms by which his plays have traditionally been given meanings. Indeed, the moves *away* from the canon may be seen as attempts to strengthen these paradigms rather than to challenge them. This seemingly contradictory process can be observed most clearly in projects specifically designed to give children access to a text, to make it 'relevant'. In line with the theory the procedures involved serve a revelatory rather than an instructive purpose. After scything through the verse a sleight of literary reductionism produces neatly baled examples of the 'timeless truths' for 'discovery' by the class. A most common strategy is to lift 'themes' from the plays so that they can be examined in a contemporary context. Many Drama teachers for example will use improvisation for this, encouraging small groups to construct dramatically parallel scenes which while hopefully reflecting the antagonisms within the text are nevertheless firmly grounded in the children's own experience. In this way Macbeth's ambitions for the crown of Scotland may be likened to a boy's desire to be captain of the football team, urged on perhaps by a sister or girlfriend. Lear's confrontation with his daughters might be reborn in a family living-room; while Romeo and Juliet at their first meeting shout to each other about the megawattage of the local discotheque. Superficially about 'access', this kind of lesson is more accurately concerned with personal and moral dilemmas contained within the text, but represented as transhistorical examples of the universality of human experience. Remove the metaphysical clutter and the arcane poetic form and Shakespeare, in the words of the tourist brochure, 'speaks to us today every bit as evocatively as he did to the audiences of his own time'. By this token what we have is Shakespeare as problem-page: the archetypes as the boy and girl next door.

On this basis it requires only a simple logical manoeuvre to justify the abandonment of the texts altogether. If what is to be distilled from them is no less than the unchanging reality of human existence then it makes sense to choose material with less literary encumbrance, where the dilemmas are more starkly arraigned. Why struggle with *Coriolanus* when *Lord of the Flies* offers such ready images of loyalty, leadership and crowd manipulation?

The *Scrutiny* movement above all gave to teachers of English a moral centre to their teaching. Under its guidance literature became a focus of value, 'a sensitive preoccupation with the whole quality of life itself, with the oblique, nuanced particulars of human experience',[14] so that meant contact with it putatively enhanced one's own humanity. In the furtherance of this moral aesthetic, now almost entirely deprived of its text-based epistemology, the liberal humanist tradition in education owes much to the development of an important parallel polemic. Also seeking the 'authentic response' to art, literature and indeed to life as a whole, the Progressive movement established itself as a force in English education by the early 1960s. In neatly shifting the emphasis from (in the slogans) a 'literature-centred' to a 'child-centred' approach the now de-textualised humanising project could be effectively rescued. Progressivism encouraged what it saw as the 'natural creativity' of children, whom it considered had for too long been fettered by restrictive adult notions of aesthetics and even moral judgement. Following Rousseau, its exponents searched for the source of moral worth not within the volumes of the canon but deep inside the soul of a child. As early as 1927 A. S. Neil was offering this interpretation of the 'Labour teacher's task': 'It is for the spiritual life, not the political and economic. It is his mission to give his pupils absolute freedom to be wise and good . . . This he can only do if he believes in children more than he believes in politics and economics. To abolish the East End of London is a psychological rather than an economic problem.'[15] This collapse of politics into psychology is fundamental to Progressivism, and its appeal to those preoccupied with feeling and experience and mistrustful of the analytic is obvious. The belief that 'political ideas are the camouflaged expressions of unconscious attitudes and passions', that there is 'a fundamental psyche which is prior to social determinations' still carries credibility, as Perry Anderson and others have pointed out with reference to developments in post-war English psychology.[16]

Progressivism was also, and indeed remains, however ambiguously, anti-intellectual, unlike the Leavisite project which had its origins at the heart of the academic establishment. As a movement of ideas it has never gained a foothold in the universities, so while it might be said to share with the Scrutineers a claim on the spiritual and emotional landscape of individual perception, its uncompromisingly psychologistic and process-orientated approach to creative literature has steered it away from the cloisters of Summerhill to the classrooms and drama studios of State education.

Drama and education

It is ironic and not without significance that a school subject closely allied to English and born out of the Progressive movement should now be participating so fully in attempts to eradicate all traces of text-based study from its corner of the curriculum. That Drama of all disciplines on the secondary timetable should have so decisively rejected Shakespeare marks a most profound, and some would say disturbing, cultural disjunction. Since its acceptance into schools not much more than two decades ago Drama has carved for itself a particular identity: drawing more from post-Freudian theories of children's play and developmental learning than from the theatre. Its popularity, compared with the more traditional subjects at least, among the less able and the socially maladjusted has led its exponents to make elaborate claims for its therapeutic and socialising potential; and more recently, with the development by Dorothy Heathcote and others of a complex methodology of role-playing, for its centrality in the education process itself.[17] In flying the flag for the non-academic, the under-privileged, and (in an overworked trope) for the working class and the poor, there is fierce resistance among many Drama teachers to the imposition (as they see it) of examinations on to a practice which is described unfailingly in the psychologistic and process-orientated language of Progressivism. This is nowhere better exemplified than in recent responses to the new GCSE syllabuses in Drama. The Northern Examining Association's Drama GCSE, with its optional list of prescribed texts (which includes *A Midsummer Night's Dream*) has been lambasted in the educational drama journals for its irrelevancy to 'education, drama or the needs of the students', and for the fact that in its 'theatre skills based syllabus . . . there is no mention of sensations (sensate experience) or feeling nor of the nature of artistic reflection'.[18] The syllabus of the Southern Examining Group, the only other Mode I to include an optional Shakespeare question, has been similarly singled out for censure: 'If I were a teacher in the area of the Southern Examining Group I would start to look pretty energetically for a better alternative. . . .'[19]

By way of offering an alternative more in keeping with the methodology a group of Leicestershire drama specialists has produced a Mode III syllabus which has gained much favour among practitioners. However, its startling paucity of content and lack of vision illustrates with fearful clarity the deadliness of this kind of post-progressivist agenda. The Leicestershire syllabus sees Drama as "a problem solving activity" and aims "(a) to promote an understanding and expertise in those activities met in drama learning and the creation of drama fictions, (b) to foster confidence in adopting a view to human problems, ideas and attitudes, and (c) to develop competencies met within socially

interactive processes".[20] Critical though one might be of Leavis's decontextualised and transcultural invocation of 'life', it is difficult not to think
that this dreary scheme might benefit from a few vitalist injections! What
is abundantly clear is that parents who might wish for their children even
a passing acquaintance with our dramatic culture will have to look
elsewhere than the school drama studio, at least until educational drama
extricates itself from this teleological cul-de-sac.

Ideology and the subject

In rejecting Shakespeare, and indeed texts in general (except as a kind of
lucky-dip of themes and universals), Drama teachers have responded
like many of their colleagues in English departments to an increasing
impatience among their pupils with respect to the iconography of bourgeois culture. Induction into the hegemony of the dominant class – the
mere reproduction of a social order – is the central project of any State
education system: and sympathetic teacher-resistance is more likely to
be carried on as a guerrilla campaign – as a 'subversive activity'[21] – than in
an institutionalised form. Thus it is that in some schools, teachers, often
at some professional risk, offer their classes direct challenges to established cultural formations and to the ideology of the market place. For
most, however, the manifest inappropriateness of standard liberal-
humanist readings of Shakespeare and others to vast numbers of
working-class children, has led them to adopt a form of cultural relativism where they see themselves as responding to the 'needs' of individual students or social groups; the category of 'needs' never distinguished conceptually from a much larger group of preferences, including wants, desires, drives and mere choices. Apart from the most obvious
(the 'need' of ethnic minority children to learn English for example),
these needs are invariably expressed, once again, in psychologistic terms,
and identified on a class or ethnic basis. Thus (it is claimed) working-class
children 'need' books related to their own circumstances and class
background. Literature is no longer to be seen as a respected canon but
as an infinite number of undiscriminated texts to be assessed only on the
grounds of their personal and social 'relevancies'. After all (the argument
goes) who are we, middle-class teachers, to impose our literary values on
working-class children, when their needs are so patently different? It
is characteristic (as we have seen) for the complex social and political
divisions within our society to be reinterpreted in terms of a collective
psychology: but while these are no doubt honest attempts to halt the

increasing alienation of whole sections of our society, they nevertheless not only patronise but unavoidably reinforce cultural divisions. More alarmingly 'needs' are now being openly categorised in relation to an accommodation with 'the real world', that most useful euphemistic construction for the present crisis of capitalism. Thus from a document tabled at a recent conference of drama advisers, rather than dull 'academic' training, children should be encouraged to develop attributes more relevant to their 'needs' – such as 'job retention skills' and 'adaptability awareness'.[22]

Despite the undeniably right-minded intentions of conscientious educationalists the liberal humanist tradition fails once again to effect the precipitations of consciousness it so ardently desires, and through which it sees the evolution of a better world. In its propensity for accommodation rather than confrontation, for sensitivity to the needs of others rather than action against injustice and wrong, it is not only often ineffectual in the face of prejudice, ignorance, brutality and oppression; but functionally the potential servant of any dominant ideology which seeks to protect its interests through the institutionalising of such practices. Its advocates claim that its moral transcendentalism holds it aloof from the vulgar position-taking of the political world and thus makes it an indispensable insurance against bias and 'ideological dogmatism'. However, as Terry Eagleton has pointed out, freedom from a commitment to specific objects of subjective belief is replaced by 'a form of subjectivity which is, apparently, an end in itself, which works, apparently all by itself, and which is its own justification'. He draws our attention to the 'intransitivity of the familiar shibboleths' of the liberal humanist soul as inherited by the tradition of Literature, and argues that its task is 'to produce an historically peculiar form of human subject who is sensitive, receptive, imaginative and so on . . . *about nothing in particular*'.[23]

Drama in schools has followed and indeed overtaken English in its commitment to this particular kind of self-justifying and self-congratulatory subjectivity. In its self-righteous rejection of a formal prospectus – theatre skills, dramatic texts, and so on – it has dedicated itself exclusively and precisely to the production of Eagleton's 'peculiar form of human subject'. English in schools at least has still a commitment to the fundamental skills of reading and writing, and texts, however they might be read, do on many occasions become the focus for creative response and class debate. While Eagleton's criticism is directed at an ideology of Literature, it applies with even greater clarity and force to educational drama. The ideological siding into which that peculiar set of pedagogic practices has relentlessly shunted itself denies not simply the text, but even much of the vocabulary by which drama and theatre are given meaning. Thus in the much lauded Leicestershire syllabus the word 'theatre' significantly fails to appear; and 'drama fictions' stands for what most of us might reasonably understand as plays. With these prohibitives semantic restraints alone it is difficult to imagine how Shakespeare, or the theatre he served and helped to define, could have anything but incidental relevance. With the passing of GCE O level, induction into the work of a playwright whose dominance over the literary pantheon of the nation is held to be unassailable has become the privileged occupation of an increasingly tiny minority.

Cultural power

While the simple response of many cultural utilitarians is 'good riddance', such easy equations fail to take account of the complex relationship between culture and power which Gramsci first mapped out for us.[24] In championing alternative cultural forms – youth culture, black culture, working-class culture – and rejecting the feudal and bourgeois traditions as good only for the museum cellars, teachers are, to any egalitarian, rightly identifying with those at the bottom of the heap in our divided society. They are profoundly mistaken however if they believe that by the simple gesture of ignoring the iconography of the dominant culture its self-evident irrelevance will result in its withering away. The child in the school party reared on rock music and the packaged simplicities of television, who gazes uncomprehendingly up at the ceiling of the Sistine Chapel, is in significant ways as powerless as his ancestors who stood for centuries in churches across Europe amid the cadences of the Latin Mass.

We are made by the totality of our culture. We may be of the impression that that which is nearest to us – most seemingly 'relevant' – exerts the greatest influence: but greater and less immediately obvious forces are at work on us. For the peasants of Medieval and Renaissance Europe the signs and meanings of the Roman Catholic church had become so deeply rooted in a collective consciousness that they had long ceased to be recognised as such. The day's toil, the moments of revelry on appointed dates, the economics of an existence grubbed from the land, were all unquestioningly measured against an elaborate yardstick of faith, morality and convention as skilfully protected as it was ruthlessly exploited by those who administered it, Georg Lukács wrote on this score: 'if from the vantage point of a particular class, the totality of existing society is not visible; if a class thinks the thoughts imputable to it and which bear upon its interests right through to their logical conclusion and yet fails to strike at the heart of that totality, then such a class is doomed to play only a subordinate role.'[25] Not to understand Michelangelo's contract with the Church, not to be conscious of Shakespeare's role as a Tudor propagandist, not to hear the pulse of Enlightenment Freemasonry in Mozart or of Bonapartism in Beethoven, not to recognise the cultural totality within which they and others stood as beacons, is to be 'condemned to passivity', powerless in the face of forces which one is only equipped to describe as immutable. As Trotsky saw clearly, the revolution is not simply a matter of swapping dominant cultures, sweeping the detritus of the bourgeois hegemony out of the museums to be replaced by the icons of the proletariat: 'the working-class cannot begin the construction of a new culture without absorbing and assimilating the elements of the old cultures'.[26]

Teaching Shakespeare in a way which perpetuates mystification and which deliberately sets out to obscure the construction of the Shakespeare myth, if successful, can offer to some of our children, at least, membership of the cultural ascendancy. For most of those inducted into the Myth however, this membership is likely to prove of a somewhat provisional kind. The Time-Life literati and the Friends of the National Theatre are the self-appointed minders of an ideological consensus for which cultivation means fluency in the language of Western European art in its Authorised Version. Acquiescence in socially accepted modes of cultural discourse comes as part of a status package for the 'nouvelle petite-bourgeoisie', the computer technologists, media producers, PR-persons and diverse managers of our changing society. The apparent immutability of the bourgeois canon, its celebration of the eternal paradoxes of human nature and the uniqueness of our individuality, must provide intellectual reassurance too for a class far from secure in its sense of its own identity and adrift in a world of moral uncertainty.

It is with this dispiriting ethnography that English and Drama teachers must now engage, for although a tiny minority will pass through the State education system well versed enough in the Shakespeare myth to gain a place on the outer precincts of the corridors of management, the inexorable retreat of Shakespeare before the armies of cultural relativism is likely, in the long term, seriously to reduce that number or even to eliminate it altogether. Meanwhile in the private sector the long established process of class initiation will continue unabashed, rung up on the termly account as an integral part of the knowledge transaction. Shakespeare is most definitely not an *optional* item on the bill when the affluent middle class buy into a 'good education'. His currency value is assured and their investment is safe. They are, after all, paying for Antonio's education; Caliban, as usual, will have to take what he can find.

Government moves to provide a more relevant 'skills-based' education for the mass of our children, while superficially appealing, are designed further to drive a wedge between this narrow guardianship of our national culture and the majority of the people. The worried liberal-left in the teaching profession has perhaps been too easily persuaded to connive at these seemingly benificent manipulations of the curriculum, and too easily forgets the struggle for the principle of comprehensive education in the days when the nation's young were neatly divided at the age of eleven. The smartly-turned-out hotel receptionists and hypermarket cashiers of TVEI and CPVE and YTS[27] are the compliant service class of tomorrow, non-unionised and badly paid, trained for the telephone and the till, and as doomed in their subordination as the mute congregations of the Middle Ages.

The Shakespeare myth

As the history of Christianity abundantly demonstrates, knowledge is traditionally kept mysterious by those who possess it. To demystify Shakespeare is to begin to provide access for all to a form of understanding which has been systematically abandoned to the forces of privilege. Teachers in schools, negotiating knowledge at the intersection of private lives and history, have the opportunity to reclaim for new generations the lost ground of our social memory. The obsessive individualism which has for too long stood in the place of an adequate socialist theory of education, and for which the pupils' 'need to succeed' is the dominating, but ultimately self-defeating criterion, can lead only to a collective isolation from the structures of meaning by which our world may be understood and reclaimed. In a crucial sense, Shakespeare tells us who we are; not as he reveals the 'universal dilemmas of mankind', the unchanging truths of the liberal imagination, but in his relationship with us, through the Shakespeare myth itself. The plays continue to provide us with examples against which our own lives are sorted, judged and given meaning, not *despite* the bardolatry but *because* of it. We inhabit a culture which just happens to have been shaped by the economic and moral collisions of Elizabethan England: it is less than surprising that our concepts of dramatic literature and its function should have been determined by a voice that so effectively gave those conflicts expressive resonance. We seek meaning from within our history. The pre-conceptions or prejudices which we bring to the texts are what make understanding possible; it can be plausibly argued that they are a condition of knowledge, providing the fundamental structure of our relationship with our historical tradition. (Thus, attempts to 're-discover' Shakespeare as he really was, to prise him free as it were from the grip of twentieth-century distortion and to relocate him in an Elizabethan context[28] are as misconceived as the decontextualised Shakespeare of the Scrutineers.) As the hermeneutician Hans-Georg Gadamer has put it, 'understanding is never subjective behaviour towards a given 'object', but towards its effective history – the history of its influence'.[29] In schools the wide variety of options now available within the new sixteen-plus examinations opens up possibilities for the reappropriation of this powerful iconography. Coursework-based curricula with internal, moderated assessment allow teachers the freedom to develop more contextualised approaches to the plays and to explore with their classes notions of Shakespeare as cultural product. For despite his formulated elitism, Shakespeare is, in a very real sense, common knowledge. If nothing else, children know his name, and few of secondary age will not be able, if pushed, to list two or three plays or to recite half-a-dozen disassociated lines of verse. No other writer has so extensively penetrated our common vocabulary. The Martin Droeshout engraving of the poet has stared at us from a thousand advertisements and is instantly recognisable, a gift for marketing agencies wishing to endow their client's products with a specious old world authenticity. These are some access points to the myth which are truly shared, and through which teachers may begin to wrest back control of the meanings of our cultural life on behalf of those they teach. The proffered alternative is a mute agenda of socially contained awarenesses and skills, a curriculum tailor-made to the needs of underprivilege, and dedicated to the perpetuation of powerlessness.

Notes

1 Some readers will doubtless not remember or will have escaped acquaintance with those small, dusty, heavily-expurgated cloth-backed editions, first published by J. M. Dent in the 1920s, but reprinted right up until the 1950s. On the fly-leaf was printed Milton's 'A good book is the precious life-blood of a master spirit'. The general editor of the series was Sir Arthur Quiller-Couch, first Professor of English at Cambridge.

2 For a useful analysis of some of these questions see A. Sinfield, 'Give an account of Shakespeare in education . . .' in *Political Shakespeare*, eds. J. Dollimore and A. Sinfield

(Manchester: Manchester University Press, 1985), pp. 134–54.

3 See P. Anderson 'Components of the national culture', in *Student Power*, eds. A. Cockburn and R. Blackburn (Harmondsworth: Penguin, 1969), pp. 268–76.

4 The Newsom Report *Half our Future* (1963) identified the fifty per cent or so of secondary pupils who effectively failed the system, and advocated 'an education which is practical, realistic and vocational'. It also examined the 'problem' of working-class alienation from formal education.

5 It is not perhaps surprising that the support for the teaching of Shakespeare is strong within the independent sector, closely allied as that minority institution always has been with the universities and little troubled as it is with the aspirations of the under-privileged.

6 The London & East Anglia Group, the Northern Examining Association, the Welsh Board, the Midland Examining Group, and the Southern Examining Group.

7 The top twenty per cent of the ability range took GCE O levels, which replaced School Certificate in 1951, on a subject by subject basis. These were organised by eight examining boards, all but one of which (the Associated Examining Board) were associated with the universities.

The Certificate of Secondary Education (CSE) was operated from 1965 for the next forty per cent down the ability range. Marked on a five-point scale, Grade 1 was the equivalent of an O-level pass and Grade 4 represented the 'expected level of a 16-year-old of average ability'. While of considerably less currency value than GCE O levels their strength nevertheless lay in their more imaginative methods of assessment and control by teachers.

8 On 20 June 1984 the Secretary of State for Education, Sir Keith Joseph, announced the introduction of a single system of examinations at sixteen-plus, based on national criteria, with effect from 1988. Industrial action in schools caused by government cut-backs resulted in a boycott by teachers of all preparation for the new system. Despite nation-wide opposition to the timetable for the introduction of the new examinations, the government pressed ahead, and the first pupils began to study the GCSE syllabuses in September 1986.

9 The Northern Examining Association's Drama syllabus has come in for fierce criticism in this respect.

10 School Certificate was until 1950 the national examination at sixteen-plus. It contained a prescribed set of subjects all of which had to be passed by candidates for successful certification.

11 See Sinfield, p. 153.

12 T. Eagleton, *Literary Theory* (Oxford: Blackwell, 1983), p. 33.

13 Recent volumes of *English in Education* are the locus for this discussion. See also *The English Magazine* published by the ILEA English Centre.

14 T. Eagleton, p. 27.

15 A. S. Neil, in *Educational Worker* (January 1927). Quoted in K. Jones, *Beyond Progressive Education* (London: Macmillan, 1983), p. 33.

16 See P. Anderson, pp. 251–4. Also L. Hudson, *The Cult of Facts* (London: Jonathan Cape, 1974).

17 Notable examples are B. J. Wagner, *Dorothy Heathcote: Drama as a Learning Medium* (London: Hutchinson, 1979), and G. Bolton, *Drama as Education* (London: Longman, 1984).

18 D. Morton, Leeds Drama Adviser, in *Leeds Drama*; reprinted in *2D*, vol. 5, no. 2 (summer 1986) – 'Other people's stories: GCSE and drama', pp. 66–9.

19 J. Spindler, 'Four out of ten for new exam' in *Drama Broadsheet*, vol 3, issue 3. *Journal of the National Association of Teachers of Drama* (summer 1985), p. 7.

20 'A draft syllabus from Leicestershire' in *Drama Broadsheet*, vol. 4, issue 3 (summer 1986), p. 5.

21 N. Postman and C. Weingartner, *Teaching as a Subversive Activity* (Harmondsworth: Penguin, 1971).

22 For the full awfulness of this arid agenda turn to *NADA News 1983: Conference Issue*, published by the National Association of Drama Advisers.
23 T. Eagleton 'The subject of literature', in *The English Magazine* (spring 1985), p. 5.
24 See A. Gramsci, *Selections from Prison Notebooks*, ed. Q. Hoare and G. Nowell Smith (London: Lawrence & Wishart, 1971), pp. 57–8, 246, 271, and *passim*.
25 G. Lukács, *History and Class Consciousness* (London: Merlin, 1971), p. 52.
26 L. Trotsky, *Literature & Revolution* (Ann Arbor, Mich: University of Michigan Press, 1960), p. 226.
27 Technical & Vocational Education Initiative; Certificate of Post Vocational Education; Youth Training Scheme.
28 See J. Russell Brown, *Free Shakespeare* (London: Heinemann, 1974).
29 H.-G. Gadamer, *Truth & Method*, trans. W. Glyn-Doepel (London; Sheed & Ward, 1975), p. xix.

John Hodgson
Interviewed by Christopher J. McCullough

You have said that 'the qualities needed for the best acting are also those needed for the fullest living'.[1] *What do you believe children should gain from an experience of educational Drama?*

I have always felt that acting was an important way of learning. While we have science laboratories for the study of the world around us, we do not recognise that there is a facility for the study of human kind built into every one of us through the medium of acting and impersonation, which afford an opportunity to experience and explore ourselves, in relation to the world around us, through using the body, voice, and imagination. The process of acting can also bring us in contact with ideas present in great literature, ultimately allowing us to understand conflicts and how we might resolve them.

What place do you think this 'drama as discovery' method should occupy in the educational system as a whole?

There is, first of all, the use of drama as a teaching method for other subjects; role play, for example, in history or language lessons. But I see a much more important role for drama as the core activity to any school curriculum. Dalcroze said that every child should have a sense of rhythm and music; I would go further and say that even more fundamentally, every child should have a confidence in expression through the body, the voice, and through interaction with other people.

'Drama' can mean so many different things: it can be a means to achieving richer living through improvisation and role playing; or it can be theatre history and the realisation of texts in performance. The two concepts are bound up with one another; the main difference being that the former does not rely upon a public celebration of the work. The learning situation built around the movement of a dramatic text into theatre is an important area that needs developing in schools: so few people (and not many English teachers amongst them), simply don't know how to 'read' a dramatic text. Reverence in the approach to the text, acquired from a literary background, usually means that we miss the nine-tenths of information that is not directly on the page. Something that may look good as literature may not work in the theatre and vice versa.

Shakespeare is marketed by most institutions as a powerful cultural token. For the theatre Shakespeare represents the highest achievement in poetic drama; for examination success, Shakespeare provides the most stringent cultural test, ensuring that the successful candidate is well deserving of entry to enlightened and ordered society. Is there not a danger that in perpetuating a 'Shakespeare' of the establishment within the education system, drama teachers – a group that generally likes to see itself as a liberating or liberalising force – can be party to a form of cultural oppression?

The root of the problem is that Shakespeare has become literature. The danger occurs when we forget that Shakespeare was a man of the theatre; he was an actor who also happened to write plays. The more one discovers about the nature of the Elizabethan theatre – the pattern of collaboration between writer and acting company, the amount to be learned from the so-called 'bad Quartos' – the more one realises how we are freed from the tyranny of the idea of literature. The study of Shakespeare can be a liberalising force so long as we can discover its real nature as theatre. Actors, whether they be Elizabethan or sixteen-year-olds in school, happily challenge the idea that words are especially sacrosanct in the form found on a page.

Do you think the teaching of Shakespeare as theatre should challenge what goes on in A and O level English teaching?

Very much so. I think that we should leave behind the chasing of historical meanings; much of the time they are superimposed meanings anyway. We should be looking for the relevance of the plays today, and be focusing on the relationships between characters, and the universality of the values.

What do you mean by the universality of the values?

Times change, but people find themselves in very similar predicaments. Parents still find it difficult to accept their daughter's choice of boyfriend; there is still racial prejudice in the world; jealousy is still a powerful motive; there are still power games and rivalry. It is much more important for us to play around with these universal values, allowing young people in schools to see the relevance of the plays to their own lives, than it is to go chasing obscure literary references.

Would you advocate the removal of Shakespeare from the A level English syllabus?

No, I would never do that, but I would advocate a radical change in the way that it is taught. So much depends on how much of a sense of theatre the English teacher can muster: while the plays can still be seen to have literary value, the emphasis should be theatrical, rather than literary. In a sense if we could extend our concept of dramatic literature to involve the experimental (in the sense of theatre practice), we may be able to do English Literature a great service. We may be able to find a way forward if people discovered more about oral and written traditions, and the way in which they vary and interact.

The activity that I find most stifling is literary theory: instead of looking at a play as a practical expression of human responses, written down in one form at one particular time, we are led by theory into abstract concepts that have little to do with real human experience. As theatre, the play has the potential to be rediscovered in human terms, any number of times. Frequently I find myself unwillingly directing a play because it is on the syllabus, but without fail I find I can rediscover it through the process of rehearsal. I think I am bored with the play at the outset; it is, say, *Macbeth* and I do not want to do it again; then I begin, only to find, damn it! there is much more to be discovered. Print has too often become the absolute. It is a terrible misunderstanding of the nature of the text because it sometimes seems so so barren on the page.

Given that you believe Shakespeare should be performed in schools, would you outline what you consider to be the best way to approach the task?

I feel that it is important that the first contact with the play avoids any form of close textual analysis: you mustn't sit the kids down to read the text, that is the quickest way to lose their interest. It is far more useful for the teacher to have thought about a few themes from the play and for the class to explore them in a modern-day context, through games and improvisation. Then it is time to return to the play to see what Shakespeare made of the problem. The way to alienate them is to start off with difficult texts and unfamiliar sentence construction. I have found that contemporary riots provide the way into *Coriolanus*: Ian Paisley gathering his mob together and going out with sticks is very little different from the mob actions in the play. The pupils can examine contemporary newspaper reports and see that what this man Shakespeare is writing about is what are, to them, familiar experiences. They must work from the angle of understanding certain human problems and then, when they have a clear idea of the problem, go on searching for it in the text.

Much of your work seems to place importance on the experience of dramatic forms within reconstructed historical contexts: 'Students experience aspects of the history of drama by being involved not just with plays but also with song, dance, poetry and prose of the period . . . they re-enact, in costume, aspects of Elizabeth I's visit to Kenilworth . . . they reconstruct Elizabethan theatre'.[2] Is this relocating the works of Shakespeare into a context of history, or into a dimension of isolated and privileged aesthetics?

We try to make an historical context which is a 'living' historical context, rather than an academic one. The danger in an academic approach is that the students get so distanced from the events that they are never able to see in history a unity between then and now.

Going to Harvington Hall serves as a marvellous 'visual aid' to demonstrate sixteenth-century religious persecution; our visit to Kenilworth shows us how Elizabeth's visit may have affected the performance of the players there. At Bromsgrove House the students re-enact life there using the facilities (such as an earth floor and an open fire etc) to gain a real sense of what life was like.

Is it not very easy using such methods of historical reconstruction to slip into a distorted and oversimplified view of history? In Stratford-upon-Avon there is a son et lumière exhibition called The World of Shakespeare which perpetuates the Edwardian myth of Elizabethan England as a golden age.

We do spend time working on documents like Henslowe's *Diaries* which give us plenty of evidence. We have students working on material from such sources and coming up with documentary drama. It is important that we try to experience life as it was then. Through our theatre work we create a context for the experiential rather than rely upon second-hand experiences from books. We take students to Southwark in order that they might walk around the area of Shakespeare's theatres, getting them to use their historical imagination, which then may be employed in their creative learning work. We take a lead from Glynne Wickham on his point regarding the reconstruction of the Globe: the problem is that once it is built everybody will say that's it, and the once living theatre experience will become fixed and sealed just like the printed word on the page.

It would seem to me though that the plays of Shakespeare were the product of a society violently divided, and that the drama, far from being a popular, national art, was from the 1590s increasingly 'professional' and exclusively directed at a minority of the population. You have argued that 'when the theatres in England were closed in 1642 the drama became severed from its roots. It had been concerned with expression, experience, doubts and certainties in the lives of all classes of people'.[3]

The Elizabethan theatre clearly was a popular theatre, interesting to all strata of society, from the apprentice to the monarch. That the theatre was centred in London is, to some extent, true, but there is evidence to show that when the plague pressured them out, the companies did make provincial tours.

The closure of the theatres in 1642 should be a significant event for anyone concerned with drama in education. When the theatres returned with the restoration of the monarchy they were indoor, élitist, and really a foreign import from France. This is where I believe that many drama teachers and head teachers have a real problem; they all tend, far too often, to think of theatrical performance in terms of proscenium arch stages and all the paraphernalia that goes with them. This form of theatre is based on the form and values of Restoration theatre and to force Shakespeare into these theatrical structures is to do Elizabethan drama a great disservice. Going around schools I am amazed at how many halls still have the proscenium arch with all the borders, curtains, and footlights that go with such an arrangement. To perform Shakespeare under these conditions is to rob the drama of all its exhilarating action and dynamism, created on the popular open stage of the public playhouse.

Before 1642 the theatre was the product of natural indigenous growth and not an artificial import, and as such, part of a natural feeling for drama common in this country.

Do you see any link between the work of the Choir Schools and the exclusive private-playhouse Boy Companies, and the development of the tradition of the 'school play'? Does 'theatre-in-education' have a longer and more conservative lineage than you suggest?

It seems more likely to me that the school play evolved from the nineteenth century and not from an earlier period. The Boy Companies I see as more professional organisations, often serving as training grounds for the adult companies. School plays, and in particular, school productions of Shakespeare, tend to be disastrous, because in using the structures of the proscenium (or picture-frame) stage they employ an imported theatrical form that divorces play and players from their audience. We need an appropriate theatre for our schools, based on the values of Shakespeare's public playhouse. Teachers could find another inroad to Shakespeare by examining, as we do at Bretton Hall in our replica Elizabethan playhouse, the dynamics of that sort of theatre; a theatre where the actor has an informal, intimate and direct relationship with the audience. Schools could tackle this in the simplest of ways by just marking out sections on the floor to delineate acting and audience areas. Of course, all of this has been done before, by Caldwell Cook[4] before the First World War. His work in converting his classroom into an acting space is something that may be emulated by drama teachers today.

One of the greatest compliments ever paid me came from a headmaster who angrily telephoned to say that drama was "the most dangerous subject on the curriculum". While I don't believe it is our business, in education, to stir things up to change the system, it is, I maintain, our duty to challenge and develop individuals to an awareness of how, when and why they may choose to do it. To this, and several other aims, Shakespeare in Education can make a valuable contribution.

Notes

1 John Hodgson and Ernest Richards, *Improvisation: Discovery and Creativity in Drama* (London: Methuen, 1966, Eyre Methuen, 1974), p. 11.
2 Bretton Hall College of Higher Education, *Prospectus* (1986), p. 16.
3 John Hodgson, ed., *The Uses of Drama: Sources Giving a Background to Drama as a Social and Educational Force* (London: Eyre Methuen, 1972), p. 216.
4 Caldwell Cook, a teacher at the Perse School in Cambridge before the First World War, is regarded as one of the architects of educational drama.

Michael Croft
interviewed by Christopher J. McCullough

You are known as the founder and director of The National Youth Theatre. Would you give a brief account of its origins and original objectives?

The National Youth Theatre grew out of the work I had done in South London, in the early 1950s, as a teacher at Alleyn's School for boys. I spent six years there and during that time developed Shakespearean production to the point where pretty well half the school got involved. I chose to do histories and Roman plays because they meant I could include a large number of pupils in the cast. This attitude had a tremendous effect on the boys and ultimately on the school community. Now, whether that would have happened without Shakespeare, I don't know. However, all my dramatic work there was wrapped up in Shakespeare.

In 1956 when I gave up teaching some of the Alleyn's boys asked me if I would carry on working with them during their holidays. When I agreed, Shakespeare was the automatic choice; theirs as well as mine. You may say that The National Youth Theatre, in its early days, became a projection of the 'school play' but, like my school productions, I didn't intend it to be only for the benefit of the precious few; I wanted it to appeal to young people generally, whether they wanted to be actors or not.

Would you then argue that Shakespeare possesses certain qualities that make the plays equal in appeal to all generations and classes of people?

My experience was that ninety per cent of the lads I taught in those days had no particular interest in drama at all. Shakespeare was absolutely a closed book to them. The idea of getting involved with Shakespeare, and actually enjoying it, never occurred to them. They were, mostly, tough Cockney boys, very anti-drama and anti-culture; as the average working-class boy is until he has the chance to take part in some form of culture that interests him.

Once the whole process had started, I saw that these 'rough diamonds' were perfectly capable of getting up and speaking often quite difficult poetic lines, and would work away at their speech and diction until they produced a result in which they all took pride. Now my theory is that this was due in part to the poetic quality of the plays with which we were working. I think this is where the magic of Shakespeare took over – to the point where these youngsters got so proud of their lines that when I came to cut any of them, they weren't at all pleased. It was exciting to see these boys who could hardly speak their native prose or express a coherent thought in conversation, get up on a stage and project the lords and messengers in *Anthony and Cleopatra* as though they had been doing it all their lives.

It really is time we gave the lie to these trendy educationalists – and they are on the increase in the drama field – who think that Shakespeare, or any written play more then ten years old, is too difficult for young people to perform. They fail to recognise that young people welcome a challenge, and even need one. Shakespeare offers a challenge on two fronts: the need to master an unfamiliar form of dramatic speech; and the ability to work in a team over long periods of time. These two elements together provide the most wonderful form of theatre for young people.

Would you pose improvisation against the tradition of English classical acting?

We have a tremendous tradition, but being English it is not an easy one to pin down. The glory of the English tradition is, in fact, its diversity, its lack of formalism, its pragmatism. The English actor is a pragmatist, not a theorist. He has rarely articulated his method of working. For nearly five decades we had the wonderfully diverse talents of Olivier, Gielgud, Richardson, Guinness and Redgrave. They all had one thing in common: a supreme feeling for the language of Shakespeare. Their approach was neither academic nor cerebral, but poetic and intuitive. They understood the basic Shakespearean priority that unless the actor makes sense of the poetry (and that means getting the sound right too) the pursuit of psychological detail will avail him little. The basic wisdom that I received long ago from Richardson was, 'Let the words do the work before you start playing about with them.' This is the fundamental advice that I give to the National Youth Theatre actors now.

I suppose that today improvisation is so widespread that it has become very difficult for the young actor to approach any part without first having to improvise his way into it. This does seem to me to be often a wasted effort. It may well be of value to young actors who would otherwise feel insecure, but it can also invite endless self-indulgence. When it comes to playing Shakespeare, or indeed any other plays which are as verbally explicit in their depiction of character and action, actors should not really be dependent on the use of improvisation.

The real danger to Shakespeare right now comes from directors with the populist approach. Improvisation usually has some logic behind it, but the populist approach throws logic to the wind. To suggest that an audience can identify events and characters in Shakespeare with those in contemporary life sounds very appealing but usually doesn't bear scrutiny, since the contemporary world is so very different from the Elizabethan world. When I heard a National Theatre director on a recent television programme comparing Richard III's state of mind on the night before the Battle of Bosworth with President Nixon's during Watergate and another (RSC) director describing Elsinore as 'Hamlet's Berlin Wall', I could not help wondering where Richard (III) kept his tape recorder, and at what point the Danish monarchy went communist. Sure, we need a popular, not an élitist theatre, but I don't think we'll achieve a popular Shakespeare theatre at all by trying to force modern parallels upon the plays which make neither dramatic, nor historical sense.

It is a cliché that Shakespeare is 'for all time', because he utters so many eternal truths and portrays so many eternal situations. But equally, it is absurd to claim that we can subject every situation in his plays to a twentieth-century treatment. We can't, because the world has changed so much. Sure we can look at fundamental human problems in the plays which may apply to our own lives today, but our solutions – with all the resources of modern science, medicine and technology – are going to be very different from Shakespeare's. We do not need the populist director forever patronising and prodding us with phoney modern parallels as to the meaning of the play, as though he thinks we are too stupid to make the connection for ourselves.

More absurd still is the director, egged on by the designer, who thinks that Shakespeare is so timeless that you can set his plays in more than one period at once.

I believe that you directed the National Youth Theatre in a 'modern dress' version of Julius Caesar some years ago. Why did you take that decision?

I do not object to updating *any* play if it can be justified from the text and I can justify it very easily with the Roman plays. With my own *Julius Caesar*, I had wanted to do it in modern dress since reading about Orson Welles's production in New York during the war. I saw strong political reasons for this treatment, but at the same time my more mundane reason was to get everybody out of togas; they create a dreadful anonymity in which you can lose sight of the characters and their status. I also saw the value of highlighting the workings of a military dictatorship in modern terms, so it seemed logical to put the actors into modern uniform: Caesar as a Tito-like figure, the flamboyant Antony as a para-trooper, Decius as a police chief etc. When I turned to *Coriolanus* in the early 1960s, I found that updating was even more successful. I chose a pre-First-War setting with a Prussian army background. The nationalism and militarism of the play took on an extra dimension; so did the rabble-rousing role of the tribunes who could be seen as early marxist-agitators. Modern dress, to my mind, is only offensive when it is completely at odds with the intention of the text, or when you alter the text to make it suit the setting. I believe you must justify it logically, not through every scene of the play, but through the main body of it. The critical comment I have treasured most highly was made by Harold Hobson years ago when he said (on the BBC), 'Unlike Guthrie, who uses it for effect, Croft uses modern dress entirely to illuminate the meaning of the play.'

You are both a director and a teacher; how do you combine these two roles with regard to the young actors in your National Youth Theatre productions?

When I start any production with the National Youth Theatre I usually have some ideas about the play, but I have to make them clear to the actors and convince them that they will work. My work with young people means that I have to teach and instruct, as much as 'direct' them. While I will listen to any ideas they can give me I have to keep in mind that they are still finding their way through difficult and unfamiliar territory. Most of my actors are at school and have had little experience, but want to learn. Some of the older actors are at university and may have directed their own productions. Some have a very cerebral approach and are used to discussing every detail or nuance of speech at great length. Some are just self-indulgent. Fine: after all this is what university life is for, in McNeice's words, 'time for soul to stretch and spit'; to think big and boldly. So, they may have to be brought back to basics, and at that point I can become a pretty strict teacher and insist that they study what Shakespeare actually wrote; not just their own parts, but the play as a whole, before they impose their own interpretations on it.

The professional theatre too is in need of stricter tuition in Shakespeare, and what they call in Europe, 'text directors'; with noble exceptions like John Barton at the RSC, they are pretty thin on the ground in this country. Too many of our younger directors think they have to 'jazz up' Shakespeare to avoid boring the audience; especially the younger audience, to whom they play down. The professional theatre needs to re-discover the great editors and critics such as Granville Barker, Dover Wilson, and of course Bernard Shaw. These were exceptional writers, but were also practical men of the theatre; giants of their time. I first discovered Harley Granville Barker when I was in the sixth form at school. Here was a man who could write excitedly about the plays and the characters, and describe the action vividly scene by scene on the printed page. It was a revelation to me. Before I direct Shakespeare now, I always go back to Granville Barker's *Prefaces* to check my bearings, irrespective of what I might do later in the production.

You have spoken of basic principles in Shakespearean production. What do you consider them to be?

Before the actor can interpret or illuminate a part at all, or let his dramatic imagination take wing, he must master the language. His first need is for clarity. This isn't just a question of sense, but of sound as well; if you get one wrong the other's likely to be wrong too. Shakespeare's language is poetic, rhetorical, highly figurative, imagistic. He leans heavily, indeed rejoices in, the endless use of metaphor, antithesis, hyperbole, repetition, play on words; in long, highly developed 'purple' periods. It is useless for the actor to approach the verse (or the prose for that matter), as if it were naturalistic. Unfortunately this is exactly how many young actors still do approach the plays. To achieve clarity the actor must first understand the poetic devices in force; to be able to unwrap an extended metaphor, unravel a complex image. If the actor can't understand them – the jewels in his speeches – how can he expect the audience to understand him? By the same token, he needs to discover the rhythms of Shakespearean speech. Not in a narrow metrical sense, although he should learn about the metre and know where one line ends and another begins – but more in the sense that he needs to make sure he is playing the score Shakespeare wrote. In regular blank verse you would think this was pretty obvious to intelligent actors. They should be able to play by ear at least, but some of them are tone-deaf when it comes to Shakespeare (and the directors often seem no better). The good Shakespearean actor is one who has obtained mastery of the verse to the degree that it sounds as clear and spontaneous as natural speech. Do you know that there are good young actors going to drama school and not being taught these basics? Every year I see members of the National Youth Theatre go off to our leading schools and come back often speaking Shakespeare worse than when they went. They may well be trained in film and television technique, but they are certainly not being prepared for classical theatre.

You place great emphasis on the social and educative value of being part of the 'company'; describing membership as being an 'experience in living'. Is the Shakespearean experience a means by which young people are united across the barriers of class and experience?

My idea of the Youth Theatre is to provide, in a very broad sense, the same exercise in community living that the school play should provide. It brings together young people from all over Great Britain, whatever their social or educational background. We cut automatically across colour, creed, class, sexual or ethnic prejudices, to give young people a rare chance of learning to live together. The theatre has a unique and powerful ability to provide this dynamic social experience. Our members are brought together in the common endeavour of preparing performances that must be put to the public test. The rehearsal period has to happen quickly during the school holidays, and the play has to be given public and critical exposure in front of audiences who, while they are not hostile, can be pretty cool and acerbic. This is the big test. It is this big challenge that knits the company together and provides a focus for them all. It's a more powerful challenge than playing for the local team. The team plays every week, it becomes a routine matter; you want to win, sure, but it is a less powerful challenge than that of the big show that you only do once in a while. The social effect of all this activity often shows itself afterwards. The whole enterprise provides an experience in heightened living, and Shakespeare is an essential part of the heightening process. For a few short weeks our youngsters, although they don't often know where the next meal will come from, work together in a common effort and live on poetic heights. The exposure to all that is happening around them enhances their experience with us. That is why I, in the end, stand by my Shakespearean platform.

The educational world seems intent on making it increasingly difficult for young people to actually enjoy Shakespeare. They still have it forced upon them on the examination plate, which has the result of putting most of them off Shakespeare for life. It is therefore all the more important that we should encourage them to enjoy Shakespeare through performance. In the National Youth Theatre young people can come and see their own age group getting up there and speaking Shakespeare with gusto, as if it was their own natural language, and this at least helps them to realise that it's not as boring and as difficult as it seemed in the classroom. In a way that is the best service we can provide to young people and to English literature. My firm conviction is that Shakespeare, and the arts in general, should be non-examination subjects. They should be taught for pleasure only (call it 'appreciation') and the treatment left to the discretion of the teacher. The good teacher could then share his or her enthusiasms with their pupils. The result might mean far fewer O levels, but instead we might see thousands of young people develop a lifelong taste for Shakespeare.

Boxing the Bard:
Shakespeare and television
Graham Holderness

Elizabeth by the grace of God Queen of England, etc., to all Justices, Mayors, Sherriffs, Bailliffs, Head Constables, Under Constables, and all other our officers and ministers, greeting. Know ye that we of our especial grace, certain knowledge and mere motion have licensed and authorised, and by these presents do licence and authorise, our loving subjects, James Burbage, John Perkin, John Lanham, William Johnson, and Robert Wilson, servants to our trusty and well-beloved Cousin and Counsellor the Earl of Leicester, to use, exercise and occupy the art and faculty of playing Comedies, Tragedies, interludes, stage plays . . .[1]

Elizabeth by the Grace of God of the United Kingdom of Great Britain and Northern Ireland and of our other Realms and Territories Queen, Head of the Commonwealth, Defender of the Faith:
TO ALL TO WHOM THESE PRESENTS SHALL COME, GREET-INGS! . . .
   NOW KNOW YE that We, by our Prerogative Royal and of Our especial grace, certain knowledge and mere motion do by this Our Charter for Us, Our Heirs and Successors will, ordaine and declare as follows . . .[2]

The second quotation, as the Miltonic powers and titles invoked indicate, is not an address from the first Elizabeth to her loving subjects, or (as the first quotation is) a licence granting liberty to a sixteenth-century acting company. It is a proclamation, dated 1981, of Elizabeth, the second of that name, formally granting a Royal Charter to the British Broadcasting Corporation.

WHEREAS in view of the widespread interest which is taken by Our Peoples in broadcasting services and of the great value of such services as a means of disseminating information, education and entertainment, We believe it to be in the interests of Our Peoples in Our United Kingdom and elsewhere within the Commonwealth that the Corporation should continue to provide broadcasting services pursuant to such licences and agreements in that behalf as Our Secretary of State may from time to time grant and make with the Corporation.

This formal act of authorisation, issued by the highest levels of the State, draws on the linguistic, cultural and political heritage of the first Elizabethan Age: and in return for the powers thus clothed in ornate language and rich cultural currency, the Corporation has consistently, and more than any other broadcasting institution or medium, preserved in active and perpetuated forms the most striking and singular product of that earlier age, the cultural phenomenon we know as 'Shakespeare'.

Institution

Although it could be argued that the founding fathers of the BBC chose incorporation by Royal Charter rather than Parliamentary Statute in order to secure political independence rather than antique dignity, the parallel with the Elizabethan theatre is irresistible. In the space of some thirty years at the end of the sixteenth century a varied, heterogenous and pluralistic medium became a virtual (and after the Restoration an actual) State monopoly.[3] When the BBC was granted its first Royal Charter in 1927 and 'public service broadcasting' was born, a relatively new technological medium with enormous and hugely varied possibilities (some of which are only now about to penetrate British society) was shaped into a national institution. The BBC emerged, like the Elizabethan theatre, in a postwar cultural crisis in which there was a pressing need for the development of a new sense of national identity:

The very condition for its existence coincided with the need for a new definition of the nation . . . In the wake of the scramble for colonies, the first imperialist war, the growth of American capital and the partition of Ireland, it was evident that 'Britishness' was not simply something present and permanent, it was something to be produced in a continual process of cultural reformation. The BBC does not reflect or represent an already fully-formed national consciousness, a coherent national identity, rather it is one of several material agents or 'national' instititions which produce and reproduce that very identity.[4]

The guiding intelligence and moral zeal behind the construction of the BBC as a kind of national church were those of John Reith, who was appointed as the Corporation's general manager, later its Director-General, and subsequently elevated to the peerage for his services to the establishment. Reith's Memorandum to the Crawford Committee, set up in 1925 to prepare plans for the new broadcasting monopoly, represents a concise statement of principles which still lie at the root of the theory of public service broadcasting. Echoing his Arnoldian inheritance, Reith articulated his vision of the new medium penetrating not only the cultural but the moral, intellectual and spiritual life of the nation: 'the

Broadcasting Service should bring into the greatest possible number of homes in the fullest degree all that is best in every department of human knowledge, endeavour and achievement – the Service must not be used for entertainment purposes alone'. The Reithian Sunday was the most intense focus of his evangelical fervour for moral improvement: 'the programmes which are broadcast on Sunday are therefore framed with the day itself in mind ... I believe that Sabbaths should be one of the most valuable assets of our existence – quiet islands on the tossing sea of life'.[5] There were to be no transmissions during hours of worship except where the transmission was of a complete church service. The BBC tradition of promoting edifying material on Sundays persists to this day: the BBC/Time-Life Shakespeare productions were all broadcast, perhaps in memory of Lord Reith, on Sunday evenings.

Regarded as an institution, the BBC has often seemed little more than an agency, if not a department, of government. Established as a supposedly independent body, in its early years it operated aggressively to identify the interests of the state and the interests of the people. In the General Strike of 1926 the Corporation acted as an instrument of centralised propaganda. 'There could be no question about our supporting the government in general' said Reith, 'since the BBC was a national institution, and since the Government in this crisis was acting for the people . . . the BBC was for the Government in the crisis too'.[6] The identification of Government and people was clearly a strategy of ideological conciliation; the identification of the BBC with the people a ludicrously inappropriate populist gesture: 'Whatever its aspirations at the time, the BBC could hardly be said to be speaking for Britain, still less to it. Its relative newness, its conception of its role as the guardian of high culture and morality, its self-denying ordinance against dealing with 'controversial' matters, all militated against a true involvement with the deeper and more varied levels of the society.'[7]

In fact as an institution the primary ideological function of the BBC remains that of constructing a coherent vision of a unified nation calculated to elide political, economic and cultural realities: 'The BBC is a national institution in so far as it consistently promotes the illusion of a unified and integrated political region with a system of common values and beliefs. Its very existence perpetuates this myth'.[8]

Medium

Television, as Marshall McLuhan observed, is an inherently *social* medium: it invites group rather than individual participation. It is easy to mistake the particular forms in which a medium is commercially and politically exploited for the character of the form itself: there is no necessary relationship between the medium itself and the dissemination of small receivers for use within individual homes. When we see a group of people watching a sporting event on television in a pub, we see the medium itself making for lively social interchange rather than isolated individual absorption. As it is, television operates as a medium of collective participation within that fundamental social institution the family (however constituted) and within that basic space of social living, the home. Secondly, television is a universal medium to a far greater extent than the theatre or even literacy: as an oral and visual form it is accessible even to the unlettered, its complex visual dialect easier to learn than spoken or written language. It can therefore claim more than any other cultural form (using 'cultural' here in the specialised sense) to be a national communications medium: the primary system of an authentically 'national' culture. More so than print (even popular newspapers) certainly more so than other 'cultural' discourses such as literature and theatre, television has succeeded in incorporating itself into the rhythms of social life, so that the medium has become a normal part of everyday experience. The act of reading involves isolation, physical separation, withdrawal; attendance at a concert or art gallery, a visit to a theatre or cinema, involve the abandonment of ordinary patterns of behaviour, the allocation of a 'special' occasion in a cultural space separate from the concrete texture of everyday living. Television, requiring no such privileged deviation from social activity, can be regarded as a peculiarly general and populist cultural form.

Such characteristics of the medium have led some writers to draw comparisons between television *as a medium* and the Elizabethan popular drama. Terry Hawkes in *Shakespeare's Talking Animals* proposed the television medium as a successor or reconstitution of the cultural potentialities of the Elizabethan playhouse. Both television and the Elizabethan theatre offer *communual* rather than solitary experiences, permitting active and simultaneous discussion and response. The modern theatre is no longer a communal but a minority art: where television is both populist and democratic. Both television and the Elizabethan drama can be described, within their respective cultures, as 'natural' activities, not distinct from the common flow of everyday living. The 'whole experience' of cinema or theatre – surrounded and interrupted, certainly, by moments of social intercourse such as intervals – involve isolation in the darkness and imposed silence of an auditorium: the brightly-lit screen or picture-frame stage commands a hypnotised absorption into an aesthetic totality. Television interacts with known and familiar surroundings, so that the complex unity of its characteristic experience has a quality of multifariousness absent from all cinema and most theatre.[9]

Such parallels between the television medium and the Elizabethan drama have certainly been expressed consistently by those involved in producing Shakespeare for the BBC. In 1947 George More O' Ferrall wrote of his production of Hamlet: 'Why should we claim that television is especially suited to Shakespeare? Because in its method of presentation it comes nearer to the Elizabethan theatre, for which the plays were written, than the modern theatre can do'.[10] The parallel characteristics cited are diversified acting areas, swift sequence of scenes and the possibility of intimacy between actor and audience. John Wilders, Literary Consultant to the BBC/Time-Life Shakespeare series, pursued this analogy to claim that television reproduction of Shakespeare could emulate or at least approach the freedom and flexibility of Renaissance popular drama.[11]

Raymond Williams has shown[12] that in all developed broadcasting systems the characteristic organisation is one of 'sequence' or 'flow'. In all communications systems before broadcasting, the essential items were discrete, independent units: in broadcasting the real *programme* is offered as a sequence of these and other similar events, which are then available in a single dimension and a single operation.

Broadcasting in its early stages inherited this problematic, and – since in general the form of the technology developed prior to any corresponding content – operated in a parasitic way upon it: the philosophy of broadcasting was 'transmission', the *relaying* of events (musical concert, play, public address, sporting event) to a general audience. *Programming* was a matter of arranging these discrete televised events into a series of timed units, with the appropriate mix, balance and proportion.

In Williams's view the important change was the movement, inherent in the nature of the medium itself, towards a concept of sequence not as *programming* but as a continous *flow*. This is recognised instinctively in the way we talk of 'watching television' rather than watching a particular unit, and in the familiar reluctance to 'switch off' after a unit is completed. What the viewer experiences is thus not the published programme of discrete units but a planned flow which is in both form and content the real 'broadcasting'.

Boxing the Bard

BBC television began to dramatise productions of Shakespeare from its inception, the first occurring in February 1937. There was already a strong tradition of broadcasting Renaissance drama in general on BBC radio – a tradition the history of which remains to be written[13] – but BBC television, with some exceptions, has never followed this, choosing always to paddle in the safer shallows of Shakespeare.

The challenge of adapting Shakespeare for television was certainly taken up at an early stage; but a close attention to the particular forms employed can be instructive. The first complete production (of *Julius Caesar*) was broadcast in July 1938: but prior to this there had been some twenty broadcasts in the form of a series called 'Scenes from Shakespeare'. The programmes would be about twenty-five minutes in duration, comparable with other types of programme. Programming information foregrounded the *actors* rather than the play or the dramatist, in keeping with a similar emphasis for light entertainment programmes, music, comedy and so forth. Caution should be exercised in drawing inferences from this form: since before the war television broadcasting was in a very early experimental stage and the technologies relatively undeveloped. Notwithstanding, it can be suggested that initially television incorporated and assimilated Shakespeare into, and employed methods of production and transmission appropriate to, its own medium. Despite the strong and evident influence of the theatrical profession (at its strongest in the 1950s) television did not seek to come to terms with Shakespeare on grounds defined by the theatre or literary criticism. Whole plays were broken into 'scenes from', short units compatible with normal programming requirements. Duration of programme units was not in itself a technical inhibition: in March 1937 a relatively full fifty-minute version of *Macbeth* (longer than many a supposedly complete silent production) was broadcast in two halves. The format was the result of programming decisions: Shakespeare was programmed as 'entertainment' rather than as 'education' or 'information'. The emphasis on the distinctive qualities of actors, derived directly from the contemporary theatre, paralleled the star cult of 'variety' common in both the contemporary cinema and in television itself.

Initially then television approached Shakespeare in a manner very different from the broadcasting techniques we have been accustomed to. The material was treated as entertainment; incorporated into a pattern of mixed programming without any unusual emphasis or special foregrounding; and regarded as not essentially different from any other item placed within a particular programmed sequence. Nor is there any manifestation, in these early stages, of the ideological appropriation of Shakespeare which later became commonplace. On St George's Day in 1936 there was no broadcast of Henry V: instead there was a documentary about another national culture hero, King Arthur. The Radio Times of 1937 carried an enormous amount of media 'hype' around the coronation of George VI: even by the standards of contemporary media servility towards royalty, the number of programming references and exploitations of popular monarchist interest is extraordinary. There were programmes on heraldry, royal families, and even archery appropriated as 'toxophily' – the sport of kings'. There were advertisements using the occasion for commercial opportunism. There was a broadcast performance of Edward German's Merrie England. But there was no Shakespeare. Even BBC Radio offered only a paltry twenty minutes of Henry V, compared with the whole of Act 3 of Wagner's Die Walküre; and to supply a more patriotic air, 'the song of a nightingale, broadcast from a wood in Surrey'.[14]

After the war BBC television moved into Shakespeare production in a much more confident way, and by the early 1950s the modern format of BBC Shakespeare, monumentally established in the BBC/Time-Life Series, was more or less fully formed. Where the early broadcast performances integrated the productions into the programmed sequence of variety and entertainment, adapting the material to the rhythms of the medium: from the early 1950s the Corporation began to make Shakespeare broadcasts into special occasions by programming on particular seasonal dates – Twelfth Night at Christmas, Henry V on St George's Day; by using a particularly significant 'slot' such as Sunday evening; and by inserting write-ups and feature articles into the Radio Times to prepare the viewer for an isolated, special experience. In the late 1940s plays were broadcast in complete versions from studios and by outside broadcast.[15] The first production of Hamlet in December 1947 sprawled magisterially across four evenings.[16] The Radio Times carried a feature article by the producer, which claimed in his support the theatrical and academic authority of Dover Wilson and Granville Barker. The production was highlighted in the 'recommended viewing' column, 'Talk of the Week'. Hamlet was followed in 1949–50 by the other three 'great tragedies', each accompanied by supportive feature articles in the Radio Times.[17]

By the early 1950s everything possible was being done to isolate a Shakespeare performance from the flow or sequence of the medium. A special kind of privileged attention was being focused on the play by accompanying 'programme notes' and quasi-academic discussions. The practice of flanking a performance with educative ancillary material was beginning to appear: on the evening of 'Shakespeare's Birthday', 1952, to herald a production of *The Taming of the Shrew*, a panel discussion on 'Televising Shakespeare' featured producers, actors and critics.[18] In the *Radio Times* a visual technique of boxing information on the play, to separate it from the contamination of the surrounding contextual *bricolage* began to be employed.

A useful example of the latter is to be found in the *Radio Times* for 15 May 1953. The programme note on the play, a production of *Henry V*, is boxed off from the surrounding page in a design resembling a theatrical programme (and beyond that, the 'society' invitation card from which the latter derives). A short article by Michael Macowan, the BBC producer, is incorporated into the programming information, describing the acting company and its methods. The company in question was called the 'Elizabethan Theatre Company':

> With very little money, and using the barest minimum of setting and the most elementary Elizabethan costumes, a dozen to a score of young men and women, mostly from Oxford and Cambridge, set out last summer to play Shakespeare wherever they could find an audience and a place to play in. Sometimes it was an inn-yard, sometimes a college garden or the hall of an ancient house, (the kind of conditions which Shakespeare's own company met on their tours), sometimes a town hall or an ordinary theatre.[19]

This touring company, based on the principle of reviving the Elizabethan *ensemble*: playing in extra-theatrical locations, without pictorial scenery, doubling parts – was a characteristic product of what Alan Sinfield has called 'culturalism'.[20] A product of the relative cultural fertility of post-war Britain, this intervention attempted to offer an alternative to mainstream theatrical tradition, aligning Shakespeare more closely with notions of accessible popular entertainment. The production was directed by John Barton, and subsidised by (among others) the Arts Council.

The Elizabethan Theatre Company was also a forerunner of the early RSC: and without making extravagant claims for the radical potentiality of this embryo which is now a monumental national institution, it can be suggested that the kind of dramatic intervention made here was culturally a potential point of radical energy in Shakespeare reproduction; and its presentation on television a challenge to the dominant theatrical and naturalistic conventions. Thirty years later Jane Howell's productions of the first tetralogy for the BBC/Time-Life Series, based on similar principles, stood out with remarkable boldness and clarity as a radical cultural intervention.[21]

Yet this remarkable production of *Henry V* appeared as the BBC's official contribution to the festivities for the coronation of Elizabeth II. The *Radio Times*' 'Television Diary' juxtaposed 'The Elizabethan Theatre Company' against a BBC film on 'The Second Elizabeth'. A potential growth-point of post-war British culture, which was attempting by a reappropriation of Elizabethan theatrical practices to harness some of the popular energies of the Renaissance theatre, was in turn appropriated by the BBC and manipulated into a curtain-raiser for the New Elizabethan Age. An opportunity of bringing the populist and democratic medium of television into an alliance with the popular aspects of Shakespearean theatre was rendered by the operation of institutional forces little more than an ideological affirmation of historical continuity, institutional hegemony and State power.

Alternatives?

The BBC/Time-Life Shakespeare series was produced in the image of the Corporation itself: a classical monument of national culture, an oppressive agency of cultural hegemony. The nature of the product itself inevitably acts to solidify the conservative tendencies of the institution, and to inhibit resistance from within. Hence the possibilities for alternative or oppositional reproduction of Shakespeare must be sought outside the BBC.[22] Channel Four, in keeping with its generally radical-liberal approach to cultural matters, succeeded in providing an impressive piece of marginal opposition in the series *Shakespeare Lives!* (broadcast January–March 1983). Director Michael Bogdanov assembled a group of National Theatre actors and an invited audience to the Roundhouse Theatre in Camden for the filming of practical workshop sessions, punctuated by open discussion, of six Shakespeare plays. Bogdanov admitted three motives for attempting the experiment: a sense of theoretical isolation; a dissatisfaction with the apparent timelessness of Shakespeare teaching; and an impatience with the BBC's handling of Shakespeare, 'which has done the greatest disservice to Shakespeare in the last twenty-five years'.[23] In the workshops director and actors could be observed constructing sections of a play, experimenting with different possibilities, arguing amongst themselves, involving the live audience. Shakily hand-held cameras recorded the proceedings with odd-angle immediacy and strangeness: other cameras, sound equipment and technicians were visibly present as the practical infrastructure of the dramatic event. The texts are often rigidly interpreted by the director, and sections of the programmes appear to be lectures given by Bogdanov to a passive audience, using the actors as visual aids. And there is no doubt that to some extent the programmes act as mythologising agents: confirming, by an insistence on Shakespeare's modernity, the infinite and perpetual universality of his work.[24] Each broadcast begins with the statement: 'Shakespeare is the greatest living playwright'. But the forces of directorial authority and of the universalist ideology itself were inevitably weakened by the open situation: in a context of practical experiment open to question by both actors and audience, the texts became at times musical scores for dramatic improvisation, or battlegrounds for the play of conflicting attitudes, interpretations and ideas.

Agencies of cultural authority in such a context wield far less power than in the achieved finality of a BBC production. Both Jonathan Miller and Michael Bogdanov have very definite views on The Taming of the Shrew: Miller sees it as a play advocating marital obedience – 'Shakespeare . . . underwrote the idea that the state, whether it was the small state of the family or the larger state of the country, required and needed the unquestioned authority of some sort of sovereign'; Bogdanov sees it as a feminist drama, 'showing Petruchio chastened and Kate victorious'.[25] Miller covered the end credits of his production with a Puritan psalm celebrating 'the orderliness and beauty of the family', thus curtailing any potential liberty of the drama to arouse the play of meanings, by imposing the sovereign authority of scripture, the written word. Bogdanov's workshop involved a quarrel between Daniel Massey (Petruchio) and Suzanne Bertish (Katherine) disputing whether in the play the man or the woman emerges victorious. Miller, averse to any 'mixing of conventions' in televising theatre, sheared the Induction from the play altogether; Bogdanov's workshop (following his production) foregrounded it as a necessary perspective for the play's exploration of sexual politics.[26]

The 'workshop' format can certainly then be regarded as an alternative form for the televising of Shakespeare. In place of the monumental stability of a definitive version, the cultural authority of an institutional production, solidly flanked by the apparatus of special occasion, publicity promotion, ancillary introduction, linked publications; we have the provisional, tentative, unfinished debate of the practical rehearsal, and the spectacle of people struggling to make meaning out of Shakespeare. Shakespeare Lives!, despite its association with the National Theatre, made no attempt to adapt the constructed television situation to established institutional forms, but rather appropriated Shakespeare into a context familar enough from other television programmes (such as panel discussions) to give the form a certain accessibility. Where the BBC/ Time-Life Series consistently employed the institutional powers of the Corporation to emulate the high culture of a theatrical experience, *Shakespeare Lives!* unashamedly adapted Shakespeare to a specifically televisual form; and in doing so, opened up to inspection and debate both the plays and the processes by which meanings are made from them.

It should not be assumed, however, that the televised workshop is an inherently radical site of cultural production. An example of the workshop form institutionalised to the point where any radical energy the medium may possess is dissipated and lost, is the series *Playing Shakespeare*: featuring John Barton, produced by London Weekend Television and broadcast on Channel Four in 1984. The cultural and ideological provenance of the series is that crucial symbiosis of Cambridge English and Royal Shakespeare defined by Christopher McCullough as 'the Cambridge Connection'. Strictly speaking the sessions filmed and subsequently published in book form were not workshops but discussions between a director and actors. The actors 'read' rather than performed the texts: the context resembling the structured informality of a seminar rather than the active practical experiment of a rehearsal or improvisation. The object of the series, as defined by Trevor Nunn, was the exemplification and illustration of a 'method':

What the programmes, and now the published texts on the series, reveal, is the method and principle of an approach to acting Shakespeare which has been fundamental to the RSC since it was formed. This approach is not didactic or political or scholastic or literary. It relies a good deal on analysis, but just as much on common sense and pragmatism, and a sense of theatre and character; it attempts to serve the complexities and contradictions of the text, but it is also trying to make the language work, and to be alive and exciting in the theatre.[27]

The cultural context invoked here is immediately recognisable: all these principles – the repudiation of ideology, the attempt to combine a 'method' of analysis with a pragmatic 'common sense', the emphasis on a practical methodology for bringing texts to 'living' realisation – can be heard echoing up and down the ideological corridor that leads from Downing College to the banks of the Avon.

John Barton's conception of the series was as a body of 'practical guidance to actors'. The 'practical guidance' offered amounts to a series of 'practical criticism' seminars, in which a motley gallimaufry of selected

passages, irresistibly reminiscent of Arnold's 'touchstones', is subjected
to detailed verbal and metrical analysis. The texts, or rather the decontextualised gobbets, become concrete embodiments of expressive matter:
articulating the character's emotions, the actor's experience, the texture
of sensuous reality: ' "in sequent toil all forwards do contend": those
words capture the swish and chafing of the sea' (p. 108).

Despite the pragmatic common-sense approach of this method, its
undogmatic, exploratory empiricism, it is carefully directed towards the
construction of a myth. The ultimate object of exploration is nothing less
than Shakespeare's 'intentions': those elusive properties here conceived
not as pearls of high seriousness, but as 'hidden directions', guidance to
the actor which 'Shakespeare himself provided'. 'Shakespeare's text is
full of hidden hints to the actors. When an actor becomes aware of them
he will find that Shakespeare himself starts to direct him.' Barton himself,
etched in Trevor Nunn's memory as 'the young man with the Renaissance face' (Foreword), is a suitable intermediary for the transmission of
these instructions from a dead director. Any actor chilled by the prospect
of confrontation with this ghoulish revenant, the director from beyond
the grave, can rest assured that nothing harmful or disturbing is likely to
be communicated: nothing but reassuring avuncular wisdom and serene
humane understanding: 'Shakespeare is timeless in the sense that he
anatomises and understands what is in men and women in any age, and
what he has to say is always true and real' (p. 190).

The Shakespeare engendered from this coupling of Scrutiny and Stratford is easily recognisable as a manifestation of the Shakespeare myth. It
is 'not of an age, but for all time'; its preternatural intelligence and
contemplative gaze flicker between the practicalities of production and
the immutable truths of human nature, rolling from stage to 'heavens'
and back again. John Barton identifies completely with this superhuman
monstrosity: Shakespeare, he affirms, did not have a 'political philosophy', only a sense of human nature. Barton, like his fellow-director
Shakespeare, spurns the quotidian and contemplates the timeless verities of eternal human nature: 'I'm sometimes asked about my own
political views. I usually answer that they are Shakespearean . . . Shakespeare is neither right-wing nor left-wing in his philosophy and tem-
perament. In political terms he is *wingless*' (p. 190).

Television and democracy

Public controversy about broadcasting has been dominated from the beginning by assumptions about its immense potency as a medium of cultural, social and ultimately political influence and power. The incessant watchfulness of government, Parliament, party politicians and even MI5 over the BBC's appointments and its broadcasts of news and political discussion, a vigilance which has led to acrimonious accusations of political bias, bespeaks a medium of such power that the character of its product, and the mechanisms of its control and accountability are a constant site of ideological struggle and political contestation. Although the Peacock committee[28] disappointed Mrs Thatcher by declining to surrender the BBC immediately to the free play of market forces, its recommendations envisage the ultimate dismantling of the Corporation and the disappearance of the concept of State-financed public-service broadcasting. Although the voice of John Reith can still be heard in the land – 'the BBC's problem', affirmed Noel Annan, 'is to re-establish itself as a national Church of culture'[29] – technological developments in television broadcasting, such as cable and satellite, will lead inevitably, as Peacock recognised, to some fundamental revaluation of the BBC. In such a volatile situation socialists should be clear about their political priorities: should the BBC be defended as a bulwark of liberal-humanist values against the tide of commercialised barbarism? or is the 'public' the Corporation ultimately 'serves' still that powerful minority extrapolated and extolled by John Reith and by the monarchy as 'the people'?

In 1977 the Annan committee on the future of broadcasting dealt with the right of access to the medium.

There is a right to speak in a free democracy, but it does not follow from this that there is a right to be listened to. I have a right to speak, you have an obligation not to stop me; but you do not have an obligation to listen to me. It does not follow that, because by a flick of the switch you can cut me off and stop listening, that I have a right of access to the medium, since there is a limited amount of time and air space. The claim to speak on it whenever you want is, in effect, a claim to be listened to; and that is an unrealistic demand. (3.14)[30]

The argument is of course Matthew Arnold's – of what value is freedom if the possessor does not know how to use it? – as mediated by T. S. Eliot – freedom of speech is futile unless the recipient of that liberty has something of value to say. But who judges such value and such utility? who decides which utterance is futile and which worthwhile? Tony Benn, in his contribution to the Annan report, drew attention to its articulation of this liberal dilemma: who, by the terms of this common-sense view, *does* have the right to have their ideas broadcast? Benn argued that the issue should be shifted, away from a consideration of whether or not programmes were good or serious, balanced or truthful; towards a concern with the medium's ability to allow people to reflect to each other the diversity of their interests and opinions, the nature of their grievances and hopes, the variations and differences between their ideologies. Such a medium, more open to democratic access, would clearly be more effective in expressing and disclosing the contradictions within a society, and deeply subversive of the moral certainties that have formed the covert propaganda of the BBC from John Reith to the present day.

Benn's argument is followed in the Annan report by the views of Sir Kenneth Clark, endorsed by the committee (3.16). Clark denies that television debases popular taste: on the contrary it widens people's horizons, 'even whetting their appetites for art and ideas, producing works of dramatic art and familiarising people with great works of literature'. Clark's avuncular liberalism has replaced Reith's moral paternalism: but the ideological function of the medium remains curiously unchanged. In a divided society the central institution of communication is controlled by those whose interests lie in reinforcing the concept of a unified commonwealth with a stable and shared system of beliefs and values: the business of broadcasting, says the Annan report, is to produce 'visions of order in a troubled world' (3.2).

I have argued that television production of Shakespeare can disclose radical potentialities only when its forms and methodologies touch those areas of popular participation and democratic access. Despite the perennial threat of ideological incorporation, such contact can be interpreted quite broadly: to insist on explicit socialist commitment as a precondition of radical cultural work is to misunderstand the nature of cultural process in a class society. I have offered the example of the early BBC as a fruitful site of Shakespeare reproduction: although its productions emanated directly from the Reithian policy of 'mixed programming', designed to secure a homogeneous and unified audience, its practice provides a model for the manipulation of Shakespeare into accessible forms relatively free from ideological control. Where television has adapted the Elizabethan drama – as in the 1953 *Henry V* or the 1983 first tetralogy – by historically-based production techniques calculated to deliver those theatrical energies inscribed into the texts by the conditions of their original performance, it has been possible to provoke from them their residual latent content of popular experience. The most productive form yet devised can be represented by *Shakespeare Lives!*, where actual democratic participation (on however limited and selective a basis) becomes a constitutive element of the medium.

Slight as these creative initiatives may appear, they have been rigorously contained: they have developed in the interstices of an agency of cultural production and distribution which invests its power and principle energy in the reproduction of hegemonic cultural discourses. Our comparisons between the medium of television and the conventions of the Elizabethan drama should be completed by a comparison of the BBC as an institution with the Renaissance theatre by which Shakespeare's plays were written. A centralised body, close to the heart of political power in the State, financed by a combination of State patronage and a fee-paying clientèle, observed by the watchful eye of a government acutely concerned about the politics of its culture, transmits a metropolitan product throughout a supposedly 'united' kingdom. What needs now to be said of the BBC could be applied retrospectively to the institutionalised Elizabethan theatre:

The key to the BBC lies in its role as the voice or vision of the British nation. As a national institution it institutes an audio-visual impression of national unity wholly at odds with political, historical, economic and social realities. It provides the London government with the possibility of a unified utterance which denies the diffracted constituency of its vast fiefdom . . . Linguistic lines of force pulsate outwards from London via education, television, radio and newspapers. While the hegemony of the BBC persists there will be a proper way to speak, a language of transparency and clarity, the voice of pure reason. BBC English is exactly the speech of that vision.[31]

Translated into that language, Shakespeare too becomes the voice of that vision. Re-read via the grammar of an alternative, oppositional discourse, Shakespeare can become a strain in the multivocal and pluralistic polyphony of a democratic culture.

Notes

1 1574 patent granted by Elizabeth I to 'Leicester's Men'; see E. K. Chambers, *The Elizabethan Stage* (Oxford: Clarendon Press, 1923), II, pp. 87–8.
2 Royal Charter granted to the British Broadcasting Corporation, 1981.
3 See Graham Holderness, *Shakespeare's History* (Dublin: Gill and Macmillan, 1985), pp. 153–60.
4 William Maley, 'Centralisation and censorship', in Colin MacCabe and Olivia Stewart, eds., *The BBC and Public Service Broadcasting* (Manchester: Manchester University Press, 1986), pp. 35–6.
5 The evidence of Mr J. C. W. Reith to the Crawford Committee, December 1925 – see R. A. Coase, *British Broadcasting: a Study in Monopoly* (London: Longman, 1950); J. C. W. Reith, *Broadcasting over Britain* (London: Hodder, 1924), p. 196.

6 John Reith, quoted in MacCabe and Stewart, *The BBC*, p. 46.
7 Krishan Kumar, 'Public service broadcasting and the public interest', in MacCabe and Stewart, *The BBC*, p. 50.
8 Maley, in MacCabe and Stewart, *The BBC*, p. 37.
9 Terry Hawkes, *Shakespeare's Talking Animals* (London: Methuen, 1973), pp. 215–241.
10 George More O'Ferrall, 'The televising of drama', *Radio Times* (19 March 1937), p. 4.
11 John Wilders, 'Adjusting the set', *Times Literary Supplement* (10 July 1981), p. 13.
12 Raymond Williams, *Television: Technology and Cultural Form* (London: Fontana, 1974), pp. 88–90.
13 The only historical studies I know of are John Drakakis, 'The essence that's not seen', in Peter Lewis, ed., *Radio Drama*, (London: Longman, 1981); and an unpublished M.A. thesis by Margaret Horsefield, *Shakespeare on Radio* (Shakespeare Institute, University of Birmingham). Janet Clare has compiled a list of radio productions in *Theatre of the Air: a checklist of radio productions of Renaissance drama, 1922–1986; Renaissance Drama Newsletter, Supplement Six* (University of Warwick, 1986). It is evident from this list that BBC radio has broadcast some one hundred productions of non-Shakespearean Renaissance plays, to over two hundred productions of Shakespeare; BBC television has broadcast just over one hundred Shakespeare productions, and sixteen non-Shakespearean plays. Stuart Evans discusses the technical problems of dramatising Shakespeare for radio in *Shakespeare Survey*, 39 (1986).
14 Philip Brockbank informs me that he recalls listening to this broadcast. The nightingale, unpatriotically insensible to the occasion, failed to show up.
15 After the war studio production became the norm, but there were several outside broadcasts from the Open Air Theatre, Regent's Park. *As You Like It* was adapted for studio, and *A Midsummer Night's Dream* broadcast from Regent's Park, in July 1946. See Ian Atkins, 'Open air theatre to studio', *Radio Times* (12 July 1946). See also Holderness and McCullough, 'Shakespeare on the screen: a selective filmography', *Shakespeare Survey*, 39 (1986), p. 16 and p. 28.
16 *Hamlet*, produced by George More O'Ferrall, broadcast between 5 and 15 December 1947.
17 See J. C. Trewin, 'Every inch a king', *Radio Times* (20 August 1948), and 'A tragedy of darkness', *Radio Times* (18 February 1949), p. 25; and Lionel Hale, 'Othello – a play bursting with energy', *Radio Times* (21 April 1950), p. 43.
18 Panel discussion on 'Shakespeare and television', broadcast 22 April 1952.
19 *Radio Times* (15 May 1953); see p. 15 for feature article 'New Elizabethan actors'.
20 Alan Sinfield, 'Royal Shakespeare', in Jonathan Dollimore and Alan Sinfield, eds., *Political Shakespeare* (Manchester: Manchester University Press, 1985), pp. 164ff.
21 For discussions of Jane Howell's BBC productions see Holderness, *Shakespeare's History*, pp. 213–19; 'Radical potentiality and institutional closure', in Dollimore and Sinfield, *Political Shakespeare*, pp. 197–9; and (with Christopher McCullough), 'Boxing the Bard: the cultural politics of television Shakespeare', *Red Letters*, 18 (1986). See also Stanley Wells, 'The history of the whole contention', *Times Literary Supplement* (4 February 1983), p. 105.
22 For resistance from within the BBC see the texts cited in previous note.
23 Michael Billington, 'Why old Bill needs rejuvenating', *The Guardian* (30 December 1982).
24 See Michael Bogdanov, Chapter 8.
25 Jonathan Miller interviewed by Tim Hallinan, 'Jonathan Miller on the Shakespeare plays', *Shakespeare Quarterly*, 32 (1981), p. 140; and Miller, Chapter 18.
26 See the three booklets produced to accompany the series, which compare interestingly in style and approach to the two-volume publication which accompanied the BBC/Time-Life Series – Michael Bogdanov and Joss Buckley, *Shakespeare Lives!* (London: Channel 4/Quintet Films, 1983); and Roger Sales, ed., *Shakespeare in Perspective* (London: BBC/Ariel Books, 2 vols., 1982 and 1985).
27 Trevor Nunn's 'Foreword' to John Barton, *Playing Shakespeare* (London: Methuen, 1984).

28 The Peacock committee reported in 1986 on the financing of the BBC. Contrary to Tory government expectations, the committee did not recommend the introduction of advertising; but its proposals recommend the eventual replacement of the licence fee by direct subscription.

29 Noel Annan, 'A programme for the future?', *Times Literary Supplement* (12 September 1986), p. 993; 'Being employed by the BBC should mean that you accept obligations that do not affect other broadcasters . . . as a national institution . . . the BBC owes duties to the state'.

30 *Report of the Committee on the Future of Broadcasting* (London: HMSO, 1977), p. 325.

31 Maley, in MacCabe and Stewart, *The BBC*, p. 36.

This essay is indebted to Christopher J. McCullough's research into the history of the BBC.

John Wilders
interviewed by Graham Holderness

You've described elsewhere[1] *the nature of your contribution to the BBC/Time-Life Shakespeare Series. How did you come to be 'Literary Consultant'?*

In the event it proved as much a diplomatic as a professional literary job: I had to get on with a lot of directors and actors of widely different temperaments; and I think I'm not a particularly difficult person. That would seem to me an essential qualification for anyone doing this particular kind of job. I'd done some editing, so I suppose I knew a bit about textual and editorial problems, should they arise. I think it may partly have been that my primary interest in Shakespeare has always been in terms of the theatre. I'd had more experience as an actor than any other academic that I happen to know. I did a lot of acting when I was an undergraduate at Cambridge: my contemporaries were John Barton and Peter Hall, Peter Wood and Toby Robertson; as students we worked together and I acted in productions which they did. So I had a great deal of first-hand experience of Shakespeare in performance. I kept this up, taking part in the Marlowe Society's recordings of the complete works of Shakespeare. I was actually for a while a member of Equity; and to some extent torn between being an academic and being an actor.

Who were the influential figures in the background at Cambridge?

Leavis particularly; Muriel Bradbrook was certainly lecturing. A man who influenced all those of us who were involved in performance was George Rylands, who encouraged us all a great deal, and had a lot of experience; so that although he was, and is, very little known in the academic world he had a tremedous effect on a whole generation, particularly of directors.

That period at Cambridge seems to have produced a particularly active rapprochement between literary criticism and the theatre; which perhaps seems surprising, considering how little interest Cambridge English showed in drama as theatre.

That's right: somebody wrote an article called 'Scrutiny's failure with Shakespeare'. Leavis and L. C. Knights adopted a thematic rather than a dramatic approach; they tended to see drama as dramatic poems rather than as plays. I think that the big influence both at Cambridge and later at Stratford was John Barton.[2] I knew him when he arrived at Cambridge, with a battered copy of the works of Shakespeare under his arm; and he already knew the plays extremely well. It's very extraordinary to think how things were thirty-five or forty years ago, but quite a lot of Shakespeare's plays had scarcely been performed in the theatre in our lifetime, and were by a lot of people regarded as very inferior plays, deficient in the sort of poetic qualities the prevailing school of literary criticism was looking for. But what we discovered was that those plays worked on the stage. One quality we realised Shakespeare had from the very beginning was an extraordinary sense of dramatic structure, derived probably from his own experience as an actor; so that the plays play wonderfully well.

One product of that alliance between literary criticism, theatre history and dramatic practice was a new interest in the revival of Elizabethan staging conditions: I'm thinking of things like the Elizabethan Theatre Company, in which John Barton and George Rylands were both involved. You've said of the BBC series that you believe producers were right to avoid the bare studio as a televisual equivalent of the Elizabethan stage. Do you think, in retrospect, that avoidance was correct? Didn't the series run the risk of losing some of the radical energies of Elizabethan drama by substituting conventions inappropriate to Renaissance theatre?

When you move Shakespeare's plays out of the Elizabethan theatre into television, you are actually producing them in a medium for which they were not designed: and there is bound to be some kind of loss in the process. Indeed there are people who feel we should never have televised these plays at all, since they are absolutely unsuitable for television: that's a very extreme view, which I wouldn't accept but can understand. One of the strongest defenders of naturalistic setting was Herbert Wise,[3] who said that the experience of watching a play on television and that of seeing it in the theatre are quite different things. This is partly a matter of differences in the nature of the media, but also involves the different physical processes undergone by 'viewer' and 'spectator'. A visit to the theatre, say to the RSC at Stratford, may be planned months in advance; it involves travel; you enter an auditorium which is designed exclusively for the showing of a play; you join a large number of people all there for the same purpose; the auditorium is darkened and the stage lit – before the first word is spoken you have been preparing for this moment for perhaps a matter of months. There is therefore a tremendous sense of concentration and expectancy, and your whole attention is devoted to this particular experience.

Thousands of people have seen Shakespeare on the television because they have been watching *Match of the Day* or *Starsky and Hutch* and were too lazy to turn the set off, or unaware of what the next programme would be; so they happen to see the opening scene of *Hamlet*. There may be continual interruptions: telephone and doorbells ring, babies cry, distractions multiply. In such a context, Herbert Wise suggested, the director must *woo* the attention of the viewer, persuade the viewer to look, pay attention, become interested; in order to do so he must use all the visual resources of television in terms of sets and costumes and colour. On the other hand, the plays are not naturalistic plays: a realistic setting can thus be at odds with the artifice and conventions of the writing.

What I think made the Elizabethan theatre such a wonderful instrument for actors was its flexibility. The actors could choose either to recognise the existence of the audience, or to pretend the audience wasn't there; so you could have either the kind of prolonged aside in which Richard III steps towards the audience and says 'Was ever woman in this humour woo'd'; or genuine soliloquies like those of Hamlet or Angelo in *Measure for Measure* in which the actor ignores the audience and talks to himself. Television, like the proscenium arch stage, is clearly not as flexible as that.

Evidently the BBC agreed with Herbert Wise, since everything possible was done to isolate the productions from the flow of the medium, to make them into special 'theatrical' experiences.

Just as you can't, in the end, adequately transpose these plays from an Elizabethan stage to a twentieth-century screen, so it is impossible to recreate the social ethos in which they were originally performed. You can't programme them like any other broadcast because they are not like any other broadcast; the planners and administrators who have accompanied the productions with editions and articles in the *Radio Times*, talks and introductory programmes, are simply acknowledging the fact that the average non-Shakespearean viewer needs a bit of help in order to understand the plays. I think this is also related to that educational function which the BBC has had since its inception, and which was exemplified, above all, in Lord Reith: the sense of an obligation to transmit culture and education to the masses. All the educational material which went with the series was linked with that philosophy.[4]

One aspect that lies behind a lot of the problems we've been talking about is the very wide range of different audiences these productions were designed for, and the fact that the most important audience is an overseas audience, particularly American. These productions have been shown all over the United States, but also in countries – Japan, Australia, Mexico, central Europe – where people are utterly unfamiliar with Shakespeare. The Americans went in for this in a much more elaborately ambitious way, and treated it in a more seriously educational way, than we did: a firm over there sent out to thousands of schools and universities a great package of tapes, articles, texts, introductions, glossaries. Far from being integrated into the daily bread-and-butter programmes, in America the plays are actually shown on an independent educational channel. Bear in mind that the series couldn't have been mounted in the first place without a lot of money from American sponsors.

Many critics on the left have come to regard the theatre for which Shakespeare wrote as an 'ideological State apparatus' expressing and reproducing the dominant values of Elizabethan society. Would it not be possible to draw a parallel with the BBC, a central agency of national culture mediating a hegemonic ideology?

This is of course a very interesting, though very difficult question. I've read some of the things you and your colleagues have written on this, and I agree with you to this extent: if you consider, for example, Shakespeare's history plays (which must be the most political plays he wrote) it is possible to interpret them in radically conflicting ways. Regarded from one point of view – the perspective of Tillyard, which dominated our understanding of these plays for thirty-five or forty years – they are very much an expression of the Tudor homilies, with their nervous fear of political subversion and their reinforcement of the authority of the monarch. On the other hand, it is perfectly possible to read these plays in a very different way indeed (one I've tried to put forward in my own book on the history plays),[5] as plays which express a religious and political scepticism. Shakespeare recognises that in history, for every kind of gain there is a corresponding loss; and that although by the end of *Henry V* the authority of the king is firmly established, it is established at a price: the price of the kind of freedom, social variety and independence particularly exemplified by Falstaff, but exemplified also by the low-life characters – the inhabitants of the taverns, the common soldiers and so on. Within what appears to be a conservative political structure, Shakespeare was actually able to express a more radical and universal conception of politics and history than the plays ostensibly express.

The Elizabethan/Jacobean playwrights could exercise a degree of freedom, but they were also subject to censorship: they were forbidden to consider in a public playhouse questions of politics and theology which were thought to be the province of those professionally equipped to deal with them. Such political control as there was would be exercised by preventing the playwright from treating certain kinds of question: so that the effects of censorship would be registered rather in what they did not write about than in what they did. Despite all the attempts to discover contemporary political significance in these plays, Shakespeare seemed to be more concerned with politics in a much larger and less immediately contemporary sense. I would be more able to make the kind of comparison you are inviting if I were more fully convinced that it is possible to perceive in the plays the effects of the social and political conditions in which they were written.

If the question is, can the production of Shakespeare's plays within the BBC be compared, culturally and politically, to the writing and performance of those plays in the Renaissance, then the answer is yes: since although we were producing classic works officially prescribed in schools and so on, there was, within limits, freedom for individual directors to interpret them in ways that satisfied themselves. In so far as the BBC productions were the expression of some centralised, official, conservative attitude, that expression must have been largely unconscious. Directors were interpreting the plays in ways they found most satisfactory and meaningful. It may be that one director rather than another was asked to undertake a production because the producer felt he would offer a relatively safe, conservative interpretation; though the producer's choice would not have been a consciously political decision.

My wife and I had seen quite a lot of productions at Stratford one year, and then we went to see a production of Ibsen's *A Doll House*. Whereas Shakespeare is continually moving from the particular to the general, so that almost proverbial observations are constantly being made about the nature of man, the human condition, and so forth, *A Doll's House* makes you wonder whether you're giving your wife enough housekeeping money. You never ask that kind of question in the interval of a Shakespeare play.

Notes

1 See Chapter 16, note 11, above.
2 For John Barton and Cambridge see Chapter 10, n. 13, and Chapter 16, pp. 183–4.
3 Herbert Wise, director of the justly-celebrated series I, *Claudius*, directed *Julius Caesar* (1979) for the BBC/Time-Life Shakespeare series: see Holderness and McCullough, 'Shakespeare on the screen: a selective filmography', *Shakespeare Survey*, 39 (1986), p. 23.
4 See 16, pp. 174–5.
5 John Wilders, *The Lost Garden* (London: Macmillan, 1978).

Jonathan Miller
interviewed by Graham Holderness

Your work in the theatre seems to be based on a forthright commitment to directing as appropriation – not projecting or translating a text, but constructing one of a 'divergent series of alternative versions . . . at least minimally compatible with the text'.[1] Didn't the BBC/Time-Life Shakespeare series on the contrary require a maximum commitment to established versions of Shakespeare's texts, and demand definitive productions rather than free and permissive 'versions'? Did you find your own conviction and the requirements of the series contradictory?

When the BBC started to imagine such a series, there was a notion of an 'authentic' Shakespeare: something that should be tampered with as little as possible, so that one could present to an innocent audience Shakespeare as it might have been before the over-imaginative director arrived on the scene. I think this was a misconception: the hypothetical version which they saw as being authentic was actually something remembered from thirty years before; and in itself presumably widely divergent from what was performed at the inaugural production four hundred years ago. I thought it was much better to acknowledge the open-ended creativity of any Shakespeare production, since there is no way of returning to an authentic Globe theatre version. But we should recognise what Shakespeare had in mind: we should realise the author's intention. That in itself of course is a very unstable notion: authors are usually hard put to say what they meant by their plays. Apart from the prompting of unconscious motives, a really interesting work contains a richness of meaning, a variety of allusions, which can be delivered in the form of alternative readings. Some of these alternative readings can indeed be fatuous, and it's up to a critic to demonstrate convincingly that they are fatuous. But it seems to me important to recognise that a play has an afterlife different from the life conceived for it by its author. There are all sorts of unforeseeable meanings which might attach to the play, simply by virtue of the fact that it has survived into a period with which the author was not acquainted, and is therefore able to strike chords in the imagination of a modern audience which could not have been struck in an audience when it was first performed. It is inevitable in any great work – in fact it is the mark of a great work – that it should be capable of delivering these unforeseen, accreted meanings.

When you took over as executive producer of the BBC Shakespeare series, did you more or less discard and ignore the institutional view of the series as the establishing of an authentic Shakespeare canon?

Yes; but without saying so deliberately – since I don't think the theory I'm propounding now would have been either received or understood by the people who actually inaugurated the series. They seemed conspicuously unacquainted with what had happened to Shakespeare, didn't know the academic work, and actually had an old-fashioned show-biz hostility to the academic world. I couldn't therefore make my purposes plain, and privately resolved not to think about that.

I was limited none the less by certain contractual requirements which had been established before I came on the scene with the American sponsors: there are however all sorts of ways of skinning that kind of cat, and even with the requirement that I had to set things in so-called traditional costume, there were liberties which they could not foresee, and which I was able to take.

Do you think that the commercial and economic basis of the series – backed as it was by American big business – was ultimately damaging to its cultural achievement?

No, there were many things that were damaging to its cultural achievement, not the least of which was its being on television in the first place. There is something about the character and intrinsic structure of the plays, whether intended or not, which means that they sit rather uncomfortably on anything but the unfurnished set which seems appropriate to such writing. Television forces you into a much more pictorial and scenic manner than I think is good for Shakespeare.

What then is your opinion of those productions which resisted such pressure from the medium and worked with the relatively unfurnished, un-scenic space of, say, Jane Howell's productions of the first historical tetralogy?

I don't think they really worked. The point of an Elizabethan theatrical space – or indeed of any theatrical space – is that it is inseparable from the audience space with which it articulates. The whole point about the space of the unfurnished theatre-in-the-round is that the panoramic 360° circumference of the stage includes the circumference of the audience; both sit inside the same space. This relationship is instantly lost as soon you are no longer sharing the space with the spectacle you are watching. The television is not inside a space at all: it's a notional space inside a box.

You've frequently described television as an inherently naturalistic medium, which translates everything it touches into naturalism:[2] *clearly this relates to what you've just been saying about the difficulties of fitting Shakespearean drama to the medium. But is television really so incurably naturalistic? Why should Shakespeare be assimilated to the documentary or pictorial dimension of television, rather than to all the other possible forms of the medium – news broadcasts, situation comedies, soap operas, – which use a wide variety of non-naturalistic conventions?*

The great thing about the television camera is that it is a periscope: it simply extends the range of your own natural perception to places which are either too dangerous, too embarrassing or too distant to be present at. Its only form of artificiality is when it becomes a kind of icon: as in the case of cartoons, which are only on the surface of the screen, which then becomes a kind of drawing pad. It might be that you could present Shakespeare in that way: but as soon as you present it with real people it insists upon scenery, simply because the abstract space, which is said to be as possible on television as anywhere else, is quite different from the abstract space of the theatre: because it exists in a beyond to which you don't have any access at all. You can argue that the audience have no access to the stage either, because they are embarrassed or prevented by decorum from walking on to the stage. That is a matter of convention: in television you cannot walk into the space, and it doesn't change its appearance as you change the position of your head. You are not looking at a world happening; you are looking at a picture.

But there are stage sets designed to give the impression that when the characters walk off-stage they are entering another area of a real world; and there are stage sets so provocatively abstract as to fracture that kind of illusion. When Jane Howell directed The Winter's Tale *for the BBC series, she used a set so abstract as to make it unimaginable that the actors could be entering from or exiting to a real world.*

Yes: they were confined by the world she had created with those white abstract masses. Nevertheless, a white abstract set on the stage is very different from a white abstract set on the box, in that you can see on the stage the limits of its abstraction; you can see that no matter how enclosed it is, it is not hermetically sealed, since there comes a point where the decor gives out and the proscenium arch begins – and that's the point where you begin too. On television that doesn't happen: the edge of the screen is not a margin shared by the space of the action and the space of the spectator; the actor knows nothing about the frame of your set; and likewise you know nothing about the edges off which the actor goes. In the theatre the proscenium arch is common to both actions.

As a director accustomed to working in the theatre, was it a problem doing productions for the BBC series and knowing that their stability and permanence of form would return to haunt your latter days?

Some people would say that regret is built into the whole process of production: that to the intelligent producer all productions are repudiable. You look back and say 'Christ, what an oversimplification! what a silly thing to have done!' The BBC productions do dog you and come back to haunt you: and I do prefer the theatre, which destroys its own artefacts. The self-consuming artefact of the theatre is in an obvious way a source of regret, since you lose your own art-work in the act of possessing it. But that is probably to your advantage: in the case of television productions, you're constantly confronted by these interpretations many years after you have adopted a richer or more complex or even an alternative view. It's rather unpleasant to be confronted by one's own previous unskilfulness or simple-mindedness.

In your recent book[3] you've offered some criticism of big institutions such as the RSC and the National Theatre. Would you include the BBC in that indictment?

I am rather against these 'national institutions': but the BBC less so, because in some odd way it is so large that it actually allows a sort of inadvertent plurality which is simply not possible in a big but nevertheless totalitarian institution like the National Theatre. I just think that these big subsidised institutions have assumed the character of British Leyland: a large national output of automobiles is turned out regularly; the firm is very efficient; the cars get onto the road, and have a fairly good record of roadworthiness. But they are standardised British products. If I were going to re-design the co-operation between the State and the arts from scratch, I would implement what I've advocated in the past: never to assign the relationship to centralised bodies which see themselves as a result as centres of excellence. Once an institution starts to see itself as a centre of excellence, a hideous institutional complacency settles over it. The claim is in any way bogus, since excellence is unpredictable and unforeseeable. The idea that the National Theatre is where it's at, or that the RSC is the centre from which all great Shakespearean production necessarily issues, seems to me complacent on the one hand and self-deceiving on the other. I got out of it because I couldn't bear the large and overweening complacency.

You've frequently expressed views on the importance of art and 'Culture' within a society, which seem to me traceable back to Matthew Arnold. You once (in an Arnoldian way) described art as a force of social unity; but qualified that assertion (with a very Arnoldian distinction), arguing that this relationship was symptomatic rather than causal: you couldn't stop the Tottenham riots by going round the area giving poetry readings; but if you have a society that doesn't value art then that kind of social malaise will be the inevitable consequence. I have felt in working on the BBC's Shakespeare output that there is often a sense of the legacy of Lord Reith: with the BBC conceived as an agent of moral regeneration and social pacification. Was anything like that at all in your mind or part of your experience when working on the series?

No, I had no view of the series as an agent of social pacification; or indeed of its adding to 'the best that has been known and thought in the world'. I think the arts have an adjuvant effect on a society, but not through any one-to-one relationship between a work of art and the audience that experiences it. I think that a society that is unfriendly to the works of the imagination is likely to be one in which people think unimaginatively about social problems. I do think that anything that encourages the life of the mind is likely to lead to people who make decisions about society acting with regard to many considerations. The life of the mind emphasises the role of the imagination, which is putting yourself in states of mind which recognise alternative ways of thinking.

A high level of artistic cultivation is not of course incompatible with political barbarism.

As we know from Germany, and indeed from other countries: high levels of cultivation in a self-regarding élite can actually be a way of guaranteeing the barbarism. We have no way at all of knowing how we stop barbarism. I just think that on the whole the more people are given an opportunity to see that there are many ways of thinking about something, the less chance barbarism has of getting a foothold. It encourages people to hold off a little, to recognise alternative ways of seeing a problem. There are other ways of imagining: possible worlds are conceivable. That I think is the only work that culture does that is to the possible advantage of society at large: it simply multiplies the possibility of seeing multiple possibilities. I may well be whistling in the dark: the forces that determine whether or not we behave barbarously or unconvivially may go ahead for reasons that have nothing to do with what we call Culture.

You've described yourself politically as 'an old-fashioned social democrat' out of sympathy with all existing political parties. Does that suggest that your cultural work is very much non-aligned, freelance, non-political?

Yes; I don't see it as work on behalf of a political standpoint.

Or as having political implications?

Not really, no. I'd find it very difficult to develop the political implications even if I thought they were there. I wouldn't know what I was doing politically.

You once said in another interview: 'I quite self-consciously use Shakespeare in order to amuse myself. I'm not doing the plays in order to honour Shakespeare. Shakespeare is not honoured by constantly and conscientiously reproducing his intentions: *Shakespeare is honoured in the complicated and plural ways in which he is attended to*'.[4] *That seems to me a very interesting mixture of piety and desecration: you talk about something called 'Shakespeare' which can be honoured; yet you say that your purpose doesn't consist in such celebration but in personal appropriation and amusement.*

It's piety only in the best sense: I do think there is some obligation to honour the achievements of the past. We've got these extraordinary, complicated, intriguing artefacts; that requires some sort of a bow in their author's direction. He was a genius. But I don't think one does service to his genius by simply adopting an inflexibly reverent attitude. That's silly. I think that any honour that may be due is more than observed, simply by our continuing to do his plays so long after his death. That's what being a classic is: he continues to preoccupy us. I have a regard, in the same way as Eliot did, for the distinguished reputations of the past. There are people who seem to have done work that continues to nourish us. I doff my hat to it, and say Shakespeare, I'm very pleased you existed. But you will only continue to exist if you lend yourself to interpretations which you couldn't possibly have anticipated or identified at the time.

We don't honour the past because that is its due: we honour the past because it's better for ourselves if we do. It puts us in touch with a wider range of human experience: to see that other people thought other things, valued other things, valued them in different ways, and used and employed symbolic resources in order to express their relationship to these values. I deplore the tendency of historical provincialism to cash out all symbolic relationships of the past into the currency of symbolic relationships that mean something to us in the present. It's like being some awful tourist who always travels with no currency but sterling.

Take *The Taming of the Shrew*: I think it's an irresponsible and silly thing to make that play into a feminist tract: to use it as a way of proving that women have been dishonoured and hammered flat by male chauvinism. There's another, more complex way of reading it than that: which sees it as being their particular view of how society ought to be organised in order to restore order in a fallen world. Now we don't happen to think that we are the inheritors of the sin of Adam and that orderliness can only be preserved by deputising power to magistrates and sovereigns, fathers and husbands. But the fact that they did think like that is absolutely undeniable; so productions which really do try to deny that, and try to hijack the work to make it address current problems about women's place in society, become boring, thin and tractarian.

Would it not be true to say that in your own production of The Taming of the Shrew *for the BBC series, you did deflect the text from whatever we can conjecture to have been its original dramatic intentions, by removing the Induction and the whole Christopher Sly framework?*

I think possibly I did. I did that for several reasons. First of all I find the Christopher Sly Induction terribly hard to do in any other format but the stage: it is a stage device, and it's frightfully hard to see it on television. It's a device that brings the audience into close identification with some person who is like them. It would be on television a little extra programme tagged on before the programme proper actually begins. On the stage it's possible to make it work much better: it's a folk style which sits rather uncomfortably in this very twentieth-century medium of domestic viewing.

Michael Bogdanov, for example, in an explicitly feminist production, not only retained but emphasised the Sly framework: because it seemed to him that the interaction of frame and content more overtly raised the issues of sexual politics.[5]

The questions about sexual politics are there in the play, regardless of the framework. I very strongly believe of that play – and I probably failed to bring it out clearly by casting someone so intrinsically comic [John Cleese] as Petruchio – that its spirit derives from Elizabethan puritanism, from a post-Marian exile's view of the household as an orderly place in which the marriage is consecrated not in the church but in the orderly procedure of domesticity; in which obedience is required, not in order to preen the male pride of the father, but simply because this is how society should be arranged given we are the inheritors of this sin of naughtiness.

You also found it necessary to make additions, such as the singing of the psalm at the end, and the establishing of that text as a scripture in the closing credits?

Yes: because that notion is so remote now, I had to give it an explicitly religious format, so people could see it as not just simply the high-jinks of an intolerantly selfish man who was simply destroying a woman to satisfy his own vanity, but a sacramental view of the nature of marriage, whereby this couple had come to love each other by reconciling themselves to the demands of a society which saw obedience as a religious requirement. I don't happen to agree with it: but one of the reasons we do these plays is because they are a form of ethnology. How did they live? What did they actually value? What did they cherish? What obligations did they feel were binding? We don't now feel that those obligations are binding in quite the same way: and I also feel that it is very simple-minded for a sort of crude *Time Out* marxism to say well, of course, the reason why they thought that is because marriage was a salient on the broad front of advancing capitalism. Certainly there are ways in which the notions of inheritance and the conveyance of property was an important part of this, but I think that comes out of the play: there the economic and cultural concerns are married closely together. What naive modern marxism leaves out of consideration is the world and the life of the imagination: how did people actually view families, daughters, children? A purely marxist interpretation would leave out of consideration these purely affectional relationships. I suppose that in most of my work I've been prompted as much by considerations of the family as a purely affective structure as I have by families as complex institutions for preserving the status quo with regard to the inheritance and transfer of property.

Both are true, of course.

Yes, I think both are true. We should take both into consideration. I think that's what being a good ethnographer is: the reason why I admire the work of the French marxist historians of the *Annales* school, is that their marxism is beautifully assimilated to a broad view of what it was actually like to live out your life – and your imaginative life – at that time. This searching for the *mentalité* of a particular period, the concern for example of the *Annales* historians and of people like Lévi-Strauss, would be incomplete if we only took into consideration the political dimension – the way in which these institutions preserved certain ways of guaranteeing the status quo.

Notes

1 Jonathan Miller interviewed by Helen Crich Chinoy, 'The director as mythagog', *Shakespeare Quarterly* (winter 1976), p. 12.
2 See Ann Pasternak Slater, 'An interview with Jonathan Miller', *Quarto*, 10 (September 1980), p. 9; and Tim Hallinan, 'Jonathan Miller on the Shakespeare plays', *Shakespeare Quarterly*, 32 (1981), p. 134.
3 Jonathan Miller, *Subsequent Performances* (London: Faber and Faber, 1986).
4 Slater, 'Interview', p. 12.
5 See above, pp. 91–2.

Afterword
Terry Eagleton

When I went up to Cambridge in the early 1960s as a working-class student, one of the very first lectures I attended was delivered by a dashing young don (now a rather less dashing professor at one of the newer universities) who recounted a squirmingly paternal anecdote about how his little son, listening to Shakespearean dialogue on television, had been enthralled by the playwright's *eloquence*. He was enthralled, in fact, by exactly what put me off. Shakespeare made me uneasy at that time because, like the middle classes, he tended to talk too much. In my northern industrial town we chalked up a rate of about ten words an hour, most of them what the linguists would call 'phatic'; down in Cambridge the air was thick with convoluted syntax, elaborate expressiveness, lexical dexterity, rhetorical virtuosity. (The aristocrats were rather less lexically dexterous, but compensated in decibels.) Shakespeare's inability to shut up, his grating habit of rattling on through sub-clause after sub-clause with not an emotional nuance or conceptual aspect left unelaborated, struck me as peculiarly tactless and overblown, an excessive garrulousness for which the closest analogy seemed that endless middle-class gushing and twittering. *Krapp's Last Tape* seemed to me decidely preferable to *Coriolanus*. Shakespeare showed me two things: first, that language was power; secondly, that I had neither.

I see now, as I didn't in late adolescence, that Shakespeare's astonishingly unmodernist faith in discourse does indeed have a lot to do with middle-class confidence – not of course with the gushing and twittering but with the historically productive energy of an emergent social class. Even so, any society which survives by structural injustice must secrete rhetoric as readily as it equips an army; and this is one reason why those who hold the views of the contributors to this book can never thrill innocently to such verbal resourcefulness as mere 'eloquence'. Each step in the evolution of an elaborated code deepens its cognitive, forensic powers, but by the same token thickens the possibilities of mystification. Caliban knew that language was ambivalently emancipation and enslavement; and there is much to be said for a Caliban school of Shakespearean criticism.

What is perhaps most striking for us now about Shakespearean discourse is its elision into a single idiom of what for us are the essentially differentiated languages of poetic rhetoric and political power. The latter language in late capitalism is factual, instrumental, strategic, bureaucratic; poetic rhetoric provides the 'spiritual' or 'human' symbolism which can then serve to cloak such prosaic realities. What then seems curious to modern ears in Shakespeare is that *everything* seems to be rhetorically inflected, even the discourses of pragmatic manipulation. This rhetorical intensification allows us a peculiarly sharp insight into the nexus of language and power, for which a single term is 'ideology'. For the humanists, Shakespearean language is not especially 'political' (apart from where it is obviously so) precisely because it is 'poetic'; but the truth is that the more poetic it waxes, the more political it becomes. The currents and motions of power in Shakespearean language are merely the other face of its intricate rhetorical resources. Indeed it is hard to think of another writer (though Henry James suggests himself) whose language is so slippery, so erotic, one is tempted to say, with the currents and microtactics of power and desire, and all this shamelessly, flamboyantly on view. The discourse of Shakespeare is unabashedly perverse, bending constantly away from some 'normative' referent, staggering and deferring the signified, luxuriating in its sumptuous transgression of strict semantic economy. It is this libidinal excess which humanism recuperates, gullibly, as 'human richness' or 'sensuous concretion', blind to the mastery, violence and manipulation implicit in any such idiom.

The incongruous combination of rhetoric and pragmatic calculation is still alive and well in the Shakespeare industry, as readers of John Drakakis's account of the Southwark project in this volume, or of the interview with Sam Wanamaker, will no doubt appreciate. All of the writers in this book are alert to the fact that Shakespeare is today less an author than an apparatus – that his name (itself, as Simon Shepherd suggests, interestingly unstable) is merely metonymic of an entire politico-cultural formation, and thus more akin to 'Disney' or 'Rockerfeller' than to 'Jane Smith'. Indeed one of the deepest ironies of the Shakespeare industry is that just when the historical individual Shakespeare (about whom we knew of course precious little in the first place) has been buried more or less completely out of sight by the processes of mechanical reproduction (from calendars and tea mugs to new directorial interpretations), the scholars are still wistfully striving to ascertain the authenticity of this or that fragment of text. Their labours are in vain in at least this sense: that even if they discovered after all that Shakespeare was Christopher Marlowe or a wandering Kentish tinker, it would be a brave man or woman who would try at this late date to close down Stratford. The apparatus has long achieved autonomy of whatever individual gave rise to it in the first place; if the shrines of Knock and Lourdes could be brought into existence by a non-person, a construct of such institutions rather than an authorial source, then the Shakespeare industry may equally continue to constitute and reconstitute its own 'founder', in an inviolably self-referential gesture.

There is, however, an undeniable contradiction at the very heart of this apparatus, one interestingly analogous to a central contradiction in capitalism itself. This is the fact that though the industry needs some unimpeachable authority or 'authenticity' on which to ground itself, its constant recycling of commodities tends inevitably to undermine such authority. In Walter Benjamin's terms, it must on the one hand preserve a certain 'aura', at the same time as economic pressures force it into a frantic 'mechanical reproduction'. In a somewhat parallel way, bourgeois society needs for ideological reasons to evoke some absolute authority (Truth, God) at exactly the point that its restless technological evolution threatens to put such transcendental guarantees into permanent question. On the one hand, Shakespearean criticism must in Drakakis's words place the works in an eternal present, 'divesting them of their historical and conjunctural determinants, and regarding them as the transparent vehicles through which 'Shakespeare' the dramatist speaks directly to us'. On the other hand, the American tourists clearly cannot be heard complaining that the Hamlet they have just seen was a carbon copy of the one they saw five years ago, if the industry is financially to survive; and so that ceaseless proliferation of sameness-in-difference which Benjamin terms 'fashion' proceeds apace.

There is a similar paradox at work in the texts themselves. What we call 'unique' or 'authentic' in Shakespeare, the genuine article, is really no more than his extraordinary ability to parody himself. Shakespeare is continually serving up uncannily accurate Shakespearean parodies, many of them so lifelike as to be positively startling – though it's also true that he quite often botches the job and comes up with some crude, creaking imitation of the real thing. Shakespeare is even more ridiculously Shakespearean than Pinter is Pinteresque, which is to say that his distinctive 'authenticity' lies in shameless self-plagiarism. There is never any mistaking the genuine article, for Shakespeare never fails to steal from his own texts. His utter uniqueness, his quintessential identity, lies in the fact that he never gives us anything we have not in some sense heard before. In this way Shakespeare is the quintessential commodity, at once ever-new and consolingly recognisable, always different and eternally the same, a magnificent feat of self-identity persisting through the most bizarre diversions and variations. He Shakespeareanises everything, as the commodity converts difference to the homogeneous; and just as the commodity emits, along with its use-value, a kind of silent lateral message ('I am wealth power, status'), so it is impossible to read or watch Shakespeare without hearing, in the very thick of the 'human life' of the drama, that insistent subliminal message: 'I am Shakespeare'. This is the message which many of the punters want to hear, pervasive throughout whatever 'use-value' the performance may have for them; and it is one strong enough to survive the fancy interpetations of the 'progressive' directors. Shakespeare's unique distinctiveness lies in his instant recognisability; we have always-already known his voice, this style, and it is to our own always pre-given recognition that we are listening. The aura, it would appear, can survive a thousand mechanical reproductions.

It is for this reason that the kind of radical Shakespearean criticism represented in this book cannot rest content with intervening in the question of 'interpretation'. Indeed one glance at the dismally regressive opinions of the various 'fashionable' directors assembled here would be enough to persuade one of the restricted value of that. Terry Hands reminds us in his interview of 'how little we have evolved in the last five centuries in language, thinking, clothes or even physical behaviour'. Hands, who for all I know speaks like Beowulf, believes in burning witches and wears knee-breeches, also believes, unsurprisingly, that politics are 'childish', and subscribes cravenly to the Great Man theory of history. Critics are supposed to be a grey unworldly bunch, and theatre directors glamorously avant-garde; but in this volume at least, the boot is truly on the other foot. Michael Croft sings the praises of Granville Barker and rejects the whole notion of a popular theatre; Sam Wanamaker records his faith in literary geniuses who 'express the human condition in a form recognisable to all people', and holds up the Reaganite Michael Caine as an instance of pride of origin. Jonathan Miller, a little more alert to the theoretical leanings of his interlocutor, discourses learnedly of hermeneutics and ethnography, but his liberal pluralism always seems to baulk, strangely enough, when it comes to marxism and feminism. Such frames of interpretation, the implication runs, automatically close off hermeneutical richness, as Miller's own bland Hampstead bohemianism of course does not. These are the very top dogs of the industry, the managing directors and executives of the whole shebang; and their collective ideological consciousness, all the way from strident elitism and abstract universalism to the depoliticising eclecticism of a Miller, makes for depressing reading. Depressing, but hardly surprising: for they did of course get where they are today partly because they hold precisely these views.

In that connection, as more than one interviewee mentions, and, as Christopher McCullough demonstrates in his essay, the Cambridge English school bulks interestingly large. A hidebound, patrician British theatre, like a sclerotic British establishment in general, urgently required some managerial modernisation, a dose of mildly modernist experimentation and technological updating; and the liberal humanism of a Leavis, fiercely hostile to a moribund ruling-class culture – but also, of course, to the political radicalism which alone might truly dismantle it – supplied the seedbed for the new, tougher-minded, more 'vital' young executives. David Hornbrook, in another context, demonstrates how that same ideology has remained the controlling factor in the schools.

If the struggle for radical theory in the educational institutions is important, it is for one reason because a British theatre of the future might be informed by such values in just the way that Scrutiny shaped the consciousness of some of the present generation of directors. There is, however, one vital difference. If it was possible for Cambridge English to make such headway in a broader public context, it was partly because its target was always the text, rather than the apparatus itself. But the Shakespeare industry, as the essays in this collection suggest, interlocks with almost every major structure of late capitalism: commerce and finance (Holderness), popular culture (Longhurst), education (Hornbrook), communications (Holderness), sexuality and the family (Ann Thompson, in her excellent review of recent feminist Shakespearean criticism). If this is indeed the case, then radical interpretations and productions of Shakespeare, though often conjuncturally valuable (they would at least offend a Hands or Croft, no bad thing), cannot finally be the answer. The answer, I believe, is exactly the one proposed by this volume, which consists in replacing the study of Shakespeare with the study of 'Shakespeare'. The question is not, in David Lodge fashion, how far can you go in critical interpretation? We can leave that to the Crofts and the Millers, the rather-more-conservative and rather-more-liberal, to fight over. The question is, How far can you go in critical interpretation given the political, cultural and ideological constraints and determinants signalled by the name 'Shakespeare'? To find a genuine new range of use-values for the texts would involve, as a laborious preliminary operation, challenging and dismantling their present exchange-values. It is the strength of this collection that it addresses itself precisely to that most difficult, but also most potentially productive, of tasks.

Contributors

GRAHAM HOLDERNESS is Head of Drama at Roehampton Institute, London. His publications include *Shakespeare's History* (Dublin: Gill and Macmillan, 1985); *Shakespeare: the Play of History*, with Nick Potter and John Turner (London: Macmillan, 1987); and *Hamlet* (Milton Keynes: Open University Press, 1987).

SAM WANAMAKER, actor and producer, is Executive Vice-Chairman of the Shakespeare Globe Trust.

JOHN DRAKAKIS is Lecturer in English at the University of Stirling, and editor of *Alternative Shakespeares* (London: Methuen, 1986).

DAVID MARGOLIES is Lecturer in English at Goldsmith's College, University of London, and author of *The Function of Literature* (London: Lawrence and Wishart, 1969), and *Novel and Society in Elizabethan England* (London: Croom Helm, 1985).

JOHN PETER is Theatre Critic of *The Sunday Times* and author of *Vladimir's Carrot: modern drama and the modern imagination* (London: Andre Deutsch, 1987).

DEREK LONGHURST is Principal Lecturer and Course Leader in Communications Studies at Sunderland Polytechnic, and general editor of a series of cultural studies, *Cultural Forms and Popular Fictions*, to be published by Allen and Unwin.

ANN THOMPSON is Lecturer in English at the University of Liverpool. She edited *The Taming of the Shrew* for the New Cambridge Shakespeare (Cambridge: Cambridge University Press, 1984), and is author (with John O. Thompson) of *Shakespeare: Meaning and Metaphor* (Brighton: Harvester, 1987).

MICHAEL BOGDANOV has directed Shakespeare for the National Theatre and the Royal Shakespeare Company, and is currently co-director of the English Shakespeare Company.

SIMON SHEPHERD is Lecturer in English at the University of Nottingham. He is author of *Amazons and Warrior Women: Varieties of Feminism in Seventeenth Century Drama* (Brighton: Harvester, 1981) and *Marlowe and the Politics of the Elizabethan Theatre* (Brighton: Harvester, 1987).

CHRISTOPHER J. McCULLOUGH is Lecturer in Drama at the University of Exeter. He has published several articles on Renaissance drama in performance, and is working on a study of Bertolt Brecht.

TERRY HANDS is Artistic Director of the Royal Shakespeare Company.

ALAN SINFIELD is Reader in English at the University of Sussex. He is author of *Literature in Protestant England 1560–1660* (London: Croom Helm, 1982); editor of *Society and Literature 1945–1970* (London: Methuen, 1983); and joint editor with Jonathan Dollimore of *Political Shakespeare* (Manchester: Manchester University Press, 1986).

DAVID HORNBROOK is Special Lecturer in Drama in the School of Education at the University of Bristol, and author of a challenging and controversial series of articles on educational drama in *New Theatre Quarterly* (1986).

JOHN HODGSON is Head of Drama at Bretton Hall College of Further Education. He is the author (with Ernest Richards) of *Improvisation: discovery and creativity in drama*, (London: Methuen, 1966), and editor of *The Uses of Drama* (London: Eyre Methuen, 1972).

MICHAEL CROFT was Director of the National Youth Theatre until his death in 1986.

JOHN WILDERS is Dean of Graduates at Worcester College, Oxford, and author of *The Lost Garden* (London: Macmillan, 1978).

JONATHAN MILLER, director, producer and broadcaster, is the author of *Subsequent Performances* (London: Faber, 1986). He is currently Artistic Director of the Old Vic.

TERRY EAGLETON is Fellow of Wadham College, Oxford. His many publications include *Shakespeare and Society* (London: Chatto and Windus, 1970) and *William Shakespeare* (Oxford: Blackwell, 1986).

Index